COUNSELING PSYCHOLOGY: A HISTORICAL PERSPECTIVE

SERIES IN COUNSELING PSYCHOLOGY
John M. Whiteley, University of California, Irvine
Arthur Resnikoff, University of California, Irvine
Series Editors

Helene K. Hollingsworth
Editorial Assistant

APPROACHES TO ASSERTION TRAINING - Order No. 71-001
Editors: John M. Whiteley, University of California, Irvine
          John V. Flowers, University of California, Irvine
THE BEHAVIOR THERAPIST - Order No. 71-007
Editor: Carl E. Thoresen, Stanford University
CAREER COUNSELING - Order No. 71-003
Editors: John M. Whiteley, University of California, Irvine
          Arthur Resnikoff, University of California, Irvine
COUNSELING ADULTS - Out of Print
Editors: Nancy K. Schlossberg, University of Maryland
          Alan D. Entine, State University of New York at Stony Brook
COUNSELING MEN - Order No. 71-006
Editors: Thomas M. Skovholt, University of Minnesota
          Paul G. Schauble, University of Florida at Gainesville
          Richard Davis, The Western Ohio Council for Educational
            and Behavioral Programs—Lima, Ohio
COUNSELING WOMEN - out of Print
Editors: Lenore W. Harmon, University of Illinois at Urbana-Champaign
          Janice M. Birk, University of Maryland
          Laurine E. Fitzgerald, University of Wisconsin, Oshkosh
          Faith Tanney, University of Maryland
DEVELOPMENTAL COUNSELING AND TEACHING -
Order No. 71-004
Editors: V. Lois Erickson, University of Minnesota
          John M. Whiteley, University of California, Irvine
THE HISTORY OF COUNSELING PSYCHOLOGY - Order No. 71-008
Editor: John M. Whiteley, University of California, Irvine
THE PRESENT AND FUTURE OF COUNSELING PSYCHOLOGY -
Order No. 71-005
Editors: John M. Whiteley, University of California, Irvine
          Bruce R. Fretz, University of Maryland
THEORETICAL AND EMPIRICAL FOUNDATIONS OF RATIONAL-
EMOTIVE THERAPY - Order No. 71-002
Editors: Albert Ellis, Institute for Rational-Emotive Therapy
          John M. Whiteley, University of California, Irvine
THE COMING DECADE IN COUNSELING PSYCHOLOGY -
Order No. 71-009
Editors: John M. Whiteley, University of California, Irvine
          Norman Kagan, University of Houston
          Lenore W. Harmon, University of Illinois at Urbana-Champaign
          Bruce R. Fretz, University of Maryland
          Faith Tanney, Washington, DC

COUNSELING PSYCHOLOGY: A HISTORICAL PERSPECTIVE

JOHN M. WHITELEY
UNIVERSITY OF CALIFORNIA, IRVINE

Published by: Character Research Press
266 State Street
Schenectady, NY 12305

Distributed by: American Association for Counseling
and Development
5999 Stevenson Avenue
Alexandria, VA 22304

Order No. 71-010

International Standard Book Number 0-915744-37-6
   (paperback)
Library of Congress Catalog Card No. L.C. 84-72259

Some of the material in this book originally appeared in
The Counseling Psychologist, the official publication of the
Division of Counseling Psychology of the American Psycho-
logical Association.

Typesetting
by
Helen C. Cernik

Published by:

Character Research Press
266 State Street
Schenectady, NY 12305

SERIES FOREWORD

The books in the series in Counseling Psychology reflect the significant developments that have occurred in the counseling field over the past decades. No longer is it possible for a single author to cover the complexity and scope of counseling as it is practiced today. Our approach has been to incorporate within the Series the viewpoints of different authors having quite diverse training and perspectives.

Over the past decades, too, the counseling field has expanded its theoretical basis, the problems of human living to which it addresses itself, the methods it uses to advance scientifically, and the range of persons who practice it successfully—from competent and skillful paraprofessionals to doctoral-level practitioners in counseling, psychology, education, social work, and psychiatry.

The books in the Series are intended for instructors and both graduate and undergraduate students alike who want the most stimulating in current thinking. Each volume may be used independently as a text to focus in detail on an individual topic, or the books may be used in combination to highlight the growth and breadth of the profession. However they are used, the books explore the many skills that are available to counselors as they struggle to help people learn to change their behavior and gain self-understanding. Single volumes also lend themselves as background reading for workshops or in-service training, as well as for regular semester or quarter classes.

The intent of all the books in the Series is to stimulate the reader's thinking about the field, about the assumptions made regarding the basic nature of people, about the normal course of human development and the progressive growth tasks that everyone faces, about how behavior is acquired, and about what different approaches to counseling postulate concerning how human beings can help one another.

John M. Whiteley
Arthur Resnikoff

CONTENTS

APPRECIATIONS

The author is deeply indebted to a number of individuals for the care with which they read this history of counseling psychology in its earlier versions, the helpfulness of their suggestions on how to improve it, and in many cases, their willingness to provide background materials which were previously either unknown to me or had been otherwise unattainable. In alphabetical order, these cherished professional colleagues are: Irwin A. Berg, Carole B. Bernard, Janice M. Birk, Edward S. Bordin, Steven D. Brown, Helen V. Collier, William C. Cottle, Bruce R. Fretz, Raymond Hummel, Norman Kagan, Gloria J. Lewis, Harold B. Pepinsky, C. Winfield Scott, Donald E. Super, Albert S. Thompson, David V. Tiedeman, Leona E. Tyler, Scott Whiteley, and C. Gilbert Wrenn.

The preparation of the manuscript which covered a historical period of over 80 years with numerous references would not have been possible without the dedicated and resourceful assistance of a number of immediate colleagues:

> Helene Hollingsworth, who has been in charge of all phases of manuscript preparation and production;

> Lori Sypherd, who has mastered the intricacies of the word processor on which drafts were revised and final copy prepared;

> Norma Yokota, who found references I inadvertantly lost and references I had been unable to find as part of supervising the preparation of the bibliography;

> Jane DuKet and Claudia Holt, who typed portions of the manuscript and tables and assisted with proofreading;

> Connie Cannon, a technical editor, who served as a thoughtful critic of the writing style in earlier versions of the manuscript; and

> Helen C. Cernik and Herman Williams of Character Research Press, who were responsible for typesetting and printing.

To each of you I am extraordinarily appreciative. This effort would not have been anywhere near as extensive, detailed, accurate, or clearly stated without your dedicated assistance.

In the transition from journal issue to book, the following colleagues contributed to refining the presentation: Robert Anderson, Irwin A. Berg, Carole B. Bernard, Robert Brown, Linda Brooks, Helen V. Collier, Shula Lazarus, Marylu K. McEwen, Harold B. Pepinsky, C. Winfield Scott, Albert S. Thompson, and C. Gilbert Wrenn.

John M. Whiteley
University of California, Irvine

Introduction

HISTORICAL PERIODS IN THE DEVELOPMENT OF COUNSELING PSYCHOLOGY

This historical perspective on the development of counseling psychology as a profession is organized around seven identifiable historical periods, each of which is accorded a separate chapter. Within each of the seven periods, central professional issues, organized activities, theoretical developments, and research advancements will be presented and discussed. The societal context of each period will be sketched to provide a perspective on how social and economic forces have influenced the profession.

THE HISTORICAL PERIODS

The first period (1908-1950) contained the diverse initial roots and seminal influences from society and organized psychology which led to the establishment of counseling psychology as an applied specialty. Five initial roots which have been identified are the work of Frank Parsons and the growth of the vocational guidance movement, the mental health movement, the study of individual differences in concert with the psychometric movement, the development of counseling and psychotherapy from nonmedical and nonpsychoanalytic perspectives, and the social and economic forces and developments in society. While counseling psychology became a separate division within the American Psychological Association during this period, it had yet to accomplish many of the tasks necessary for viable status as an applied, scientific specialty.

The second period (1951-1956) provided the inaugural definitions of the profession and initial standards for training. This period was extraordinarily important and productive. The name of the division was changed from "Counseling and Guidance" to "Counseling Psychology," and official statements were created and adopted on doctoral and practicum training and specialty definition. Reviews of counseling psychology topics began appearing regularly in the *Annual Review of Psychology*. It was a prolific period in the development of scientific literature on counseling theory, diagnosis, and therapy.

The somewhat overlapping third period (1954-1962) was a time when there were a number of different viewpoints expressed on the status of counseling psychology and its proper focus. While the third period began with the appearance of the first issues of the *Journal of Counseling Psychology*, this was not a time of positive accomplishment for organized counseling psychology. It was marked by significant conflict concerning the status and proper focus of the specialty. The fruits of all but one of the major attempts to address the fundamental problems of the status and proper focus of the profession languished unpublished for 20 years. Division 17 failed to become significantly involved with those activities supported with federal funds which blossomed after Sputnik. Major accomplishments during the third historical period were those of conceptualizers and researchers.

The fourth period (1963-1967) contained one of the single most important years in the history of the young specialty: 1964, the year of the Greyston Conference. Counseling psychology was at a crossroads at the time the fourth period began. The Greyston Conference provided greater clarity on identity issues, substantive bases, and needed directions for the future. Research issues and theoretical problems identified in the 1950s were better understood as a consequence of research in the 1960s. Behavior therapy and existential approaches to counseling were but two of the major theoretical matters debated at this time.

The fifth period of history (1968-1976) closely resembled the time between 1954 and 1962 when a number of alternative directions for the profession emerged and when there was a spirited debate over the central mission of the specialty. This period began with the appearance of the most comprehensive statement yet developed of the specialty definition. Counseling psychologists were assigned a three-part role which was composed of the remedial/rehabilitative, the preventive, and the educative/developmental. The theoretical and research literature underwent a steady increase in methodological rigor and design sophistication. There was a dramatic change in prevailing social attitudes including a growing search for wellness and a preoccupation with self-help.

The sixth historical period (1977-1983) was characterized by an intensive period of rethinking on two topics: professional identity and the role of the specialty. This period was greeted by a general consensus on professional identity, a positive legacy of theoretical and empirical developments with promising programmatic research in progress, and a supportive attitude of society toward the profession. Organized counseling psychology initiated four activities: a refinement of its identity statements, a projection of the role of the profession into the 21st Century, the further defining of applied specialties within organized psychology, and the Next Decade Project (a definition of challenges in the areas of the conceptual bases of education and training, definitional concerns, the marketplace conditions for professional practice, and needed directions and developments in scientific affairs).

The seventh historical period (1984—) is already shaping up as another era when the principal influences on counseling psychologists are coming from outside the professional specialty. A number of significant challenges have been identified for the profession in the waning years of the 20th Century. The task is to address those challenges actively and to anticipate needed changes at the very time when the immediate pressures on members of the profession are ones of maintaining the status quo and operating within a stable framework of specialty definition and guidelines for training and practice.

THE SUBSTANTIVE INFLUENCES

The history of counseling psychology as an applied-scientific specialty in organized psychology may be understood in terms of the forces of society operating upon it and of the activities of its formal organizational structures. It may also be understood in terms of its substantive history: the development of its most influential ideas, its theories concerning aspects of the human condition, and the approaches which have developed for understanding what it is that assists human beings to change their behavior and lead more fulfilling lives.

This second approach to understanding the history of counseling psychology has been organized in terms of the two constellations of theories which have most fundamentally affected its development and professional practice: the constellation of theories of personality, counseling, and psychotherapy; and the constellation of theories of vocational psychology, occupational choice, and career development. While it is beyond the scope of this general history to review the development of the theories themselves, a presentation of when representative seminal theoretical publications first appeared provides an indication of substantive influences on the thinking of counseling psychologists.

Theories of personality, counseling, and psychotherapy will be considered together. The reason is that theorists often covered topics in both personality theory and counseling or psychotherapy within a specific article, monograph, or book. It is not practical or necessary to try to separate these contributions as to whether they are attempting either to explain and understand human beings (personality) or to change them (counseling or psychotherapy).

While counseling psychologists have been influenced by a wide range of theories of personality, counseling, and psychotherapy, there have been a number of basic schools of thought which have been predominant over time. Those judged most influential on counseling psychology are: psychoanalysis, Adlerian therapy, client-centered therapy, behavior therapy (and its derivative, behavioral counseling), rational-emotive therapy (the most influential on counseling psychology of the cognitive therapies), gestalt therapy, transactional analysis, and existential theory and therapy.

In selecting among the voluminous writings of the major schools of personality theory, counseling, and psychotherapy, there has been an anticipation that the coverage would be representative, though not complete. When there exists a central founder or major disciple, an attempt has been made to present sample titles from his or her writings. For each author, the topics or titles covered are followed by the year of publication in order to reflect chronology of appearance and, therefore, when initial impact began on counseling psychology.

For any period in the history of counseling psychology, the impact of a theory of personality, counseling, or psychotherapy is essentially cumulative: The central writings up to that point in time are available for study and are undoubtedly covered in the formal graduate and in-service (and convention) training programs.

Some of the schools of personality, counseling, and psychotherapy have influenced counseling psychology since its inception (such as psychoanalysis which dates from the turn of the century). Other schools of thought more closely parallel the development of counseling psychology as an organized profession, such as client-centered therapy, which dates from the 1940s. Still others, such as rational-emotive therapy, gestalt therapy, and transactional analysis (which underwent extensive development in the 1960s and 1970s), began in a more systematic fashion in later periods. The coverage of theories of personality, counseling, and psychotherapy concludes with the end of the fifth historical period (1976). Contributions to the literature after that point in time were judged to be too recent to properly assess their influence on counseling psychology.

A second constellation of theories which have had a substantive impact on counseling psychology are those directed to explaining aspects of vocational psychology, occupational choice, and career development. As with the theories of personality, counseling, and psychotherapy which have had pre-eminent influence on counseling psychology, the principal theories of vocational psychology, occupational choice, and career development emerged during different historical periods. Some of the theories, such as the trait and factor, trace their origins to the first historical period prior to 1950 and have remained influential. Others, such as the social learning approach, did not appear in the literature in systematic form until the middle 1970s and have therefore only recently begun to be the subject of systematic empirical inquiry.

While scholars in the field of career development, vocational psychology, and occupational choice such as Osipow (1983) and Brown and Brooks (1984) differ somewhat in how they categorize this constellation of theories, there is a high degree of consensus on which have been the most influential on counseling psychology. Influential theories are associated with the work of the following researchers and their associates: Anne Roe, John Holland, Donald Super, David Tiedeman and Robert O'Hara, John Krumboltz, and Eli Ginzberg. Additional influential theories, the psychoanalytic/psychodynamic and the trait and factor, are somewhat less identified with principal parentage since they date from an earlier phase in counseling psychology's first historical period.

Finally, there have been other influential contributions to counseling psychology in the general area of vocational psychology, career choice, and career development which do not fit neatly within a theoretical orientation, such as the pioneering work of Frank Parsons (Parsons, 1909) and the first edition of the *Dictionary of Occupational Titles* compiled by the staff of the United States Employment Service in 1939. It is beyond the scope of this general history of counseling psychology to deal with the evolution of the constructs within each principal theory or with those contributions within vocational psychology, career choice, and career development (such as relevant tests and measurements and instrumentation) which are not integral to the basic influential theories.

Chapter 1
Formative Influences in the First Half of the 20th Century: The First Historical Period

Counseling psychology as a contemporary applied-scientific specialty in psychology has grown to its current status from numerous and diverse roots in the 20th century.

HISTORICAL ROOTS OF COUNSELING PSYCHOLOGY

The diverse initial roots include the work of Parsons and his associates in Boston and the growth of the vocational guidance movement. The impetus for this initial root may be traced to the diversity of careers available as a consequence of the growth of U.S. industry, the rapid expansion of secondary school enrollments, and the floundering in the labor market of many young men and women. These trends combined to create new conditions of educational opportunity and occupational choice. Parsons and his associates in Boston provided vocational assistance to young people through the Bread Winners Institute, a branch of Civic Service House. This service, in turn, led to the founding of the Boston Vocational Bureau in 1908. The purpose of the Vocational Bureau was to relate occupational aptitudes and interests to the vocational choices and job seeking of young men (Parsons, 1909). Parsons also started a counselor training program designed "to fit young men to become vocational counselors and manage vocational bureaus in connection with Young Men's Christian Associations, schools, colleges, universities, public school systems, associations, and business establishments anywhere in the country" (Miller, 1961, p. 27).

In March of 1910 the organized vocational guidance movement achieved national prominence with the convening of the First National Conference on Vocational Guidance sponsored by the Boston Chamber of Commerce. The National Vocational Guidance Association was founded in 1913. The needs for guidance at the time were identified as:

economic   the need for a better and more efficiently selected body of employees in industry;

1

educational   the need for wise choices of education programs by pupils; and

social   the preservation of society. (Miller, 1961, pp. 31-32)

A goal of the vocational guidance movement was to improve the vocational choices of young adults through the provision of guidance services in community agencies and in the public schools. Such services were oriented primarily toward more systematically matching individual occupational aptitudes and interests to appropriate jobs. This progressive political reform movement was aimed at eradicating poverty and substandard living conditions spawned by rapid industrialization and the consequent migration of people to major urban centers at the turn of the 20th Century.

A second root of counseling psychology is the mental hygiene movement. An early 20th Century force in this movement was a book by Clifford Beers (1908), *A Mind That Found Itself*. He documented his personal experiences with a mental breakdown and subsequent commitment to a mental hospital. The conditions under which mentally ill persons were confined were brought to the attention of the public by this book, and it served to increase interest in mental hygiene. In addition Beers helped found the National Committee for Mental Hygiene in 1909. Concern with mental health has continued to expand throughout this century, and since its inception, counseling psychology has been deeply involved with this issue.

A third historical root of counseling psychology is the psychometric movement and the study of individual differences. Concomitant with the rise of the vocational guidance movement were developments taking place in France that would serve to move vocational guidance into mainstream psychology for the first time. Specifically, the psychometric movement and the study of individual differences, stimulated by Alfred Binet's (Binet & Henri, 1895; Binet & Simon, 1905; Binet, 1907) work on the measurement of intelligence, provided the impetus. Those interested in the objective assessment of aptitudes and interests now had a vehicle and method with which to begin the task.

During World War I, psychologists under the direction of Walter Dill Scott (a founding father of industrial-organizational psychology) in the Army's Committee on Classification of Personnel were given the task of developing methods to place civilian recruits into appropriate military jobs. This "on-the-job training" with psychometric methods served participating psychologists well as they left the military. Postwar activities of such "applied" psychologists were oriented largely to the psychometric study of individual differences in personality, interests, and abilities, and to the analyses of abilities and skills required in specific jobs.

Super (1955a) has provided an excellent history of the transition from vocational guidance to counseling psychology and of the vocational guidance and psychometric movements' roots. While World War I caused a partial merging of these roots, Super observed:

> That the merger was only partial was made clear by the different emphases, in the 1920s, of educators such as John Brewer (1932), with his stress on exploratory experiences in guidance, and of psychologists such as Clark Hull (1928), with his hopes for psychological tests as the basis of vocational counseling. (Super, 1955a, p. 4)

The depression of the 1930s had the consequence of increasing attention to both the job placement and educational functions of vocational guidance. As Super summarized the situation of the late 1930s, "The union of education, of social work, and of psychometrics in the vocational guidance of youth and adults was now somewhat more complete" (Super, 1955a, p. 4).

The 1956 report of the Committee on Definition of the Division of Counseling Psychology illustrates well how developments in psychometrics and individual differences influenced the profession:

> the psychometric movement and the study of individual differences got under way, bearing fruit in the 1930s in programs such as the occupational ability pattern research of the Minnesota Employment Stabilization Research Institute (Paterson & Darley, 1936). Psychometric research workers joined forces with proponents of vocational orientation, and the revitalized vocational guidance movement proclaimed that "vocational guidance is now possible" (McConn, 1935). Individual differences in aptitudes and interests could now be studied in relation to occupations, and students and clients could be given adequate information about occupational opportunities and requirements. (APA, 1956, p. 283.* Also in Whiteley, 1980c, pp. 93-94).

The psychometric movement itself served to greatly increase society's appreciation of individual differences in intelligence, aptitudes, interests, and personality types. The interested reader is referred to Anastasi (1954, 1958) and Cronbach (1956, 1969) for an extended treatment of the intertwined development of the psychometric movement and the psychology of individual differences.

A fourth historical root of counseling psychology is the development of counseling and psychotherapy from nonmedical and nonpsychoanalytic perspectives, particularly stimulated by Carl R. Rogers' book, *Counseling and Psychotherapy* (Rogers, 1942a). Prior to the appearance

---

*This and all other quotations from this source are from *American Psychologist, 11*, 282-285. Copyright 1956 by the American Psychological Association. In the public domain.

of Rogers' work, psychotherapy was dominated by the view that only properly trained psychiatrists were qualified to perform psychotherapy. At the same time, the major focus of counseling psychology was in the areas of assessment and diagnosis stimulated by the psychometric movement. Super (1955a) noted that all three textbooks on counseling methods published in the 1930s dealt exclusively with diagnostics. However, the appearance of Rogers' book with its explicit assumption that one could perform psychotherapy without a medical degree (or any degree at all, for that matter) almost overnight expanded counseling psychology's focus to include personal counseling and psychotherapeutic activities. In fact, the early 1950s saw the publication of 10 textbooks on counseling methods, and only three retained their exclusively vocational, diagnostic, and assessment emphases (Super, 1955a).

In the 1940s, the impact of developments in theories of psychotherapy on counseling psychology was not necessarily direct. The reasons for this were articulated by the Committee on Definition of the Division of Counseling Psychology in 1956:

> In the 1940s, the influence of the psychoanalytic concepts of repression and anxiety and their significances for the understanding of behavior began to be felt. As those who worked with problems of personality and emotional development communicated with those who worked with problems of educational and vocational planning and adjustment, the unity of the task became apparent. As personality and learning theory became clarified, and as their role in counseling was more widely recognized, it became apparent that earlier concepts of counseling as restricted to the matching of individual abilities and interests with occupational requirements needed to be modified. At the same time, psychotherapeutic methods were being modified and described in terms that made them usable in everyday counseling situations. (APA, 1956, p. 283. Also in Whiteley, 1980c, p. 94)

Once the direct relevance to the conduct of counseling sessions was established, theories of psychotherapy had a much greater impact on counseling psychology.

In writing a commentary on a book about the history of counseling psychology, Fletcher (1981) indicated that insufficient attention has been given to the importance of several developments of the 1930s. The first was the role of the Occupational Analysis Section of the United States Employment Service, including the construction of the *Dictionary of Occupational Titles*. The second was the rise in counseling and testing at universities in the United States.[1] The third was the impact of Army and Navy programs during World War II concerning selection, classification, testing, and psychological screening.

A fifth historical root of counseling psychology is the social and economic forces and developments in society which have had an impact on the profession. Schwebel (1984) provided a very useful service to those who have an interest in how movements in social history (rather than developments of a professional or scientific nature) predominated in shaping the first historical period. He drew attention to a number of the conditions which prevailed after World War II that coalesced to generate counseling psychology:

> Among those conditions were (1) the personal and career problems of adjustment faced by vast numbers of veterans, including those handicapped during the war; (2) the influx of new types of students to higher education as a result of the G.I. Bill of Rights, an influx comparable to the compositional changes in the secondary school earlier in the century; (3) increased acceptability of psychological services by the general public, and in fact, their hunger for them, an appetite that was exploited by many a charlatan, as revealed by Steiner (1945); (4) growth in size, status and influence of the APA; and (5) recognition of the need for a scientific basis for professional practice at a time on the one hand, when the federal government and private foundations were enlarging their financial support for research and, on the other, when American universities were commencing their drive to become centers of research. (Schwebel, 1984, p. 285)

This was the first time there was an active concern about the need to develop a scientific basis for professional practice.

Thus, by the end of the Second World War a largely social and political reform movement (vocational guidance), the mental hygiene movement, three influences from organized psychology (psychometrics, the psychology of individual differences, and psychotherapy), and the effects of two world wars merged to produce a field of applied-scientific psychology that had greatly outgrown its vocational guidance roots, and which provided a unique blend of service orientation and research activity.

POSTWAR INFLUENCES (1946-1950): THE VETERANS ADMINISTRATION

World War II, as noted in the previous section, created an "unprecedented demand for psychological services" (Pepinsky, Hill-Frederick, and Epperson, 1978). During the war psychologists were involved in helping create a wartime army from the ranks of civilian draftees and volunteers. After the war, psychologists helped meet a massive demand to return veterans back into civilian life by assisting them with problems of personal and vocational adjustment.

The Veterans Administration was given the public mandate of taking on this task by the creation of two new major programs of rehabilitation: educational and occupational, and emotional. Their decision to involve counseling psychology in achieving the public mandate was to have a major positive impact on the profession. The reason for establishing the "Counseling Psychologist (Vocational)" position in the VA was indicated by Vice Admiral J. T. Boone, Chief Medical Director of the Veterans Administration. He stated that:

> the medical job is not really complete until the veteran has been restored to a life as socially productive and personally satisfying as possible and that it has become increasingly clear that vocational problems and conflicts are often inextricably interwoven with illness. (*Counseling News and Views*, 1952, Vol. 5, No. 1, p. 16)

In a related development, the education and training issues were addressed by the VA's Division of Vocational Rehabilitation and Education, which contracted with colleges and universities for assistance in order to better fulfill the unprecedented need for services. Pepinsky (1984, in press) described the time well:

> Toward the end of the War, the USA's Veterans Administration was assigned the mission of assisting millions of veterans to return to civilian life. Lack of sufficient adequately trained personnel for this work within the VA forced it to seek outside help. The VA's Division of Vocational Rehabilitation and Education thus supplemented its internal counseling services by contracting with colleges and universities to provide for the vocational-educational "advisement" of ex-service men and women, so as to guide them into appropriate programs of education or training. As Mitchell Dreese pointed out in 1949, numerous community and college counseling centers, recently established, owed their existence to initial subsidy by the VA.*

As can be inferred from this, the VA had a direct impact on community and college counseling centers. Pepinsky et al. (1978) expanded on the training impact:

> If the services were to be performed—so went the reasoning among psychologists who were politically active at the time—there also must be persons trained to offer them. Older, established programs of graduate training, as the University of Minnesota, The Ohio State

---

*This and all other quotations from this source are from "A History of Counseling Psychology" by H. B. Pepinsky. In R. Corsini (Ed.), *Encyclopedia of psychology*. Copyright © 1984 by John Wiley & Sons, Inc. Reprinted by permission.

University, and Teachers College, Columbia University, were re-constituted, expanded, and formalized. (Pepinsky et al., 1978, p. 485. Also in Whiteley, 1980c, p. 50)

The emotional concerns of veterans were addressed by another unit within the Veterans Administration, the Division of Medicine and Neurology. Pepinsky (1984, in press) described the chronology:

> Under a second mandate, to assist returning veterans with "emo-tional" problems, the VA's Division of Medicine and Neurology also had established within its hospitals and outpatient clinics the post of Clinical Psychologist, a move accompanied by the public announcement in 1946 of the Division of Clinical Psychology—No. 12—as yet another charter division of the reorganized APA. Con-currently, too, a number of doctoral training programs for clinical psychologists were established within universities' departments of psychology. In 1950, Victor Raimy's report of an APA-sponsored conference on *Training in Clinical Psychology* was published. It recommended the content, standards, and modes of doctoral training for that specialty.
>
> By 1950, negotiations were underway among representatives from the APA's Division 12 and 17 and the VA's Central Office staff in Clinical Psychology to create in the medical setting yet another position for psychologists. That could happen if the Division of Counseling and Guidance[2] were to explicate and upgrade its standards for training and practice to the level which Clinical Psy-chology had set for itself. The staff person would help emotionally disturbed veterans to obtain and maintain suitable gainful employ-ment outside the hospital. Since the proposed activities ostensibly required something other than knowledge of neurological impair-ment and psychopathology, the new position would serve as a lever to move all of psychology out from under psychiatry's control.

The theme of establishing counseling psychology as outside the domain of psychiatry was not new. But the theme of establishing it as distinct from clinical psychology was just beginning, and in 1952 the Veterans Administration formally established a new Counseling Psychologist position.

THE AMERICAN PSYCHOLOGICAL ASSOCIATION

The move to establish counseling psychology as a separate discipline, however, did not occur solely within the Veterans Administration—it was within the American Psychological Association itself. Nineteen forty-six was a watershed year in this regard. Pepinsky et al.'s (1978) description is as follows:

If 1946 was a time of accelerated change for institutionalized psychology, it was also marked by organizational change within the American Psychological Association. No longer was the association to be dominated by persons who prided themselves on being "pure" psychologists and for whom "professional practice" was an object of contempt. At the historic convention in Philadelphia, a merger having been effected between APA and the American Association for Applied Psychology, the APA itself was reorganized into a conglomerate of divisions. Nearly half of these had distinct implications for professional practice—for example, the Divisions of Clinical Psychology (12), Consulting Psychology (13), Industrial Psychology (14), Educational Psychology (15), School Psychology (16), Counseling and Guidance (17), Psychologists in Public Service (18), and Military Psychology (19). To mark the occasion further, Carl Rogers—an avowedly applied psychologist—was introduced at the annual convention as President-Elect of the APA. (Pepinsky, et al., 1978, p. 485. Also in Whiteley, 1980c, p. 50)

DIVISION 17 AND INITIAL DEFINITIONS

The founding of Division 17 of the American Psychological Association has been described in several sources (Super, 1955a; Scott, 1980; Pepinsky, 1984). The initial creation of Division 17 stemmed from the 1943 Joint Constitutional Committee of the APA and the American Association of Applied Psychology. In a ballot mailed to 6,000 psychologists in 1944, the returns from 3,680 members identified personnel psychology as second only to clinical as an area of interest. Hilgard (1945) concluded that "the center of gravity of interests of psychologists has shifted toward applied fields" (p. 22-23). Scott (1980) cited Anderson (1944) in noting that write-ins for guidance, vocational, and education "presumably influenced the choice of the title 'Division of Personnel and Guidance Psychologists' as the first official name of Division 17" (Scott, 1980, p. 26). Scott (1980) remains the best source of information on the key events immediately following World War II which established Division 17, and the interested reader is referred to that source for details.

The principal affiliations of counseling psychologists, as distinct from clinical psychologists, were in effect then and remain largely in place today:

As noted here and earlier, Division 17 came into being as a charter division of the APA under the title of "Counseling and Guidance." That was in recognition of common ground among founding parents —for example, Hugh Bell, Edward Bordin, John G. Darley, Mitchell Dreese, Frank Fletcher, William Gilbert, Milton Hahn, Francis

Robinson, Winfield Scott, Dewey Stuit, Donald Super, Edmund Williamson, and Gilbert Wrenn, who were university teachers and administrators or, like George Bennett and Harold Seashore, who were in the business of producing and selling psychological tests. Almost all of these persons had overlapping memberships in two non-APA organizations: the American College Personnel Association (ACPA)—centered on student personnel work in colleges and universities—and the National Vocational Guidance Association (NVGA)—largely concerned with vocational guidance activities at the junior and senior high school levels. Although several of that group also were members of the APA's Division of Clinical Psychology, relatively few were visibly identified with clinical as well as counseling psychology. (Pepinsky et al., 1978, p. 485-486. Also in Whiteley, 1980c, p. 50-51)

Division 17 of the American Psychological Association has had five names during its history,[3] beginning in 1944: the Division of Personnel Psychologists (Pepinsky, 1984), the Division of Personnel and Guidance Psychologists (Scott, 1980), the Division of Counseling and Guidance Psychologists (Scott, 1984), the Division of Counseling and Guidance (Pepinsky, et al., 1978), and after August 29-30, 1951, Counseling Psychology (Wrenn, 1984). (This latter designation became offical APA policy at the time of the 1953 annual convention.)[4]

The original purposes of Division 17 remain of historical importance and merit repeating:

The purpose of the organization shall be:

a. to extend the techniques and methods of psychology to counseling and guidance activities in vocational, personal, educational, and group adjustments, including the disciplinary and behavioral problems encountered in educational institutions;
b. to promote high standards of practice in the psychometric, diagnostic, and therapeutic phases of counseling and guidance, as they are carried out in educational institutions, governmental agencies, private practice, and in the community, non-profit agencies that are spreading throughout the country;
c. to encourage and support scientific and professional inquiry into all aspects of counseling and guidance;
d. to assist in the formulations of professional standards and ethical codes for workers in the field of counseling and guidance;
e. to assist in the promulgation of adequate scholastic and professional training requirements for workers in these fields;
f. to collaborate with those clinical psychologists who are primarily attached to medical activities in arriving at definitions and work-

ing relationships between these related psychological specialties. (Scott, 1980, p. 29)*

The second statement of purpose of Division 17, appearing in 1949, was as follows:

1. The name of this organization shall be the Division of Counseling and Guidance of the American Psychological Association.

2. The purpose of this Division is to bring together psychologists specializing in counseling and guidance and to further the development of practice and research in this field. Such an organization has a unique contribution to make in the professional and technical development of counseling and guidance, supplementing the promotional and organizational work of kindred associations whose membership includes professional workers in other fields.

The interests of the Division are classified and described under three major headings:

a. Scientific Investigation

(1) to encourage surveys of research in the field of counseling and guidance, summarizing present knowledge and practices;
(2) to isolate problems in special need of investigation in this area; and
(3) to encourage research projects pertinent to administration and practice in this field, defined in section *b*, by members of the Division and by other appropriate groups.

b. Administration and Practice

(1) to extend the application of the methods and techniques of psychology to counseling and guidance in educational, vocational, and personal adjustment, whether in educational institutions, industrial or business enterprises, government agencies, social agencies, or in private practice;
(2) to promote high standards of practice in the use of individual and group psychometric, diagnostic, and counseling techniques; in the use of educational, occupational, and related information; and in the development of organizational patterns and administrative procedures in the above types of organizations and practice;

(3) to assist in the formulation and observance of a code of ethics for professional psychologists, and to cooperate with other professional associations in the development of a similar code for counseling and guidance workers; and

(4) to formulate appropriate requirements of professional education and experience for specialists in counseling and guidance and to promote their adoption, in cooperation with kindred professional associations and agencies.

c. Dissemination of Information

(1) to organize and promote pertinent meetings and conferences, with or without its positive recommendation;

(2) to encourage the preparation and publication of critical reviews of research and practice in counseling and guidance;

(3) to encourage the preparation and publication of manuals and other aids;

(4) to facilitate the exchange of information and experience within the membership of the Division; and

(5) to promote public understanding of counseling and guidance. (*Counseling News and Views*, 1949, Vol. 1, No. 3, p. 19-20)

The notion that the Division membership was composed of psychologists was one which was frequently amplified upon in subsequent statements. A third bylaws change occurred in 1954 (Scott, 1980, p. 29-30) which incorporated the name change from counseling and guidance to counseling psychology.

From its inception, therefore, counseling psychology has had a broad charge to promote "educational, vocational, and personal adjustment" in a variety of settings which include education, business, government, social agencies, and private practice. Nearly 40 years later these themes and settings remain constant.

Finally, in *Counseling News and Views*, the official newsletter of Division 17 from 1948 to 1968, President Hugh Bell articulated chief concerns of counseling psychologists at the time:

In thinking of the school year 1948-1949 and the work of our Division, these are some of the problems on which I feel we should be working:

1. Meeting the demand for new personnel workers.
2. Providing in-service training for individuals now on the job.
3. Developing more effective standards for admission to graduate study in personnel work.
4. Raising training standards by providing more meaningful internship experience, adapting training procedures to different age

levels and different kinds of counseling activities, and coordinating training activities within a given institution.

5. Coordinating our plans and procedures with the National Vocational Guidance Association and the American College Personnel Association.
6. Keeping the public informed on what personnel work is and the part it has in a community service program. (*Newsletter*, 1948, Vol. 1, No. 1, p. 1)

This inaugural newsletter of Division 17 merits a detailed scrutiny as it serves as a benchmark from which to understand the later growth of organized counseling psychology. The Committee on Counselor Training was just getting started, as is reflected in its annual report:

The Counselor Training Committee activities for the year just passed have consisted largely of getting organized. Since it has been impossible to have a face-to-face meeting, all decisions have been reached by correspondence. The Committee sponsored a symposium on the training of counselors at the 1948 A.P.A. meeting. A status study of training offered in the guidance field is being set up. The Committee is working closely with the National Vocational Guidance Association Committee on the preparation of a manual entitled THE PROFESSIONAL PREPARATION OF COUNSELORS. Many of the Committee members are also members of this NVGAC. (*Newsletter*, 1948, Vol. 1, No. 1, p. 4)

The close association with the National Vocational Guidance Association is obvious.

The Committee on Research was also just getting started. They had three projects for the year:

1. To stimulate the preparation of a survey of the research in counseling for publication in the *Psychological Bulletin*.
2. To prepare an outline of needed research in the field which would come down to specific proposed experiments, such that a number of members of the division would be stimulated to actually perform them. The Committee thought it would use a 10-year perspective in its planning with the idea that perhaps at the end of 10 years a future committee would survey the degree to which the proposed research has been followed up and set up a new proposal.
3. To act as a potential coordinator of attempts to duplicate the suggested research projects by investigators in different areas of the country working in rather diverse settings. (*Newsletter*, 1948, Vol. 1, No. 1, p. 4)

The *Psychological Bulletin* was viewed as the appropriate outlet for research publications, and the need to create an outlet more specific to counseling was recognized. Such a research journal for counseling psychology was first to appear six years later.

   In terms of the composition and distribution of Division 17 members in 1948, Mitchell Dreese (Secretary of Division 17) reported on a survey he did in cooperation with Mary Josephina Carroll. Several tables are of historical interest. At the time of this survey, slightly over 50% of the membership were employed in institutions of higher education with another 19% employed by the Veterans Administration. Only 5% were in private practice.

Table 1.1

**Occupations of Members of the Division
of Counseling and Guidance in 1948**

Occupation	Assoc.	Fellows	Total	Percent
College or University Instructor in Counseling and Guidance	40	27	67	13.06
Director or Counselor in College or University Guidance Center	116	61	177	34.50
Clinical Psychologist in College or University	9	4	13	2.53
Director or Counselor in City Public School Guidance Program	11	6	17	3.31
Director or Counselor in County Public School Guidance Program	11	0	11	2.15
Director or Supervisor of State Guidance Program	14	2	16	3.12
Veterans Administration, Rehabilitation and Training Division, Central, Branch, or Regional Office	75	10	85	16.57
Clinical Psychologists, Veterans Administration	12	2	14	2.73
Employee Counselor A. Business or Industry	13	3	16	3.12
B. Federal Service	6	1	7	1.37
Personnel Administrator A. Business or Industry	16	6	22	4.29
B. Federal Service	12	5	17	3.31
Public Welfare Agency	20	5	25	4.87
Private Practitioner	14	12	26	5.07
Total	369	144	513	100.00

At the time of this survey, 79% of the membership were men; 21% women. Four hundred eighty-five of the membership had Master's degrees; 282 had earned the doctorate. The doctoral degrees had been earned at 54 different institutions, though six institutions accounted for 54% of the total: Columbia (16%), Ohio State University (9%), Minnesota (9%), New York University (8%), Iowa (6%), and Yale (6%).

Organizational affiliations and expressed research interests provide further clues to the thinking and interests of Division 17 members, as Table 1.2 indicates.

Table 1.2

**Professional Organizations in Which Members of
Division 17 Commonly Hold Membership**

(As reported on the 1948 APA Yearbook Questionnaires)

Organization	Assoc.	Fellows	Total	Percent
National Vocational Guidance Association	155	51	206	40
American Association for the Advancement of Science	48	42	90	18
American College Personnel Association	45	36	81	16
American Psychological Association (Designated by State)	52	29	81	16
American Association of University Professors	17	14	31	6
Academy of Science (Designated by State)	15	14	29	5
National Educational Association	16	6	22	4
American Educational Research Association	7	14	21	4
Psychometric Society	8	9	17	3
American Statistical Association	11	5	16	3

(*Newsletter*, 1948, Vol. 1, No. 1, p. 10)

Forty percent of Division 17 members had an organizational affilia-
tion with the National Vocational Guidance Association, followed by the
American Association for the Advancement of Science (18%) and the
American College Personnel Association (16%).[5]

The expressed research interests covered a wide array of topics, as
Table 1.3 indicates. While this table does not inform the reader about
research actually conducted, it illustrates that research interests of
Division 17 members were centered on vocational counseling, personnel
psychology, psychology of personality, physiological psychology, and
aptitude measurement.

Table 1.3

**Expressed Research Interests of the Members of
the Counseling and Guidance Division of APA**

(Based on 1948 APA Year Book Data)

Expressed Interests	Assoc.	Fellows	Total
Abnormal Psychology	16	7	23
Adjustment	24	13	37
Applied Psychology	1	0	1
Children			
Adolescents	4	4	8
Juvenile Delinquents	8	2	10
Exceptional	7	1	8
College Students	17	10	27
Corrective Education	21	11	32
Counseling	51	12	63
Educational Counseling	45	11	56
Personal Counseling	18	2	20
Psychological Counseling	11	0	11
Techniques of Counseling	5	7	12
Veterans Counseling	2	0	2
Vocational Counseling	98	23	121
Emotions	3	3	6
Experimental Psychology	10	5	15
Industrial Psychology	51	23	74
Marriage Prediction and Counseling	4	2	6
Medical Psychology (including Psychosomatics)	6	7	13

Table 1.3 (Continued)

**Expressed Research Interests of the Members of
the Counseling and Guidance Division of APA**

(Based on 1948 APA Year Book Data)

Expressed Interests	Assoc.	Fellows	Total
Mental Hygiene	10	6	16
Military Psychology	2	3	5
Personnel Psychology	76	54	130
Philosophical Psychology	2	0	2
Physiological Psychology	35	40	75
Prison Psychology	1	0	1
Psychology of Education	13	4	17
Psychology of Maturity	3	2	5
Psychology of Personality	32	52	84
Psychometrics	31	15	46
Psychotherapy	51	18	69
Clinical Methods	16	7	23
Group Therapy	11	3	14
Projective Techniques	59	13	72
Research, General	12	10	22
Statistics	12	5	17
Test Techniques	24	23	47
Tests & Measurements	29	8	37
Achievement Tests	28	14	42
Aptitude Measurement	64	18	82
Attitude & Opinion	15	12	27
Diagnostic Testing	29	14	43
Intelligence	16	10	26
Interest	17	11	28
Special Abilities	6	3	9

Vewsletter, 1948, Vol. 1, No. 1, pp. 10-12)

CONTROVERSIES OVER THE DESIGNATION OF A NAME

The search for a definitive name began early as is shown by Milton Hahn's statement in the Feburary 1949 issue of the *Newsletter of the Division of Counseling and Guidance*. This statement is important because it outlined the objections to the name of Division 17 (Counseling and Guidance):

Last September at the Executive Committee meeting of Division 17, there was a discussion of the proposed new constitution of the division. At that time we considered the relevancy of the present division title, *Counseling and Guidance*. Not only did some of us present feel that this title is ambiguous and inappropriate, but such a feeling seems to exist among members of the division not at the meetings.

Because the word 'clinical' has acquired a quite narrow meaning in the APA, a large group of psychologists has been left without an appropriate professional name. The individuals in this group are those who usually are affiliated with educational institutions at the college level; as yet we have only a small secondary school representation in Division 17. The literature identifies us as *clinical* psychologists, but within the APA the *Division of Clinical Psychology* is composed of psychologists who either are medically oriented, or whose primary interest is nonmedical psychotherapy. We differ from these psychological brethren in our basic training patterns, our interests, and, to some degree, the types of institutions or private practice in which we engage. Perhaps we can be described as clinical psychologists who usually work with clients within the normal range of adjustment, diagnose in all major problem areas and, using the interview as our major therapeutic tool, apply most of our time for therapy with problems designated as education-vocational. We also find ourselves engaged in therapy with clients having poor emotional and social adjustments not requiring depth therapy. We tend to be quite eclectic in the choice of our diagnostic tools and techniques. The breadth of our diagnostic endeavors appears to me to offer a suitable name for the division.

What are the objections to the present title of the division? There are several. First, 'counseling' is a generic term which includes a wide range of efforts ranging from the professional level to such part-time, nonprofessional endeavors as summer camp 'counselors.' Secondly, the term does not serve a meaningful descriptive purpose. We cut too broadly if we speak of 'counseling psychologists,' and we encounter also some semantic difficulties.

A third objection often voiced, is the inclusion of the term 'guidance' in the division title. General usage tends to attach guidance to the curriculum and co-curriculum of the secondary school.

The 'guidance' worker functions as a quasi-administrative intermediary between and among the secondary school administration, teaching staff, curriculum, the students and community. His formal preparation for professional practice tends to center in professional education with a minor concentration in psychology. This group of educational specialists has an excellent national organization of its own — the *National Vocational Guidance Association*. This organization has established a clear prior claim to 'guidance.' At the college level we are increasingly finding the clinical psychologist as a counseling specialist within the framework of the *student personnel program*, not a college or university 'guidance' program. Some of us believe that we confuse the issue of names for other organizations and fail to describe ourselves accurately if we employ the term 'guidance' in our divisional title. The term 'guidance psychologist' has a strange ring.

Perhaps we can be described best by our functions as *generalized specialists* or *specialized generalists*? It is difficult to identify us by our therapeutic tools and techniques because of our almost complete reliance on the interview. It is, perhaps, from our eclectic and widespread collection of diagnostic tools and techniques that a name can be drawn. For purposes of generating discussion, I propose that the Committee on the Constitution for Division 17 consider the title, *The Division of General Clinical Psychology* or *Clinical Counseling* (*Newsletter*, 1949, Vol. 1, No. 2, p. 3)

The objections Hahn raised to the name of Division 17 appear to summarize the concerns of many members, as there remained a continual reappraisal until a new name was officially adopted in 1953.

As part of a continuing concern with the definition of the specialty, Bordin (1949) offered a viewpoint on the matter:

The assumption which shall be made here is that the area of Division 17 can be differentially defined as being concerned with the clinical treatment of psychological problems of the normal or near-normal individual. Although not necessarily confined to interview treatment, this is the dominant focus of treatment programs as now seen by the members of this group.

Let us examine this definition to determine to what extent it enables us to establish the uniqueness of the Division, starting with the relation to Clinical and Abnormal. The dominant concern of that Division is the professional and technical problems of the clinician working in the medical psychiatric setting. Thus, in thinking about training programs and about certification, this Division has represented the needs of psychologists working in close relation to psychiatrists, psychiatric social workers, and other medical practitioners. Theoretical discussions in this Division are likely to deal with the diagnosis of psychiatrically defined disorders or with psychological effects of physiological disorders, e.g., psychological evidences of brain damage as reflected in the Wechsler-Bellevue or the TAT. Research is also dominated by concern with the abnormal. Now, it might well be argued that diagnosis and treatment of the normal and near normal can only be artificially distinguished from that of the abnormal, and future research and theory construction may well substantiate this position. Certainly, the line between "near normal" and abnormal must always be vaguely drawn. Yet, at the present time the diagnostic and treatment emphases in counseling are considerably different from those in clinical work with the abnormal. In addition, since most counselors operate more or less independent of a medical relationship, there is a rather different orientation toward the types of problems faced in inter-professional relationships. (*Newsletter*, 1949, Vol. 1, No. 2, p. 4)

The centrality of the concern with problems of normality has continued to appear in subsequent statements defining the parameters of counseling psychology.

The quest for a divisional name was paralleled by a search for a newsletter name. Vol. 1, No. 2 of the *Newsletter* marked the appearance of suggestions for the permanent name of this publication. The list of possible titles suggested by the membership reflects the diversity of opinion within the Division:

Counseling Cues
Guidance News
Guidance Gains
Guidance Glimpses
Guidance Grapevine
Guidance Grist
Counseling Channels
Counseling Commentary
Counseling Chords
Counseling Lines
Counsel-Lines
C and G News
Counseling News and Views
(*Newsletter*, 1949, Vol. 1, No. 2, p. 2)

Counseling News and Views was selected as the title, after a mail ballot, and the publication continued as a source of professional communication within counseling psychology for the next two decades.

The inaugural issue with the *Counseling News and Views* title appeared as Vol. 1, No. 3. Noteworthy in this issue was a response to Milton Hahn's suggestion of titles for the Division as *Division of Clinical*

Counseling or *Division of General Clinical Psychology*. The initial reaction on whether to change the name was as follows:

1. Rejection of "guidance" in the title, 14 to 1
2. Inclusion of "counseling" in the title, 14 to 5
3. Desire for a modification of the present title, 14 to 1
   (*Counseling News and Views*, 1949, Vol. 1, No. 3, p. 4)

The sentiment for change was clearly very strong, and it persisted until a satisfactory solution was reached with the choice of *Counseling News and Views*.

Finally, writings by officers or former officers of Division 17 began to reflect the primacy of psychology in considerations of policy and practice for Division 17. Bell (1949) provided an example in a contribution titled "The Psychologist as a Counselor."

> In the new By-Laws of the Division of Counseling and Guidance appears this statement: "The purpose of this Division is to bring together psychologists specializing in counseling and guidance and to further the development of practice and research in this field."
>
> This formulation of purpose for Division 17 places emphasis upon the fact that our Division is composed of *qualified* psychologists, individuals who by reason of their interests, abilities, and training meet the high professional standards of psychologists as a group. The importance of having highly qualified psychological counselors is pointed out in a recent statement by Malcom Willey. He writes, "The surest safeguard against adverse campus reactions to student counseling . . . is sound scholarship, grounded in research and caution in claims of infallability." Thorough scholarship as it applies to the study of human behavior is, then, the first requirement for a psychologist who specializes in counseling.
>
> But the counselor must be more than a recognized student of human behavior skilled in research, statistics, and experimental design. He must also possess an abiding desire to be of intelligent help and assistance to human beings. The counselor must have a spontaneous interest in people as persons and have the desire to assist them in the fullest possible realization of their potentialities. Without scholarly training, a counselor is only a blind do-gooder; but without warmth of human helpfulness the counselor becomes a cold precision instrument ineffective in translating his scholarship into the lives of the individuals with whom he comes in contact.
>
> In addition to sound scholarship and a helpful attitude towards students' problems, the psychological counselor must have a clear understanding of the limits of his field of specialization, plan and carry out his work in such a manner that related professional groups may readily discern the boundaries of his field so as to coordinate

their activities with his. In the paragraphs which follow, an attempt is made to describe briefly the field of operations of the psychologist who specializes in counseling.

It seems to me that the psychological counselor's field of work may be characterized as follows: (1) He works primarily with normal individuals; (2) he is a specialist in the interpretation of standardized tests, particularly group tests; (3) his counseling activities include the fields of educational, vocational, and personal adjustment; (4) he is a specialist in personality appraisal; and (5) he serves as a source of referrals to specialists in other areas related to his own.

The work of the psychological counselor differs from that of the clinical psychologist and the psychiatrist in that the human problems with which he is concerned are primarily *situational* as contrasted to problems in which there is some personality disorganization or deterioration. The latter problems naturally fall in the province of the psychiatrist. The counselor working with normal individuals assumes that there is no serious personality disorganization present in the lives of the individuals with whom he works and directs his effort towards helping individuals work out satisfactory life adjustments. If he detects signs of personality disorganization in a client, he turns the case over to a psychiatrist for diagnosis and treatment. The psychological counselor recognizes that the job of appropriate care for the neurotic, and the pre-psychotic and the psychotic is clearly outside his field and he devotes his time to normal individuals whose adjustment problems relate to their everyday living. (*Counseling News & Views*, 1949, Vol. 2, No. 1, p. 3-4)

The late 1940s were a period in the history of counseling psychology when there were frequent attempts, as with the above contribution, to distinguish the role of "psychological counseling" from that of clinical psychology and psychiatry.

Two activities commencing in 1949 reflect the attempts to define psychological counseling in the context of the other helping professions. The first activity was the Ann Arbor Conference, sponsored by the University of Michigan and Division 17, and funded by a Public Health Grant. The purpose of this conference was to "consider the most desirable plan for the training of counselors whose background is to be primarily psychological" (p. 1).[6] The report notes that psychologists were "particularly concerned with a clearer definition of the relationship between counseling and clinical psychology" (p. 1).[7]

The second activity was disclosed in the presidential message from John Darley (1949) which touched on the theme of defining counseling psychology in the context of other helping professions. After noting that clinical psychologists "appeared to be anxious to exclude other psychologists from personal service functions" (p. 2), he drew attention to the charge of a new divisional committee:

The purpose of the new committee is to consider definitions of the fields and functions of clinical psychologists, counseling and guidance psychologists, industrial psychologists, and other areas of professional application. This committee grew out of discussions held at the Boulder conference on graduate education in clinical psychology where relations between the clinical psychologists working in a medical framework and psychologists working in guidance and educational programs was a frequent topic of discussion. *Counseling News and Views*, 1949, Vol. 2, No. 1, p. 2)

Three decades later, at the time the Next Decade Project of Division 17 was set in motion, the issues with psychiatry were largely settled. Issues with clinical psychology remain at the state and national level after more than 30 years, as well as problems of exclusion from third-party payments in private practice and full licensure.

The founding of the *Annual Review of Psychology* was noted in the March 1950 issue of *Counseling News and Views* (Vol. 2, No. 2, p. 5). The *Annual Review of Psychology* has provided an opportunity for relevant literature to be carefully reviewed; it is a most important repository of the development of theory and research over three decades.

By 1950, there were changes in the composition of the membership and the settings in which they worked. A small increase in the membership of Division 17 occurred, as well as an upward shift in the proportion of members who held the doctoral degree. By 1950, 62% of the membership had earned a doctorate. Women constituted 20% of Division 17's membership. In the 1950 survey of employment locations of Division 17 members conducted by Winifred Scott (1950), there were changes from the previous sampling. The percent employed by the Veterans Administration declined to 12% (from 16%), and there was a decline of the percentage of counseling psychologists in private practice, from 5% to 3%.

Another perspective on counseling psychology as this first period in its history drew to a close is in terms of the status of the profession itself. Super (1984b) summarized that status as follows:

we were a group of practitioners in search of an identity, representatives of an applied field in search of a theoretical base. We had no established specialty name; our tools were those of vocational psychology, psychometrics, and applications of the theory of individual differences. The one clear fact about us was what we did: vocational assessment and counseling. No one else did it; the clinical psychologists who used our tools used them reluctantly and with little knowledge of the world of work; the vocational counselors who used them did so with little knowledge of psychometrics or of individual differences. (Super, 1984b, p. 279)

Table 1.4

**Employment of Division 17 Members
in Relation to Highest Academic Degree,
Fellowship and Diplomate Status, and Sex in 1950**

Place of Employment	N	% of 611	Ph.D.s	MA.	BA.	Fellows	Diplo-mates	Men
College & University	321	53	75	24	1	33	29	83
Elementary & Secondary Schools	33	5	39	61	0	21	24	52
State Department of Educ. (incl. Voc. Reh.)	7	1	0	100	0	0	40	100
Other Federal Agency	20	3	65	35	0	40	45	90
V.A.	75	12	48	49	3	16	21	92
Counseling or Psychological Agency	44	7	61	34	5	27	30	80
Hospital & Clinic (non-VA; Prison)	15	2	60	40	0	20	20	67
Private Welfare Agency	10	2	30	70	0	0	0	40
Business or Industry	27	4	48	52	0	27	31	81
Private Practice	16	3	56	44	0	25	19	50
Other (N=11) Unknown	43	7	42	49	7	23	16	81
Total Number	611		381	218	11	169	163	492
% of Total Membership	100		62	36	2	28	27	81

(*Counseling News and Views*, 1950, Vol. 3, No. 1, p. 11)

CONSTELLATIONS OF SUBSTANTIVE
THEORETICAL DEVELOPMENTS

As was stated in the introduction, there are two constellations of theories which have had a pre-eminent influence on counseling psychology: a constellation of theories of personality, counseling, and psychotherapy; and a constellation of theories of vocational psychology, occupational choice, and career development.

As a final perspective on the first period in the history of counseling psychology, the substantive theoretical developments as reflected in major articles, monographs, and books for each constellation will now be represented. Table 1.5 presents examples of important contributions to personality theory and theories of counseling and psychotherapy up to 1950. Influential on counseling psychology in its first historical period were theories of psychoanalysis, Adlerian psychotherapy and theory of personality, behavior theory and therapy, the beginnings of client-centered therapy, and humanistic and existential theory and therapy.

Table 1.5

Representative Contributions to Personality Theory
and Theories of Counseling and Psychotherapy
in the First Historical Period
(Up to 1950)

Psychoanalysis

Fenichel, Otto	The psychoanalytic theory of neurosis (1945)
Freud, Anna	The ego and the mechanisms of defense (1936)
Freud, Sigmund	Studies on hysteria (1895)
	The interpretation of dreams (1900)
	Three essays on sexuality (1905)
	The problem of anxiety (1926)
Fromm, Erich	Man for himself (1947)
Fromm-Reichman, Freida	Principles of intensive psychotherapy (1950)
Jung, C. G.	Symbols of transformation (1911)
	The archetypes and the collective unconscious (1934)

Adlerian Psychotherapy (Theory)

Adler, Alfred	Study of organ inferiority and its physical compensation (1917)
	The neurotic constitution (1926)
	The education of children (1930)
Dreikurs, R.	The challenge of marriage (1946)
	The challenge of parenthood (1948)
	Fundamentals of Adlerian psychology (1950)

Table 1.5 (Continued)

**Representative Contributions to Personality Theory
and Theories of Counseling and Psychotherapy
in the First Historical Period
(Up to 1950)**

Behavior Theory and Therapy

Bekhterev, V.	General basis of the reflex action of man (1928)
Dollard, J. & Miller, N. O.	Personality and psychotherapy (1950)
Guthrie, E. R.	The psychology of learning (1935)
Hull, C. L.	Principles of behavior (1943)
Jacobson, E.	Progressive relaxation (1938)
Pavlov, I. P.	Conditional reflexes (1927, 1941)
Salter, A.	Conditioned reflex therapy (1949)
Skinner, B. F.	The behavior of organisms (1938)
Thorndike, E. L.	The psychology of learning (1913)
Tolman, E. C.	Purposive behavior in animals and men (1932)
Watson, J. B.	Psychology from the standpoint of a behaviorist (1919)

Client-centered Therapy

Rogers, C. R.	Counseling and psychotherapy (1942)
	The use of electrically recorded interviews in psychotherapeutic techniques (1942)
	The nondirective method as a technique for social research (1945)
	Significant aspects of client-centered therapy (1946)
	Dealing with social tensions: A presentation of client-centered counseling as a method of handling interpersonal conflict (1948)

Humanistic and Existential Theory and Therapy

Buber, M.	Between man and man (1948)
Husserl, E.	Ideen zu einer reinen phanomenologie und phanomenologischen philosophie (1950)
May, R.	The art of counseling (1939)
	The meaning of anxiety (1950)

The early years of the first period in the history of counseling psychology saw the appearance of many of Sigmund Freud's seminal writings in psychoanalysis, including: *Studies on Hysteria* (1895), *The Interpretation of Dreams* (1900), *Three Essays on Sexuality* (1905), and *The Problem of Anxiety* (1926). Otto Fenichel's exhaustive treatment of psychoanalytic theory, *The Psychoanalytic Theory of Neurosis*, appeared in 1945.

The origins of Adlerian psychotherapy have been traced to 1911 (Mosak & Dreikurs, 1973) with a number of important publications by Adler appearing during counseling psychology's first period (Adler, 1914, 1917, 1926). Books and articles by Rudolf Dreikurs began to influence counseling psychologists in America with the publishing of *The Challenge of Marriage* (1946), *The Challenge of Parenthood* (1948), and *Fundamentals of Adlerian Psychology* (1950).

Behavior therapy in the United States has been traced (Goldstein, 1973) to the translation into English in 1927 of the works of Ivan Sechenov (1829-1905) and Ivan Pavlov (1849-1936). John B. Watson's influential book, *Psychology from the Standpoint of a Behaviorist*, appeared in 1919 (Watson, 1919). Subsequent learning theories offered by Guthrie (1935), Hull (1943), Tolman (1932), and Skinner (1938), among others, served as catalysts for extensive applications of behavioral psychology to problems in psychotherapy during the first historical period.

Client-centered therapy had its beginnings during the latter part of the first historical period. Meador and Rogers (1973) indicate that the real "crystallization of the core" of client-centered therapy occurred between 1937 and 1941, with the first formal paper presented in 1940 and the first book, *Counseling and Psychotherapy*, published in 1942 (Rogers, 1942a). A comprehensive, chronological bibliography of Carl R. Rogers' writings appears in Rogers (1980).

Table 1.6 presents examples of important contributions to vocational psychology, occupational choice, and career development up to 1950. From this second constellation of theories, contributions from the psychoanalytic/psychodynamic and trait and factor schools influenced counseling psychology in its first historical period. The "Life space/Life span" model associated with Donald E. Super and associates made initial contributions to the literature during this historical period.

As Super (1984a, in press) has noted, the pioneers of career development came from four disciplines:

> differential psychologists interested in work and occupation, developmental psychologists concerned with "the life course," sociologists focusing on occupational mobility as a function of social class, and personality theorists who viewed individuals as organizers of experience.

Table 1.6

**Representative Contributions to Vocational Psychology,
Occupational Choice, and Career Development
in the First Historical Period
(Up to 1950)**

Psychoanalytic/Psychodynamic

Bordin, E. S.	A theory of vocational interests as dynamic phenomena (1943) Diagnosis in counseling and psychotherapy (1946)
Brill, A. A.	Basic principles of psychoanalysis (1949)
Hendrick, I.	Work and the pleasure principle (1943)

Trait and Factor

Paterson, D. G.,
  Elliott, R. M.,
  Anderson, L. D.,
  Toops, H. A., &
  Heidbreder, E.
	Minnesota occupational rating scales and counseling profile (1941)

Paterson, D. G.,& Darley, J. G.	Men, women, and jobs (1936)

Paterson, D. G.,
  Gerken, C. A., &
  Hahn, M. E.
	The Minnesota occupational rating scales (1941)

Strong, E. K., Jr.	Vocational interests of men and women (1943)
Viteles, M. S.	Industrial psychology (1932)
Dodge, A. F.	Occupational ability patterns (1935)

Life Space/Life Span (Donald Super and Associates)

Super, D. E.	Occupational level and job satisfaction (1939) Avocational interest patterns: A study in the psychology of avocations (1940) The dynamics of vocational adjustment (1942) Appraising vocational fitness (1949)

From differential psychology he singled out Strong's work on vocational interests, the application of intelligence and aptitude tests during World War I, and practical applications during the Great Depression of the work of the Minnesota Employment Stabilization Institute spearheaded by Donald Paterson. Understanding how individuals came to acquire abilities and interests was a contribution from developmental psychology. Singled out was Buehler's (1933) study of life histories where she focused on experiences leading up to, and associated with, careers. Environmental influences on occupations were illuminated by such contributions from occupational sociology as Davidson and Anderson (1937). Warner, Meeker and Elles (1949) were viewed as less directly career oriented, but as providing a sociological background for studies of career development.

SUMMARY

Five initial roots of counseling psychology are: The work of Frank Parsons and the growth of the vocational guidance movement, concern with mental health, the psychometric movement and the study of individual differences, the development of counseling and psychotherapy from nonmedical and nonpsychoanalytic perspectives, and the social and economic forces and developments in society.

Immediately after World War II counseling psychology became a division of its own within the APA, and was at once separate from clinical psychology and not under the control of psychiatry—at least within the Veterans Administration. Yet, the profession had many tasks still undone. It lacked prescribed standards of training, education, and an agreed upon specialty title and definition. The tasks were cut out as far as developing a viable profession was concerned. These tasks were addressed for the first time during what has been identified as the second period in the history of counseling psychology. Two constellations of substantive theories were presented which have pre-eminently influenced counseling psychology: theories of personality, counseling, and psychotherapy; and theories of vocational psychology, occupational choice, and career development.

FOOTNOTES

[1]Cottle (Note 1) indicated that an impetus for the rise in counseling and testing at universities was two laws passed by Congress: "The first of these was P.L. 16 *requiring* testing and counseling of disabled veterans of World War II. The second was P.L. 346 providing optional testing and counseling of all other World War II veterans who requested it. Both of these had a tremendous impetus on the development of college counseling centers. They funded the start of many centers and provided the universities with money to subsidize counselors working in the centers who were also working on doctorates in psychological counseling and testing. The practicums arising from this activity provided excellent training for a new nucleus of members for Division 17."

[2]The Division of Counseling and Guidance was one of the early names of Division 17.

[3]There is some difference of opinion as to the exact number of names which Division 17 had between 1943 and 1953. Scott's (Note 2) view is that there were four correct names. In a communication dated September 13, 1983, he offered supporting references as follows:

Division of Personnel and Guidance Psychologists.
　Anderson, 1944, in Scott, 1980.
Division of Counseling and Guidance Psychologists.
　APA Yearbook 1946-47; November 1948, News Letter, p. 1 (Division 17).
Division of Counseling and Guidance.
　News Letter (Division 17) February, 1949, cover page.
Division of Counseling Psychology.
　Counseling News and Views, November, 1953, 6:1, p. 5.

In a subsequent communication dated July 2, 1984, he provided more detail as follows:

Verifiable names of Division 17 and applicable dates:
　From 1946 through 1950, the APA called Division 17 the Division of
　　Counseling and Guidance Psychologists.
　　APA Yearbook, 1946-47, p. 10
　　1948 Directory, p. 358.
　　1949 Directory, p. vii.
　　1950 Directory, pp. vii, 252.
　In 1951, the name was Division of Counseling and Guidance.
　　1951 Directory, pp. vii, 630.
　No directory was published in 1952.
　In 1953, the name became Division of Counseling Psychology.
　　1953 Directory, p. vii.
　No name change has occurred since 1953.

The intra-division name record of Division 17 follows:

Division 17's first bylaws, completed in 1946 and presumably adopted the same year (Scott, 1980, pp. 26-27), used the name Division of Counseling and Guidance. But the division probably accepted the official name from the outset (1946), for the cover page of the first issue of the first Newsletter, November, 1948, identified the division as the Division of Guidance and Counseling Psychologists.

From 1949 through 1952, according to cover sheets of the newsletter, Counseling and Guidance was the name of the Division. In 1953, as shown both by the cover sheet of the newsletter (*Counseling News and Views*) and as reported in minutes of the business meeting held September 5, 1953 (*Counseling News and Views*, November, 1953, p. 5), the Division of Counseling Psychology became the permanent name of the division.

During the first eight years of Division 17's existence, APA's official name and those used by the division were the same for four, presumably the same for two, and different for two, namely 1949 and 1950.

[4]Pepinsky (Note 3) helped clarify the *history* of naming the Division. "As I pointed out in the *Encyclopedia* article, concerns began before 1946. The first *public* announcement of the name occurred in 1946. With respect to the process of naming the Division 'Counseling Psychology,' the ad hoc committee's *recommendation* came out of the Northwestern Conference in 1951; the Division adopted the title officially—I don't have the data before me, but as I think I wrote—in 1952; that is also cited in our Committee report in 1956. You are quite correct in distinguishing this from the date of *APA's* adoption in 1953."

[5] Several reviewers commented upon the absence from this table of the American Association for Counseling and Development (formerly the American Personnel and Guidance Association) and the Association for Counselor Education and Supervision. Both AACD and ACES were founded after 1948. Both NVGA and ACPA were well-established at the time this survey was taken.

[6] *Training of psychological counselors: Report of a conference held at Ann Arbor,* Ann Arbor: University of Michigan Press, 1950.

[7] *Ibid.*

Chapter 2
Inaugural Definitions of the Profession: The Second Historical Period (1951-1956)

An important perspective on the second period in the history of counseling psychology may be gained from reflecting on the social forces which influenced the 1950s. Schwebel (1984) summarized them as follows:

> In the fifties, the career and interpersonal needs and problems of the many veterans and their families and the unprecedented growth in higher education enrollments created a ferment of research and experimentation, especially in the areas of career development and of counseling orientations. (p. 5-6)

Super (1984b) has referred to the 1950s as a time when counseling psychology applied differential psychology to the world of work and counseling processes to issues of vocational and occupational choice and adjustment.

SOCIETAL CONTEXT: KEYSTONES OF CONSCIOUSNESS

A second perspective on the growth of counseling psychology during the early 1950s is provided by what Schwebel (1984) has called the "keystone of consciousness." While social and economic forces may be highly influential on the profession and therefore need to be understood, counseling psychologists as professionals are much more influenced by the "keystones of consciousness." The first keystone refers to theories about human development (including career) and behavior (including social interactions). These theories grew in number and in depth of coverage during the 1930s, 1940s, and early 1950s. Client centered, directive, learning, psychodynamic, humanistic, and existential theories of counseling expanded dramatically during this period of time (see Tables 1.5 and 2.1).

The second keystone consists of social attitudes. These changed during this period of time to embrace an increased acceptability of seeking psychological services and a heightened demand for assistance with personal, educational, and career problems of adjustment.

NORTHWESTERN CONFERENCE

It was in this context of theory development and changing social attitudes that planning how to solve initial problems of professionalization became an essential task of counseling psychology.[1] The Northwestern Conference was the vehicle for addressing the problems of standards for practicum training and training psychologists at the doctoral level.

C. Gilbert Wrenn was the President of Division 17 (1950-51) at the time that the Northwestern Conference of 1951 was set in motion. Psychologists were invited from all parts of the country to develop the requirements for a doctoral program in counseling psychology. The work of the conference clustered around members of the Division's Committee on Counselor Training chaired by Francis P. Robinson. Wrenn (1984), who is uniquely qualified to write on the background of the Northwestern Conference, described the circumstances leading up to the conference as follows:

> In 1946 the Division of Counseling and Guidance of APA was initiated, largely through the efforts of John G. Darley, Director of what I believe was then called the Counseling and Testing Bureau at the University of Minnesota. The same gentleman was again largely responsible for the provision of a Diploma in Counseling and Guidance in the program of the American Board of Examiners in Professional Psychology (ABEPP), which started to function in 1947 again, I believe on that date! Both of these developments brought us squarely up against the problem of what to call counselors who had adequate preparation in psychology. *Counseling and Guidance* did not suggest this and in fact, many Ph.D.'s in Counseling and Guidance did not have much basic psychological preparation. Their degrees were secured in colleges of education, many of which were not yet convinced that basic and applied psychology courses were an essential part of the Ph.D. program.
>
> The heavy demand for clinical psychologists following World War II (in which many psychologists had been active in the medical programs of the several military services) was paralleled by the demand for student personnel workers and counselors in the burgeoning post-war universities. So while university psychology departments were preparing clinical psychologists who would serve in medical settings, both colleges of education and departments of psychology were preparing Ph.D.'s for service largely in educational institutions and in business. For these latter settings the Ph.D.'s having some educational and organizational preparation (as in colleges of education) were found quite suitable. This bothered the graduates of psychology departments. It also bothered many of us in

colleges of education who were troubled by the weakness in psychology of many of our programs. Both groups of professionals were
unhappy about the *Guidance* part of our label and wished for
something else. On the other hand *Guidance* (at that time) suited
those working in programs at the M.A. level, in particular, which
prepared people for secondary school programs. This was one of the
"itches" that brought about the Northwestern Conference (Wrenn.
1984, pp. 312-313)

What Wrenn referred to as the second "itch" which set in motion
the Greyston Conference was related to the continuing concern with
clinical psychology:

> The second major pressure was the desire to develop a program
> and a title which clearly differentiated us from clinical psychologists.
> They were high on the totem pole in psychology. We weren't even
> *on* the pole! Beyond this small matter of jealousy, there were many
> reasons why "counselors" in general wished to be seen as contributing
> positively in non-medical settings as clinical psychologists were seen
> as contributing in medical settings. We not only were not prepared
> for "medical therapy" service, we did not wish to be. We had our
> strengths in vocational and life planning, in developing the potentials
> of normally functioning persons, in taking into account the enor-
> mously significant factor of the various environments in the life of a
> client. We were not "intrapsychic" in our emphasis, we were con-
> cerned with the "life-space" of a client. But our titles and our
> Ph.D. programs did not make that distinction clear. This also led up
> to the Northwestern Conference. (Wrenn, 1984, p. 313)

Having set the background which led up to the Northwestern Conference, it is timely to consider its products and consequences. Perhaps
the most enduring consequence was neither anticipated nor ultimately of
benefit to the profession; namely, the sowing of the seed of a continuing
identity problem by adopting the counseling psychology title. Super
(1984b) captured the essence of this consequence when he reflected:

> Having established ourselves during the decade of the 1950s . . .
> we found ourselves still lacking, in the eyes of our fellow psycholo-
> gists on the APA's Education and Training Board and of similar
> bodies, a clear and distinct identity because our name denoted a
> process that was and is used by many other professional and lay
> people. (p. 279)

This consequence of adopting a process title is imbedded deeply now in
history and in professional identity.

Two other consequences of the Northwestern Conference, however, are of enduring positive value. The first was the specification of recommended standards for training counseling psychologists at the doctoral level. The report of recommended standards is in five parts: role and functions of counseling psychologists, selection of students, graduate training, tentative time allotments to areas of training, and further steps.

The statement on role and functions of counseling psychologists indicated that a professional goal of the counseling psychologist is "to foster the psychological development of the individual" (APA, 1952a, p. 175. Also in Whiteley, 1980c, p. 71). Counseling psychologists, according to this report, spend the majority of their time with individuals within the normal range, as opposed to those individuals suffering from severe psychopathology. Counseling is viewed as stressing the "positive and preventative." Educational institutions provide a central setting. However, in what was a statement that came close to the language frequently used to describe the usual role of *clinical* psychologists, the Committee stated that the client population served would include:

> all people on the adjustment continuum from those who function at tolerable levels of adequacy to those suffering from more severe psychological disturbances. (APA, 1952a, p. 175. Also in Whiteley, 1980c, p. 71)

Further, the training of counseling psychologists should "qualify them to work in some degree with individuals at any level of psychological adjustment" (APA, 1952a, p. 175. Also in Whiteley, 1980c, p. 71). In retrospect, this inaugural recommendation of training standards left open to interpretation exactly where the boundary lines should be drawn between clinical and counseling psychology.

Bell's (1949) statement differentiating psychological counseling from clinical psychology and psychiatry was much more precise and helpful in clarifying the emphasis and focus of the profession. While noting that psychological counselors were highly qualified psychologists first, Bell stated there must be a "clear understanding of the limits of his field of specialization." This includes a focus on situational problems in contrast to those involving "personality disorganization or deterioration" which are the province of psychiatry.

In addition to educational institutions, the settings in which counseling psychologists may function were broadly defined by the Committee on Counseling Training to include business and industry; hospitals; and community agencies such as marital clinics, youth organizations, churches, rehabilitation agencies, vocational guidance centers, and parenthood foundations. This breadth of settings has continued on through the present, though there have been shifts in the percentages of counseling psychologists who are employed in the various settings and a small increase in the number in private practice.

In what has come to be a very important statement, counseling psychologists were assigned the:

> chief responsibility for conducting the research upon which depends the possibility of more effective counseling. Any applied field needs roots in the basic scientific disciplines that lend substance to its work. It is therefore imperative that psychological counseling remain firmly established within the orbit of basic psychological science and related disciplines and that counseling psychologists acquire the research skills which make possible the enlargement of knowledge. We feel strongly that research must continue as a basic job of the counseling psychologist and that he must be trained accordingly. (APA, 1952a, p. 176. Also in Whiteley, 1980c, p. 72)

This statement was of crucial significance to the long-term strengthening of the profession.

A continuing problem remains: Counseling psychologists as a group have yet to develop fully their potential for research (Osipow, 1984; Harmon, 1982; HIll & Gronsky, 1984; and Whiteley, 1984). Among the purported reasons for this state of affairs is the fact that there is not yet sufficient emphasis on research within graduate training programs. In its section on graduate training, the Committee on Training in 1952 said that the counseling psychologist should acquire "a core of basic concepts, tools, and techniques that should be common to all psychologists" (APA, 1952a, p. 177). Also Whiteley, 1980c, p. 73). The Committee also noted the "inevitable incompleteness" of a doctoral training program and the importance of expanding postdoctoral training.

Along with research training six other areas were singled out by the Committee on Training including personality organization and development, knowledge of the social environment, appraisal of the individual, counseling theory, professional orientation, and practicum. In retrospect, the section on what research training should include provides an important clue to understanding why the profession has had such problems with its research mission. The Committee stated in part:

> At a minimum, such training should aim to develop the ability to review and to make use of the results of research. Psychological counseling is and should be founded upon basic psychological science and related disciplines. Counseling psychologists can make unique contributions to psychological knowledge because their counseling experience provides an especially fruitful opportunity to formulate hypotheses. It is therefore essential to maximize their research training. How to achieve a balance between practice and research during the training period is an unsolved problem. A flexible program of training in research that takes into account the range of research potentialities of its students will go a long way, however,

toward solving this problem. (APA, 1952a, p. 179-180. Also in Whiteley, 1980c, p. 78)

In the view of this writer, the minimum should *not* have been set at the "ability to review and to make use of the results of research."[2] Rather, the minimum *should* have been set at the ability to *formulate independently hypotheses* and *to conduct original inquiry* as well as the ability to review and make use of the results of research.

The establishment of too *low* an initial minimum competency in research has continued to plague the profession. Further, what the Committee on Counseling Training described as an unsolved problem in research training remains unsolved three decades later: establishing the proper balance between practice and research during the training period. The Committee had established a balance as follows:

Proportion of One Year's Study in the Various Areas of Training
(Total of 4 years = 400)

Core	65-70	Diversification	30-50
Personality	20-30	Professional orientation	10-20
Social environment	15-20	Practica: Field work and	
Appraisal	35-45	internship	120-135
Counseling	20-30	Research	45-50

(APA, 1952a, p. 178. Also in Whiteley, 1980c, p. 78)*

It is highly symbolic that the other product of the Northwestern Conference was a statement on practicum training in counseling (APA, 1952b). As vital as this topic of practicum training is, it could have been accompanied, or followed soon after, by a parallel in-depth statement on standards for research training in counseling psychology. This has not yet occurred. Over three decades later, the development of a detailed statement on research training is still a pressing task yet to be accomplished.

COMMITTEE ON DEFINITION

In addition to the development of standards of doctoral training and practicum, the third organized activity of Division 17 during this historical period which has had a major impact on the profession of counseling psychology was the work of the Committee on Definition. Its report,

---

*From *American Psychologist, 7*, 182-188. Copyright 1952 by the American Psychological Association.

Counseling Psychology as a Specialty (APA, 1956), appeared four years after the 1952 reports on doctoral training (APA, 1952a) and practicum training (APA, 1952b) emerged from the Northwestern Conference. In reflecting back upon the circumstances at the time of the Northwestern Conference, the Committee on Definition stated:

> A carefully stated definition of the specialty of counseling psychology was needed at that time, but none was available. Since the two statements on professional training proved to be sufficient tasks, the earlier committee contented itself with a brief description of the specialty and postponed to a later period the task of more elaborate definition. This document is the present committee's attempt to supply a more complete statement of what is counseling psychology. (APA, 1956, p. 282. Also in Whiteley, 1980c, p. 92)

The assigned task of the Committee on Definition was the development of a more explicit statement about the focus and boundaries of counseling psychology. A new scientific journal, the *Journal of Counseling Psychology*, had just started (1954), and the American Board of Examiners in Professional Psychology had very recently (1955) changed the title of the relevant specialty diploma from "Counseling and Guidance" to "Counseling Psychology." The Committee on Definition commented upon the need to differentiate between counseling and clinical psychology:

> The existence within the Veterans Administration of related operations in counseling psychology and clinical psychology and their antecedents in university programs that prepare students for these kinds of work, make highly desirable the spelling out of similarities and differences in these two psychological specialties. Such a delineation of specialty areas within the field of psychology becomes even more timely since the conference on the overlapping field of school psychology has just made its report (Cutts, 1955). Of course, it is appropriately the function of the American Psychological Association to make official pronouncements regarding its specialty fields, but its Divisions have been expected to exercise initiative in the preparation of these statements. Any formulation such as that presented here should be viewed as part of an ongoing activity within psychology and its professional association, tentative in nature, and subject to modification as warranted by changes in the science of psychology and its various applications. (APA, 1956, p. 282. Also in Whiteley, 1980c, p. 93)

The recurrent theme in counseling psychology's history of identifying similarities and differences with clinical psychology was noted as well as the responsibility of APA divisions to exercise initiative in the preparation of definitional statements.

A key statement by the Committee on Definition was as follows:

> At the present time, the specialty of counseling psychology is approaching a state of balance among emphases upon contributions to (a) the development of an individual's inner life through concern with his or her motivations and emotions, (b) the individual's achievement of harmony with his or her environment through helping him or her to develop the resources that he or she must bring to this task (for example, by assisting him or her to make effective use of appropriate community resources), and (c) the influencing of society to recognize individual differences and to encourage the fullest development of all persons within it. (APA, 1956, p. 283. Also in Whiteley, 1980c, p. 94)

The concern with motivation and emotion, developing personal resources, influencing society to recognize individual differences, and encouraging personal development to the fullest have been recurrent themes in counseling psychology. In helping individuals develop a more mature inner life, counseling psychologists draw upon theories of personality and learning and use tools which are also used by clinical, experimental, social, and school psychologists. Further, counseling psychologists were said to use varying combinations of exploratory experiences, psychometric techniques, and psychotherapeutic techniques to assist people.

In a treatment of differences from other psychological specialties, the Committee on Definition stated that because of its aim of contributing to the personal development of a great variety of people:

> counseling psychology does not concern itself only with the more extreme problems presented by individuals who are in need of emergency treatment. In other words, counseling psychology does not place special emphasis upon the development of tools and techniques necessary for intensive psychotherapy with individuals whose emotional growth has been severely distorted or stunted. Counseling psychology, then, leaves to other psychologists the major responsibility for the emergency treatment of psychological disasters. (APA, 1956, p. 283. Also in Whiteley, 1980c, p. 95)

When texts on psychodiagnostics are contrasted with texts on educational and vocational appraisal, counseling psychologists are presented as more concerned with the outcomes of activities of clients in the normal course of their lives (educational achievement, occupational success, and marital happiness). Clinical psychologists, by contrast, focus more on the analysis of an individual's inner life and predicting problems of hospital management and psychotherapeutic treatment. Counseling psychologists wish to advance the "fullest possible self-realization" of members of social groups, not just clients or deviants who are making only a minimal adjustment. The major responsibility for treating psychological disasters is assigned to other specialties. The focus on assisting individual self-realization in a variety of settings is emphasized.

The work of the Committee on Definition is presented in the second historical period because of its clear link (as a natural extension of the work on doctoral training and practicum) to the earlier Committee on Counselor Training. Also the three reports were the products of organized activities of Division 17 in contrast to the thrust of developments outside of the profession which characterized the third historical period.

The coverage of the years 1951, 1952, and 1953 within the second historical period will conclude with three sections. The next section on organized activities will be compiled primarily from *Counseling News and Views*. The following section on constellations of substantive theoretical developments will highlight contributions from theories of personality, counseling, psychotherapy, vocational psychology, occupational choice, and career development.The concluding section on other theory and research reflects the content of the first four years of coverage of counseling psychology by the *Annual Review of Psychology*, as well as significant contributions to the literature from other sources including the newly founded *Journal of Counseling Psychology*.

ACTIVITIES OF ORGANIZED COUNSELING PSYCHOLOGY

Volume 4, No. 1 of *Counseling News and Views* noted the appearance in the *American Psychologist* (APA, 1950) of the tentative draft of the Code of Ethics for Psychologists, a sign of the continued maturation of psychology as a profession. In 1951, Division 17 was the second largest within the APA.

Donald Super's presidential statement clarified the functions of the division, which included:

1. The study, and aid in the improvement, of the selection of students of counseling
2. The formulation of standards and the improvement of methods for the training of counseling psychologists
3. The support (financial) of counseling
4. Research (facilitating the planning and execution of worthwhile research)
5. Relations with other fields (Super, 1951a, p. 4)

With respect to the fifth point, Super (1951a) stated:

Many *clinical* psychologists believe that counseling is not a field in its own right, and that counseling psychologists who are worth their salt are really clinical psychologists and should be in the Clinical Division. Some educational psychologists, apparently unaware of our kinship with the clinicians, similarly feel that we are really educational psychologists and should merge our division with the Division of Educational Psychology. And not a few of us, who have worked in industry or government, tend to feel that we have more in common with members of the Industrial Division than with any other group of psychologists, even though we are aware of differences. One of the suggestions coming from the Northwestern Conference was that we work with other divisions in defining more clearly the ways in which we differ from these other kinds of psychologists, and to point out also the specialties which we have in common. (p. 4)

Thus while the issue of central identity continued to be a topic of concern, the terrain was broadened to include issues shared with educational and industrial psychology.

Super (1952a) expanded on the formal statements from the Northwestern Conference (APA, 1952a; 1952b) when he commented that "it is therefore imperative that counseling psychology remain firmly established within the orbit of basic psychological science and related disciplines." The issues he addressed remain with counseling psychology three decades later and are therefore as timely now as they were then:

What are the Related Disciplines, and, more important, how does the counselor acquire a grounding in them? The statement makes it clear that the disciplines involved are the other behavior sciences: sociology, cultural anthropology, and economics. In many counselor-training institutions students are encouraged or required to take some courses in urban or rural sociology or in the sociology of the community, in labor economics, or perhaps in cultural anthropology. They often find these courses interesting and stimulating, but it is generally only the ablest students who are able to make the necessary applications to their own work. Many students, moreover, report that a given course in labor economics or in urban sociology may be fine for majors in those fields, but that it has little of value to them.

In writing on this subject more than ten years ago in a basic text on vocational guidance, we lamented the fact that "Economists . . . have given surprisingly little attention to the vocational adjustment of individuals as an economic problem." What was true in 1942 is still true in 1952. Our cousins the sociologists and cultural anthropologists have done somewhat better than the economists, with the result that there are a number of excellent sociological studies of occupations and of work, but it was only a year or so ago that Form and Miller published what they claim to be the first treatise or text on Industrial Sociology. In so doing they reflect a growing concern with work and occupation as a social institution, and a growing number of studies of vocations and of vocational adjustment, by sociologists and anthropologists. We were both pleased and annoyed by the fact that Form and Miller build much of their book on the admittedly pioneer work of psychologist Mayon and his colleagues while attempting to stake a claim to industrial relations for sociology. Furthermore, to this observer at least, it seemed that the most important papers on occupations and work read at the last annual meeting of the APA were those of the sociologically oriented Committee on Human Development people at Chicago. And it is not just in the vocational field that we psychologists are finding that we must keep up with anthropology and sociology: the important work in personality being done by scholars from these two disciplines is even greater in volume and better known.

With this increasing volume of important work being done in the related disciplines, it becomes more important than ever for counseling psychology to establish and maintain good liaison with them. It seems to us that we have not had good liaison or cross-fertilization in the past. Academic psychology has been oriented toward biology and physics, striving to be an exact science. Clinical psychology has been oriented toward medicine, trying to establish itself as a clinical profession. Counseling and guidance have just grown, like Topsy, sometimes in the domain of psychology and sometimes in that of education but truly nurtured and loved by neither, sometimes aware of potentially important contributions from the other behavior sciences but generally looked at askance by sociologists or anthropologists who were interested only in theory or in applications of a type quite different from those which counselors might make. (Super, 1952a, pp. 3-4)

The academic disciplines Super viewed as relating to counseling psychology are sociology, cultural anthropology, and economics. The necessity to establish and maintain close relationships to each of the disciplines is stressed. He also noted that representatives of those disciplines "are not likely to make much of a contribution to the training of most practicing counselors, for the social sciences are not and cannot be sufficiently familiar with the problems faced by counseling psychologists to make the needed applications of their knowledge" (Super, 1952a, p. 4). It was necessary, therefore, in the early 1950s to find ways to bring counselors and representatives of other behavioral sciences together. That necessity remains three decades later.

In another related contribution, Williamson (1952) indicated that Division 17 had done an excellent job of studying "nearly every aspect of the development of counseling except the one of the organizational context in which nearly all counseling will be done" (Williamson, 1952, p. 8). Except for private practitioners, almost all counseling psychologists are employed in organizations. He indicated that the importance of understanding the organizational context is that vector forces with the organization "help determine the nature of the counseling functions themselves" (Williamson, 1952, p. 8). He contends it is simply incorrect to assume that the cooperating counselor is able to determine which counseling functions to implement without considering influences beyond the profession itself. Williamson explored a role for counseling psychologists in discipline and the issue of ethical concerns as two matters which are responsive to organizational pressures.

Volume 4, No. 3 of *Counseling News and Views*, published in June of 1952, was remarkable on two grounds. First, it reported a spirited attempt by the leadership of Division 17 to influence the U.S. Office of Education to reverse its plans to discontinue its Guidance and Personnel Branch (Super, 1952b). For 15 years, this branch of the Office of Education had provided leadership in the development of counseling and guidance services for public schools. In recent years,to the disadvantage of the profession, the leadership of Division 17 has not been an active force in trying to influence either legislative or executive branch activities of the federal government.

Second, Volume 4, No. 3 of *Counseling News and Views* contained a call to the membership of Division 17 to join the American Personnel and Guidance Association as an organization which should be "of vital interest to psychologists." It was presented as "logical that most members of Division 17 should also be members of APGA." In the late 1950s, 40% of the members of Division 17 were members of the National Vocational Guidance Association, and another 16% were members of the American College Personnel Association, both divisions of APGA. It is regrettable that more recently there has not been such a spirit of cooperation. In the areas of legislation affecting the helping professions and federal funding for research on human services, to note just two examples, there is clear reason to make common cause with APGA where similarity of interest exists.[3]

Volume 5, No. 1 of *Counseling News and Views*, which appeared in November of 1952, contained a report by Harold Pepinsky on a productive year for the Research Committee. It had focused on three tangible projects:

1. A study of methodology in counseling research
2. A study of the financing of current research projects
3. An exchange of current research activities

This latter project had taken the form of a special supplement to Volume 4 of *Counseling News and Views*. In Pepinsky's (1952) view, the Research Committee should serve "primarily as a stimulus to research, not as a research-conducting group" (p. 10).

OBTAINING SUPPORT FOR COUNSELING

In 1952, Division 17 had a Committee on the Support of Counseling, an initiative which has since been lost (to the detriment of the long-term enhancement of the profession). In providing a charge for it, President C. Gilbert Wrenn (Wrenn, 1952) wrote to Chair Ralph Bedell asking that the committee focus on:

> relations with various government agencies which may be concerned with either helping develop standards for or subsidizing counselor training . . . . I have letters from 4 or 5 major government agencies indicating their extreme interest in what Division 17 could do to help them . . . . We think there may be a lead there for some subsidy of counselor training. (Wrenn, 1952, p. 11)

Bedell (1952) reported that the Committee:

> soon became aware of the necessity for having a strong program for the development of counseling in order to interest private and governmental agencies in the support of counselor training activities. Organizations with money to invest in the advancement of a profession are not likely to give very serious consideration to anything short of a well-planned program of action that has support of the bulk of leaders in that profession. The conversations members of the Subcommittee had with potential sponsors of activities in counseling lead directly to the conclusion that improved standards were necessary if any request for support were to be considered seriously outside of the Division. For these reasons the Subcommittee proposed that Division 17 develop a statement of standards of counseling. (Bedell, 1952, p. 11)

The opinion of the Committee was that the "amount of support which Division 17 can encourage for counseling largely will be the result of the extent to which the Division can prepare forward-looking plans for the development of counseling and provide the machinery that may lead to the implementation of these plans" (Bedell, 1952, p. 12).

In a statement which could serve as a reminder of challenges to be faced in the 1980s, the Committee stated:

> One of the most widespread and persistent obstacles the Committee has found among officials of foundations and governmental agencies is the lack of recognition of counseling psychology as a field worthy of separate consideration at the professional level. Thus a foundation accustomed to working with such groups as sociologists, educators, or statisticians needs to be made aware of the ways counseling

psychologists can contribute to their objectives. Any approach short of a broad professional attack on common problems will almost certainly fail. On the other hand, a successful attack by Division 17 could open the way whereby the projects of many counseling psychologists might receive favorable consideration by an increasing number of foundations and agencies. (Bedell, 1952, p. 13)

The rationale for more initiative by counseling psychologists in attracting support for the profession is clearly stated and is equally applicable in the 1980s.

There was a continuing concern with the abolishment of the Guidance and Personnel Services Branch of the U.S. Office of Education. Vol. 5, No. 1 reported a resolution of the Division:

RESOLUTION: Whereas, the U.S. Office of Education has seen fit to absorb a cut in the budget for vocational education by abolishing the Guidance and Personnel Services Branch, and whereas, the action is resulting in decreased guidance and counseling services to the youth of the nation, be it resolved by the Counseling and Guidance Division of the American Psychological Association, in convention here assembled:

1. That Administrator Ewing and Commissioner McGrath be urged to take immediate steps to reconstitute an adequate guidance and counseling unit in the U.S. Office of Education, and
2. That the Division of Counseling and Guidance take such additional steps as may be necessary to ensure that adequate support be forthcoming for guidance and counseling services in the U.S. Office of Education, and
3. That the Division of Counseling and Guidance herewith offers its services as may be needed for reconstituting in the immediate future a guidance and counseling unit in the U.S. Office of Education. (*Counseling News and Views*, 1952, Vol. 5, No. 1, p. 14)

Three months later (in *Counseling News and Views*, Vol. 5, No. 2), there was talk of waiting for the change in administration of the executive branch of the federal government as a result of the 1952 election. Continuing concern with this problem was reported in Vol. 5, No. 3 which appeared in June of 1953.

In Vol. 5, No. 2 of *Counseling News and Views*, President Mitchell Dreese reported that he had received more than 20 letters from members of Division 17 recommending that the name of the Division be changed. (Despite adoption of the term "counseling psychology" at the Northwestern Conference, there was not an official change of name until 1953). The most frequent suggestion was the Division of Counseling Psychologists.

The November, 1953 issue of *Counseling News and Views*, (Vol. 6, No. 1), contained four important announcements for the membership of Division 17. First, the name of the Division had been officially changed to the Division of Counseling Psychology. Second, the forthcoming birth of the *Journal of Counseling Psychology* was announced. Third, Mitchell Dreese indicated that the Guidance and Pupil Personnel Services Section of the U.S. Office of Education was being re-established. Finally, Noble H. Kelley, Secretary-Treasurer of the American Board of Examiners in Professional Psychology, indicated that awarded diplomas would designate "Counseling Psychology" instead of "Counseling and Guidance."

CONSTELLATION OF SUBSTANTIVE THEORETICAL DEVELOPMENTS

Substantive theoretical developments appearing during the period 1951-1953 provide a perspective on counseling psychology's second historical period. Major articles, monographs, and books in the constellation of personality theory and theories of counseling and psychotherapy are presented in Table 2.1. Gestalt therapy made an appearance for the first time, and developments continued to occur in the previously introduced approaches to theory and therapy.

In the constellation of theories of vocational psychology, occupational choice, and career development, there was a new influential theory introduced, as Table 2.2 indicates. Eli Ginzberg and associates published their first major statement of general theory in 1951. There continued to be contributions to the theories which had previously made an appearance.

OTHER THEORETICAL AND RESEARCH ADVANCEMENTS

The initiation of the *Annual Review of Psychology* and its first appearance in 1950, coupled with the founding of the *Journal of Counseling Psychology* in 1954, has made it possible to review theoretical and research advancements in a much more systematic manner than would otherwise have been possible. From 1950 through 1953 there were seven relevant reviews: Bordin (1950), Berdie (1950), Pepinsky (1951), Stuit (1951), Gilbert (1952), Williamson (1953), and Wrenn (1954). (The review by Wrenn covered literature up through 1953.) As a resource in considering theoretical and research advances, the collections of the *Annual Review of Psychology*, as Zytowski and Rosen (1982) note, are "nearly exactly congruent with the life span of counseling psychology, and a working knowledge of the contents of these volumes should provide yet another perspective of counseling psychology's history" (Zytowski & Rosen, 1982, p. 69).

There are three major limitations, however, to the usefulness of articles in the *Annual Review of Psychology* as a consistent source on the

Table 2.1

**Representative Contributions to Personality Theory
and Theories of Counseling and Psychotherapy
in the Second Historical Period
(1951-1953 to prevent overlap)**

Psychoanalysis (Neo-Freudian)

Sullivan, H. S.   Conceptions of modern psychiatry (1953a)
                                   The interpersonal theory of psychiatry (1953b)

Psychoanalysis (Freudian)

Hartmann, H.   Ego psychology and the problem of adaptations
                                       (1951)

Adlerian Psychotherapy (Application to Practice)

Grunwald, B.   The application of Adlerian principles in a
                                       classroom (1954)

Behavior Theory and Therapy

Skinner, B. F.   Science and human behavior (1953)

Client-centered Therapy

Rogers, C. R.   Client-centered therapy (1951a)
                                   Perceptual reorganization in client-centered
                                       therapy (1951b)
                                   Through the eyes of a client (1951c)
                                   Communication: Its blocking and facilitations
                                       (1952)
                                   A research program in client-centered therapy
                                       (1953)

Rogers, C. R., &   Psychotherapy and personality (1954)
   Dymond, R. F.

Gestalt

Perls, F.,   Gestalt therapy (1951)
   Hefferline, R. F.,
   & Goodman, P.

Humanistic and Existential Theory and Therapy

Tillich, P.   The courage to be (1952)

Table 2.2

**Representative Contributions to Vocational Psychology,
Occupational Choice, and Career Development
in the Second Historical Period
(1951-1953)**

Psychoanalytic/Psychodynamic

Forer, B. R.	Personality factors in occupational choice (1953)
Small, L.	Personality determinants of vocational choice (1953)

Life Space/Life Span (Donald Super and Associates)

Super, D. E.	Vocational adjustment: Implementing a self-concept (1951)
	A theory of vocational development (1953)

Trait and Factor

Severin, D.	The predictability of various kinds of criteria (1952)
Paterson, D. G., Gerken, C. d'A., Hahn, M. E.	Revised Minnesota occupational rating scales (1953)
Heron, A. A.	A psychological study of occupational adjustment (1952)

Career Choice (Eli Ginzberg and Associates)

Ginzberg, E., Ginsburg, S. W., Axelrad, S., & Herma, J. L.	Occupational choice: An approach to a general theory (1951)

history of theoretical and research advances in counseling psychology. The first is that, as Magoon (1980) noted, each review covers too short a time frame to adequately represent and reflect long-term development and trends in the fields.

Zytowski and Rosen (1982) explain the second limitation as follows:

Such a compilation is unlikely to be an exact delineation of the growth of counseling psychology nor is it apt to provide the basis for an exact prediction of its future; ARP policy and author predictions enter a biasing factor into this survey. Early, ARP chapters tended to reflect the standard discipline of psychology. As the publication progressed however, some of the accepted fields, counseling psychology particularly, decreased in frequency of appearance, while special topics in the subfields of psychology appeared more and more frequently, e.g., Soviet psychology, color vision, facial expression of emotion, and the like. Table 2.3 shows the diminishing attention given to counseling psychology, and as well, documents the changes in emphasis which it has seen during the years. (Zytowski & Rosen, 1982, p. 69)

Table 2.3 helps explain their point further.

Table 2.3

Counseling Psychology in the (1950-1979) Annual Review of Psychology

Year	Volume	Titles	Author(s)
1950	1	Counseling Methods: Diagnostics	Berdie
1950	1	Counseling Methods: Therapy	Bordin
1951	2	Counseling Methods: Diagnostic	Stuit
1951	2	Counseling Methods: Therapy	Pepinsky
1952	3	Counseling Methods: Therapy & Diagnosis	Gilbert
1953	4	Counseling Methods: Therapy & Diagnosis	Williamson
1954	5	Counseling Methods	Wrenn
1955	6	Counseling	Hobbs & Seeman
1956	7	Counseling	Shoben
1957	8	Counseling	Shaw
1958	9	Counseling	Tyler
1959	10	Counseling	Berdie
1963	14	Counseling Psychology	Brayfield
1966	17	Counseling	Patterson
1968	19	Student Development & Counseling	Segal
1971	22	Student Development & Counseling	Layton, Sandeen, & Baker
1973	24	Student Development & Counseling	Pepinsky & Meara
1975	26	Counseling & Student Development	Whiteley, Burkhart, Harway-Herman, & Whiteley
1979	30	Counseling Psychology	Krumboltz, Becker-Haven, & Burnett

(Zytowski & Rosen, 1982, p. 70)

Counseling psychology as a discipline has been only occasionally reviewed by the *Annual Review of Psychology* in recent years. (Note: There were six very relevant reviews in the first four volumes. By contrast, between 1973 and 1979 there were seven volumes of the *Annual Review of Psychology* and only three relevant reviews of counseling psychology.)

The third limitation reflects the constraints placed upon individual authors; for example, the current author and his associates (Whiteley, Burkhart, Harway-Herman, & Whiteley, 1975) were assigned two fields to evaluate and cover in approximately 90 double-spaced manuscript pages: student development *and* counseling. It would be difficult to review adequately within those page constraints two years of progress on even one of those topics. Further, counseling as a generic term is broader than the applied specialty of counseling psychology. Fortunately, the appearance of the *Journal of Counseling Psychology* in 1954 and *The Counseling Psychologist* in 1969 supplement the *Annual Review of Psychology* by discerning aspects of theoretical and research advancements.

Berdie (1950) evaluated the literature on diagnosis in counseling. He contrasted the views of Rogers (1942) and Snygg and Combs (1949) with those of Super (1949). Oscar Buros' valuable series (for example, Buros, 1949), entitled the *Mental Measurement Yearbook*, was noted as strengthening the arguments of the proponents of diagnosis. The balance of this review covered surveys of techniques, abbreviated intelligence scales, tests of special aptitude, professional aptitude tests, the expanding use of interest tests, counseling uses of the Minnesota Multiphasic Personality Inventory, and the use of projective tests in counseling.

In considering diagnosis in counseling, Berdie (1950) identified a number of trends in recent publications:

(a) Individual workers are publishing comprehensive and frequently critical surveys and reviews of diagnostic tests; (b) attention given during the war to the development of brief, screening tests has continued; (c) continuing work is being done on the development of tests of special abilities; (d) professional aptitude tests are being developed in new fields; (e) implications for the interpretation of personality found in interest tests are being explored; (f) attempts are being made to develop new uses in counseling for the Minnesota Multiphasic Personality Inventory; (g) new uses of projective methods in counseling are being explored; and (h) lacunae in the research literature continued to reveal the lack of evidence concerning the validity of many otherwise carefully developed diagnostic tests. (Berdie, 1950, p. 256)

These trends have recurred over the years and still appear in the literature of the 1980s.

Where Berdie (1950) had been assigned the topic of diagnostics, Bordin (1950) reviewed developments in counseling. The year 1950, therefore, allowed a more comprehensive evaluation of counseling psychology than normally has been the case. In Bordin's (1950) view, "Writings in the field of counseling are still largely characterized by exploratory efforts at rationalizing the counseling process or some portion of it, with the non directive formulations still the center of attention" (p. 268). Thorne's (1948) directive approach was noted as being in opposition to the general trend, as was Bordin's (1948) focus on the limitations of nondirective concepts as descriptive devices. The balance of this review centered on analysis of the counseling process (both the entire process and the initial interview), and on the personality of the counselor.

Stuit (1951) focused, as had Berdie (1950), on diagnostics in counseling. Stuit noted that "it can hardly be denied that modern counseling procedures owe much to the development and use of diagnostic instruments" (p. 305). Williamson (1949) was quoted extensively on the role of diagnostics in counseling, and Rogers (1942) was presented as placing diagnosis "in better perspective" (p. 305). Counselors wishing to evaluate tests and their limitations were referred to Buros (1949) and Super (1949); Cronbach's (1949) introductory textbook was presented as an excellent source on the general principles of testing. Topics for consideration in this review included differential and special aptitude tests, measures of achievement and general intellectual aptitude, measures of interest and personality characteristics, questionnaires, check lists, projective techniques, and the counseling interview itself.

Stuit (1951) indicated that the trends noted by Berdie (1950) continued, with the most notable being the following:

(a) continued interest in the use and validation of differential aptitude tests, (b) search for better methods of assessing personal qualities, particularly interests and personality characteristics, and (c) better standardization and validation of existing tests and diagnostic devices. (Stuit, 1951, p. 314)

Pepinsky's (1951) review of counseling centered on five topics: definitions of counseling as a profession, formulation of theory and method, analysis of the counseling process, discussion of therapy in groups, and research (especially on the effects of counseling). In terms of counseling as a profession, he indicated that four texts (Hahn & MacLean, 1950; Porter, 1950; Super, 1949; Williamson, 1950) reflected the "uncrystallized" stage of the field. Publications in 1949 and 1950 indicate an enhanced concern with social and psychological factors in the counseling process. In Pepinsky's view:

The most significant development in publications on counseling during the past year has been a concerted attempt to integrate what happens in therapy with basic theory and experiments in the social sciences, especially in general psychology. Reference is made to motivation, learning, and perception, and also to the seemingly more diffused areas of personality and social organization. (Pepinsky, 1951, p. 319)

This marked a major departure from the previously more limited focus. Albert Ellis (Ellis, 1950) marked one of his initial citations in the counseling psychology literature with a critique of the Chicago nondirective counseling research group (Carr, 1949; Haigh, 1949; Hoffman, 1949; Rogers, 1949; Raskin, 1949a, 1949b; Seeman, 1949; Sheerer, 1949; Stock, 1949).

Pepinsky did not find any significant new trends in the analysis of counseling process other than those reported by Bordin (1950). Stone's (1950) study of counseling in groups was cited as an important contribution to a relatively new research area. The section on effects of counseling reported that there was a lack of agreement by counselors on what constituted a desirable counseling outcome. The debate on this topic was to accelerate during the remainder of the 1950s and the 1960s.

Gilbert's review (1952) covered the dual assignment of evaluating both therapy and diagnosis, though he was allocated essentially the same page space by the *Annual Review of Psychology* (29 pages) as had been Pepinsky (1951) and Stuit (1951) combined. Gilbert's opening comment reflected the tone of the review as a whole:

The broad view of articles and books which have appeared in this field during the past year is on the whole tremendously encouraging and in parts even exciting. While there are some wide gaps, particularly in the area of relating diagnosis to counseling and therapeutic procedures, there is a general trend towards a healthy integration of varying viewpoints which while not explicit in some instances, is implicit in the more specific statements made by the various authors. (Gilbert, 1952, p. 351)*

The trend toward unification, which he considered possibly the most important, was between experimental psychology and psychoanalytic theory and therapy. Some of the research articles on the counseling process, in Gilbert's view, suggested methodological possibilities of a potentially far-reaching nature. There was also a wealth of articles on the development, refinement, validation, and critical examination of various diagnostic instruments. By way of elaborating this latter point, Gilbert described the state of scientific development with respect to diagnostic instruments as well as the challenges yet unmet:

---

*This and all other quotations from this source are reproduced, with permission, from the *Annual Review of Psychology*, Vol. 3. © 1952 by Annual Reviews Inc.

Many of these articles show an encouraging concern for careful methodology and for testing some of the fundamental assumptions upon which the instruments are based. This is particularly true in the field of projective devices. However, it is precisely in the area of diagnosis that the greatest gap in knowledge seems to exist. Not one research article has been seen regarding the general problem of relating diagnosis to counseling in a broad way. This is understandable in terms of the great amount of original thinking and labor involved in such research, but it does leave a significant gap which will need to be filled if counseling and therapy are ever to reach a more scientific status. (Gilbert, 1952, pp. 351-352)

The section on counseling explored general professional trends, and noted the appearance of Carl R. Rogers' (1951a) book on client-centered therapy which has had such a profound impact on the profession. The first reports of the American Psychological Association's Committee on Ethical Standards for Psychology (APA, 1950, 1951) addressed the problems of how to assume the necessary professional and social responsibilities, and establish a core of ethical principles for the profession.

For Gilbert, the most meaningful and intellectually exciting contributions to the field of psychological counseling during this period were those which related basic personality theory, theories of learning, and theories of perception to how maladjustment is acquired and to what is therapeutic for alleviating maladjustment. He singled out contributions by Dollard and Miller (1950), Thorne (1950), Cameron (1950), Fisher (1950), Wrenn (1951), Robinson (1950), Mowrer (1950), Blum and Balinsky (1951), and Rogers (1951a). Across these various contributors, the similarities, differences, and agreements are noted most clearly in:

(a) the various beliefs as to the manner in which maladjustment arises, (b) the general methods of therapy which are suggested for treating such maladjustments, (c) the manner in which the transference relationship is conceived and handled, and (d) the social implications of the various theoretical approaches. (Gilbert, 1952, p. 354)

The review covered a time of exceptional scholarly output in the development of counseling psychology.

One of the most frequently quoted series of studies in counseling psychology appeared during this period (Fiedler, 1950a, 1950b, 1951a, 1951b). The problem Fiedler addressed was how to describe and quantify different types of therapeutic relationships. Such a methodological accomplishment was necessary in order to make scientific statements on important topics such as which theoretical approach is the most effective, either overall, or with different client populations, and why. Gilbert (1952, p. 360-362) reviews the Fiedler studies in detail. They have turned out to be of considerable heuristic value, and over the next two decades they stimulated widespread commentary and further inquiry.

Williamson (1953), like Gilbert (1952), had been assigned the topics of both therapy and diagnosis. His characterization of the literature, in contrast with Gilbert's, was less positive. As he stated it:

> Examination of the professional and scientific literature appearing during the period covered by this review has revealed a disappointing paucity of publications providing information derived from research on counseling. The number of persons professionally engaged in counseling during this period was large; there were 645 members in the Counseling and Guidance Division of the American Psychological Association, and many of these persons were working in colleges and universities in which were located active psychological research centers. For these reasons, and considering the research orientation so strongly stressed by many who write about counseling, one would have hoped that a greater quantity of research would have been reported. (Williamson, 1953, p. 343)

The literature itself fitted into two main categories: a psychotherapeutic orientation toward counseling theory and techniques, and an attention to choosing occupational goals based upon the diagnosis of aptitudes and interests and the selection of occupational training which will help to achieve the identified goals.

Super's (1951b) contribution was considered to be an exception to the characterization of the counseling literature because of its formulation of a conception of vocational adjustment based on self and self-perception. Ginzberg, Ginsburg, Axelrad, and Herma (1951) contributed to the psychology of vocational choice by identifying three stages in making choices and describing personality factors important in the choice process.

This review reported the beginning of what was to become an intensive two-decade period of concentrated attention on evaluating the outcomes of counseling and psychotherapy. The January, 1952 (Volume 8) issue of the *Journal of Clinical Psychology* focused on research design issues and included contributions by Ellis (1952), Thorne (1952), Berg (1952), Sells (1952), Watson (1952), and Edwards and Cronbach (1952). The interested reader is referred to this historically important issue. The balance of the Williamson review evaluated contributions to diagnosis in the area of projective techniques, objective personality testing, measurement of interests, aptitude testing, and predicting academic achievement.

This was a very important period in increasing the understanding of potential contributions of projective tests. Abt and Bellak (1950) reviewed eight different tests. Particularly noteworthy were: Lindzey's (1952) interpretative assumptions in the use of the TAT; Schneidman's

(1951) study of blind TAT interpretations by 15 clinical psychologists, and Anderson and Anderson's (1951) introduction to projective techniques. Such an extensive review of projective tests seldom appears in the literature of counseling psychology, a circumstance which deprives the field of an opportunity to remain current on diagnostic tools which aid in understanding issues in normal personality development, needs, motivations, values, personal transitions, and normative crises.

The review by Wrenn (1954) marked a change in policy by the *Annual Review of Psychology*. His assignment was to include psychological measurement only as it pertained directly to the counseling process. Further, with the addition of a review on psychotherapy now being included in the *Annual Review of Psychology*, it became essential to have some viable distinction between "counseling" and "psychotherapy." The resolution was to differentiate between research conducted in medical and nonmedical settings, but to make no effort to distinguish between definitions of counseling and psychotherapy in deciding what literature to include in the respective reviews.

Wrenn reported that counseling was making progress toward status as a profession within psychology. He focused his review on studies of instruments, procedures, and methodology in counseling research. The topic of selecting and educating counselors was well represented in the research conducted during the early 1950s; Cottle (1953) comprehensively covered the work to date. Ethical standards began to be raised. Wrenn (1952) adapted the APA standards for counselors, and Gluck (1952) constructed a code for ethical practice by drawing on the codes in social work, psychology, law, and medicine.[4]

Counseling theory continued a period of rapid development during this time period. Seeman and Raskin (1953) reviewed nearly 50 research studies on aspects of client-centered therapy. Super's (1953) theory of vocational development challenged some of the assumptions of the Ginzberg et al. (1951) occupational choice theory. Features of the client counselor relationship common to all therapies were analyzed by Black (1952). In a related line of inquiry Hahn (1953) attempted to discern the common elements across counseling theories.

Mowrer and associates (1953) made a major contribution to the development of research and evaluation methodology for studies in psychotherapy. Existing approaches to analyzing research methods in counseling were extended by Dressel (1953), Shoben (1953b), and Pepinsky (1953). Thorne (1952) identified 11 basic conditions of successful therapy, and Watson (1952) identified limitations of psychotherapy effectiveness research. These contributions have a common theme of expanding knowledge of how to study the process and outcome of counseling and psychotherapy.

A section on psychological measurement in counseling covered interest measurement, personality measures, aptitude tests, and prediction studies of academic performance. As a consequence of the aforementioned shift in *Annual Review of Psychology* policy, the literature on projective techniques was not covered.

The concluding sections of the review covered vocational choice, occupational information, and procedures in counseling. Textbooks in counseling began to appear with greater frequency during this time period, and Shartle's (1952) book providing basic occupational information was published. The thrust of Wrenn's closing commentary merits consideration:

> The past year has seen the beginning acceptance of "Counseling Psychologist" as the professional title at the Ph.D. level in this field without abandonment of the term "counselor." There has also developed an improved understanding of what is involved in professional training, in the research needed on the nonintellectual qualities presumed essential for practitioners, and in the application of a code of ethics to counseling. Professionally, this field of psychology is a little more nearly mature than it was a year ago. Knowledge and researchwise we have greatly benefited by a dozen studies of major significance. A prediction is made by this writer that some of the past year's writing on counseling and vocational choice theory, on research evaluation methodology, on the Strong Interest Blank and on the MMPI will influence thinking and research on counseling for several years to come. (Wrenn, 1954, p. 351)

Wrenn described himself as encouraged by the quality of what he read in preparing the review. His prediction that "thinking and research on counseling" would be positively influenced by the literature of this period has been borne out by subsequent development.

SUMMARY

The second historical period in the growth of counseling psychology was extraordinarily important and productive. There were major official statements on doctoral and practicum training and specialty definition. The name of the division was changed to Counseling Psychology (and the choice of a process term like "counseling" in the title which has over 300 uses has contributed to a continuing identity diffusion). The *Annual Review of Psychology* provided a forum for regular scholarly evaluation of the literature, and the *Journal of Counseling Psychology* was founded. The Veterans Administration provided major employment opportunities for counseling psychologists. This was one of the most prolific and important periods in the history of the literature on counseling theory, diagnosis, and therapy. Gestalt theory and therapy and the theory of career choice of Ginzberg and associates appeared during this period of time.

FOOTNOTES

[1] Fretz (Note 1) provides an important clarification: "The task was inevitable, given the developments of the first historical period. The task is accurately defined, though there is not necessarily a link between the task and the historical context."

[2] Several reviewers of this historical perspective have drawn attention to the fact that these particular remarks are essentially editorial in nature, and may or may not reflect the views of other counseling psychologists.

[3] Pepinsky (Note 2) offered an interesting comment on this subject: "There *are* documented historical reasons why the split between — not APA as a whole, so much because liaison was never much in evidence — Division 17 and the APGA occurred. Pulling together in cases like this one *could* be constructive all around if it were not for . . . the emphasis on competitiveness and individualism that pervades our society and its organizational life. What I am suggesting here is that while your lament may be shared by many, it may also oversimplify the genesis of any one schism within and between organizations in our society."

[4] Wrenn (Note 3) indicated that: "Division 17 was the first division to apply the embryonic APA Code of Ethics to a Division or a field. In the process of writing this, I was aware of the fact that I was interpreting counseling psychology as I changed or modified or added phrases to the APA code. I think this helped to define the field a bit."

Chapter 3
Emerging Differences on Status and Focus: The Third Historical Period (1954-1962)

The year 1954 marks the beginning of the third period in the history of counseling psychology. Coming immediately after a period of exceptional theoretical and scientific accomplishment and strides toward resolution of important professional issues, this was a period rife with disagreement over the central role of the specialty. It was not, however, a period devoid of long term contributions.

FOUNDING OF THE JOURNAL OF COUNSELING PSYCHOLOGY

One enduring contribution was the founding of the *Journal of Counseling Psychology* by Milton E. Hahn, Harold G. Seashore, Donald E. Super, and C. Gilbert Wrenn (founding Editor). It first appeared in February of 1954. Wrenn (1966) has provided an absorbing account of its early history, and Pepinsky et al. (1978) of its subsequent development. The journal was financed with capital raised from private shareholders, and existed as a private corporation until taken over by the American Psychological Association in 1967.[1]

The Table of Contents for the first issue, after a year of planning, reflects topics deemed important at the time:

A Follow-Up After Three Years of Clients Counseled by Two Methods:
  Edward W. Forgy and John D. Black

An Interest Inventory as a Measure of Personality:
  Manuel N. Brown

Career Patterns as a Basis for Vocational Counseling:
  Donald E. Super

Analysis of Counselor Style by Discussion Units:
  W. J. Dipboye

Personality Characteristics of Counselors:
II. Male Counselor Responses to the MMPI and GZTS:
  W. C. Cottle and W. W. Lewis, Jr.

Counseling as Learning: A Symposium.
Counseling as a Learning Process:
  Arthur W. Combs

Counseling from the Standpoint of an "Interactive Conceptualist":
  Franklin J. Shaw

Counseling and the Learning of Integrative Behavior:
  Edward Joseph Shoben, Jr.

Changes in Self-Ratings as a Method of Evaluating Counseling:
  Ralph F. Berdie

Research Notes from Here and There:
  Harold B. Pepinsky

Book Reviews

Wrenn categorized the content of the first three volumes as follows:

Topical Area	No. of Articles
Counseling and Personality Theory	22
Counseling Process	21
Research Theory and Method	21
Studies of Students	20
Vocational and Rehabilitation Counseling	28
Measurement in Counseling	25
Counselor and His Professional Growth	22

(Wrenn, 1966, p. 488)

The categories are reflective of important emphases in theory development and research inquiry in the 1950s. Subsequent citations in the *Annual Review of Psychology* will highlight the continuing contributions of the *Journal of Counseling Psychology* to the dissemination of new knowledge in the field.

DIFFERING CONCEPTIONS OF A DEVELOPING PROFESSION

The differing conceptions of a developing profession began with Milton E. Hahn's Division 17 Presidential Address of 1954 (Hahn, 1955). He noted that a consequence of the rapid rise in the demand for non-medical professional services was that organized professional groups (such as social case work, psychiatry, and psychology) would stake out "zones of influence" in unclaimed territory and even attempt to claim functions considered the province of other disciplines. The competition for status, legal sanction, and advantage was particularly in evidence between psychiatry, social work, clinical psychology, and counseling psychology. The purpose of Hahn's (1955) contribution was to establish counseling psychology as a "functionally unique" pattern of practice. This involved demonstrating a patterning of methods, objectives, and situations peculiar to one specialty in a circumstance where related disciplines use the "same general toolkit of methodology."

Clinical psychology was the most difficult to differentiate from counseling psychology. Hahn offered four hypotheses:

1. Counseling psychologists resemble industrial psychologists to a greater extent than they do psychotherapists.
2. Clinical psychologists have a greater personality dimension of interests in "persons and personalities" as opposed to "processes and things" than do counseling psychologists.
3. Counseling psychologists tend to have greater managerial, administrative interests.
4. Counseling psychology trainees take more readily to statistics and statistical research.

(Hahn, 1955, p. 280. Also in Whiteley, 1980c, p. 101)

As Hahn was quick to point out, these hypotheses had not been subject to empirical evaluation. He did report that three of the four years of doctoral training were very similar. Learning theory is employed differently by clinical and counseling psychologists, however, and there are different applications and implications of personality development and structure theory:

> The clinical psychologist is more concerned with the deviate whose anxiety level is disabling and disintegrative. The counseling psychologist tends to work with those whose anxieties are interfering and disruptive but not disabling. When therapy is based on learning theory, the counselor usually concentrates more on cognitive, intellectual levels and less on phenomenological constructs.
>
> Differences appear too in the applications and implications of personality development and structure theory. Here, counseling psychologists concentrate on the problems of interfering value systems and judgments and the changing of attitudes. The clinical psychologist appears to work more in the medically related areas of reorganizing basic personality structure. Although the course work is often done in the same class, what is taken from the course in terms of future practice may be quite different. Counseling has greater concern with a positive approach to trait strengths and less

concern with medically diagnosed personality deviations that demand remediation through psychotherapy. (Hahn, 1955, p. 281. Also in Whiteley, 1980c, p. 102)

Counseling is not in order with "deeply disturbed patients." Hahn concluded that despite similarities in three-fourths of doctoral training, there is little proof that clinical and counseling psychologists are being trained to do the same things. He summarized the relatively unique pattern of functions of the counseling psychologist as follows:

> First, the major concern of the counseling psychologist is with *clients*, not *patients*, from the mass of people who can support themselves and live with reasonable adjustment in our society.
>
> Second, our employment is in situations that do not place us professionally under the direction or supervision of related disciplines either as a matter of policy, law, or political or economic conditions.
>
> Third, our tools and techniques of practice are based in general more on normative approaches than are those of related disciplines.
>
> Fourth, we tend to emphasize learning theory at the cognitive, intellectual, and rational levels, although not omitting orientation to the content of psychodynamics. We help *clients* to change attitudes and value systems, but we rarely attempt the major restructuring or rebuilding of a personality.
>
> Fifth, we deal usually with anxiety states at the frustrating, interfering levels, not when disability or disintegration is indicated.
>
> Sixth, and our most nearly unique single function, we are the most skilled professional workers in the assessment and appraisal of human traits for educational-vocational-social living: the casting of a psychological balance sheet to aid our *clients* to contribute to, and to take the most from, living in our society.
>
> Seventh, we are obligated to follow our *clients* beyond the office door. Until there is *client*-accepted planning for such future action as formal education or training, vocational exploration, and social direction, the counseling process is not complete.
>
> Eighth, and last, we stress positive psychological strengths and their personal and social use as opposed to a process of diagnosing and remedying psychopathies. (Hahn, 1955, p. 282. Also in Whiteley, 1980c, p. 104)

Hahn indicated that this pattern did not appear to be duplicated by professionals in related fields.

In this period of differing views of an emerging specialty, events set in motion by the APA Education and Training Board in 1959 led to four sharply conflicting appraisals of the status of counseling psychology (Berg, Pepinsky, & Shoben, 1980; Tyler, Tiedeman, & Wrenn, 1980;

Berg, 1980; Tiedeman, 1980). The conflict was so fundamental that one of the appraisals was suppressed (see Pepinsky et al., 1978, for an account), and three of the four which resulted from the conflict did not appear in print until finally published 20 years later by Whiteley (1980c).[2]

The motivation of the APA Education and Training Board was to determine whether counseling psychology should continue to be recognized as an "independent" specialty (Pepinsky et al., 1978, p. 52). As part of their report on the status of counseling psychology in 1960, Berg et al. (1980) elaborated upon the thinking of the 1959 APA Education and Training Board in commissioning their report:

> The reason for the Board's action was a general feeling among its members that all was not well with counseling psychology. Although counseling as an activity in fields other than psychology appeared to be flourishing, as witness the provision for counseling in the National Defense Education Act, *counseling psychology* appeared, in the opinion of some members of the Board, to have lagged behind other specialty areas of psychology. Two or three decades ago, counseling psychology was immensely prestigeful as a specialty, but now it appears to be in some ways on the wane. (Berg et al., 1980, p. 105)

The first section of their report was entitled "The decline of counseling psychology" and began with the declarative statement that "there is clear evidence that counseling psychology is declining" (Berg et al., 1980, p. 105). They cited the declining numbers entering the field, the drop-off in quality of graduate students, the fact that students were entering counseling because they could not get into clinical psychology, the fact that there were no APA-approved counseling psychology internship programs, and the decline in the number of people applying for ABEPP diplomas in counseling.

If all of this was not dismal enough, they quoted two independent reports that found the scientific status of counseling psychology was "far from satisfactory" (Goodstein, Buchheimer, Crites, & Muthard, 1959), and that counseling psychology was rated by a sample of APA members as being lowest in status of all specialties in psychology requiring the Ph.D. (Granger, 1959). Counseling psychology, although growing, was lagging behind clinical psychology in its rate of growth. While recognizing that there was no single solution to the complex of problems presented in their report, one alternative suggested was the fusion of counseling and clinical psychology at the doctoral level.

The response from Division 17 was not long in coming. Seashore (1960) reported that the Executive Committee of the Division had asked Leona Tyler, David Tiedeman, and C. Gilbert Wrenn to draft a statement on the current status of counseling psychology as a field of work and study. The reasons the Executive Committee commissioned the statement were several:

> The Executive Committee of Division 17 decided in 1960 that the opinions expressed in that report did not reflect the variety of interests of the members of the Division. Furthermore, the Executive Committee felt that the report (which has not yet been officially released for general circulation) did not adequately marshal the factual evidence concerning the current status of counseling psychology which should be relevant in the deliberations of the Education and Training Board. However, the Executive Committee instructed its special committee not to write a rejoinder to the aforementioned report but rather to write a positive statement deducing conclusions from documented evidence. (Tyler et al., 1980, p. 114)

The first section of their report documented the emergence of counseling psychology. Citing the Committee on Definition (APA, 1956), counseling psychology was said characteristically to emphasize the development of an individual's perception of self, the achievement of harmony with the environment, and the encouragement of society to promote the fullest development of all persons and the recognition of individual differences. Recent accomplishments noted included: the statements on definition (APA, 1956); doctoral training (APA, 1952a); practicum training (APA, 1952b); the role of counseling psychology in the training of school counselors (APA, 1961a); the assessment of the characteristics, attitudes, and expectations of its members (APA, 1959); and the founding of the *Journal of Counseling Psychology* in 1954.

After reviewing a number of studies of counseling psychologists, the following summary inferences about the state of the profession were offered:

a. If Division growth rate is used as a criterion, then the state of health of counseling psychology resembles the state of health of psychology as a whole.

b. The newer members of the Division are reducing the average age of the Divisional membership and have a wide range of interests outside of their primary interest in counseling. It is apparent that they do not live in professional isolation.

c. Most counseling psychologists, whether new Division members, recent Ph.D.s, or writers for the *Journal of Counseling Psychology*, are employed in educational institutions. Very few label themselves other than counseling psychologists, teachers, or, for the older ones, administrators. They do *not* call themselves clinical psychologists or school psychologists, and very few are in private practice.

d. Only a small proportion of the total securing doctorates in psychology do so in counseling. Far outnumbered by those in the experimental and clinical field (perhaps they should be), they are numerically in the neighborhood of those taking degrees in social and educational psychology and considerably ahead of those taking the degree in industrial psychology. It is a "medium-sized" field which has good evidences of viability. (Tyler et al., 1980, pp. 119-120)

The survey by Granger (1959), which assigned counseling psychologists the lowest prestige of all positions requiring the Ph.D. in psychology, was quoted. Further, as of 1957 25% of Division 17 members also belonged to Division 12.

A very informative section on the distinctive characteristics of counseling psychology quoted Perry (1955) on the differences between counseling and psychotherapy. Psychotherapy is concerned with intrapersonal conflicts, while counseling focuses on "role" problems such as education, vocation, and marriage. Tyler et al. (1980) summarize the importance of counseling psychology's focus:

on *plans* individuals must make to play productive *roles* in their social environments. Whether the person being helped with such planning is sick or well, abnormal or normal, is really irrelevant. The focus is on assets, skills, strengths, possibilities for further development. Personality difficulties are dealt with only when they constitute obstacles to the individual's forward progress. (Tyler et al., 1980, p. 121)

The social demand for counseling psychologists was viewed as great and on the increase. Their statement (Tyler et al., 1980) was approved by the 1960-61 and 1961-62 Executive Committees of the Division of Counseling Psychology.

In a subsequent paper on the status and prospect of counseling psychology in 1962, Tiedeman (1980) summarized the Tyler, Tiedeman, and Wrenn rationale for continuing the existence of the Division in terms of:

1. a distinguished history of responsible accomplishment;
2. a substantial and healthy rate of growth during the immediately preceding decade;
3. a lively journal, named after our Division, which provides a publication medium for our members;
4. existing specialized training programs;
5. the possibility of qualifying for a diploma, from the American Board of Examiners in Professional Psychology, which denotes special training in our field;

6. opportunity for employment which is reasonably specific as to the necessary training and certification; and,
7. goals, purposes, and techniques which are distinctly different from their counterparts in the field of clinical psychology. (Tiedeman, 1980, p. 125)

The general thrust of the Tyler et al. (1980) and Tiedeman (1980) analyses was at variance with the subsequent outline by Berg (1980) of alternative roads for counseling psychology in 1962.[3] Berg's view was that "alternative roads are not only feasible but perhaps necessary" (p. 133). The basis for his analysis was partially rooted in the suppressed report on the status of counseling psychology in 1960 by Berg et al. (1980). Referring to the suppression, Berg (1980), reviewed the history:

This committee was appointed by the Education and Training Board and asked to report on the status of Counseling Psychology. In 1960 the Education and Training Board requested that the report be published; however, contrary to the E & T Board request, the report was not published. The reasons for this are not entirely clear. (Berg, 1980, p. 133)

His consideration of alternative roads for counseling psychology contained three possibilities: merger with clinical psychology as a fusion, not an absorption, so that a new field would emerge which would train for competency in dealing with both normal and seriously disturbed persons; the training of counselors first and psychologists second in an extension of Danskin's (1959) idea; and development of a technical level of counseling at the M.A. level. He favored the first alternative for the following reasons:

We do not know where the dividing lines are between normal and pathological states, and we already have clinical psychology extending its professional domain (particularly among private practitioners) to problems of normal persons. Furthermore, we already have solid programs which cover both specialties. Thus I should favor extending and formalizing a new program, preferably with some new name to avoid partisan semantic identifications.
    In summary, I should say that *counseling* is a rapidly growing and important professional activity; however, *counseling psychology* as a special field of *psychology* does not seem to have experienced the same growth as a psychological specialty that it has as an educational specialty — that is, its growth has been under the aegis of colleges of education. Perhaps many of the tools and techniques we deal with are historically or by custom found more often in education. The same is largely true of the research; that is, the standardized test lists of vocational requirements (*Dictionary of Occupational*

Titles), and so on, are perhaps found more often among professional educators than among psychologists. Whether such is the case or not, it is true that counseling is flourishing in colleges of education but not in departments of psychology. Thus counseling psychology as *psychology* should seriously consider some alternative roads. (Berg, 1980, p. 135)

SOCIETAL CONTEXT: KEYSTONES OF CONSCIOUSNESS

The societal context in the middle and later 1950s influenced counseling psychology in a number of different ways. A cordial relationship existed between Division 17 and the American Personnel and Guidance Association. This cordiality extended to the cooperation between the *Personnel and Guidance Journal*, the official APGA publication, and the *Journal of Counseling Psychology* (see Pepinsky et al., 1978; Wrenn, 1966).

In terms of influence on federal policy toward the provision of counseling services and the funding of training opportunities, the initiative shifted away from organized counseling psychology during this period of time. Two pieces of legislation, the Vocational Rehabilitation Act of 1954 and the National Defense Education Act (NDEA) of 1958, created a demand for more counseling positions than could be filled by the available pool of counseling psychologists. The lobbying efforts of the APGA and activity by schools of education led to major funding for the training of subdoctoral counselors to work in elementary and secondary schools. Pepinsky et al. (1978) provided the best insight into the reasons why organized counseling psychology acted as it did:

> Neither the Division of Counseling Psychology nor the APA saw fit to establish formal liaison with the APGA to aid in developing guidelines for the new programs. Instead, the APA formed a major committee to negotiate with representatives of the American Psychiatric Association on territorial disputes between the two organizations. Concurrently, an invitational conference on graduate education in psychology (there were no professional schools of psychology in those days) recommended emphasis upon the doctorate as a minimally essential level of training for psychologists. Because resources were limited, so ran the prevailing argument, there could be only token sponsorship of subdoctoral training programs. (Roe, Gustad, Moore, Ross, & Skodak, 1959)

The Division of Counseling Psychology's inaction vis-a-vis the APGA at this time is also understandable. Earlier it had endorsed the idea of the doctorate as a requisite level of training for counseling psychologists (APA, 1952a). More recently, as noted above, divisional ties with rehabilitation and school counseling were allowed to erode, while counseling psychologists in large numbers were receiving doctoral training and subsequent employment in VA hospitals. The VA had ample funds for trainees, staff, and consultants. Counseling psychology thus was able to compete successfully with clinical psychology for its share of a lucrative market for psychological services. These events contributed toward a blurring of distinctions between the two psychological specialties. (Pepinsky et al., 1978, p. 486-487. Also in Whiteley, 1980c, p. 52)

Once again, competition with clinical psychology served to divert the attention of counseling psychologists.

In February, 1958, the Division 17 presidential statement by Ralph Berdie (1958) provided an insight into the effects of a federal response to Sputnik I in the form of the National Defense Education Act:

Never before has action of the national government promised to touch so closely and directly upon issues of professional interest to the members of the Division of Counseling Psychology. Impending government actions in the areas of testing, counseling and guidance, scholarships, and the distribution of manpower are topics of daily headlines. Members of Congress and of the Administration reiterate that if our national defense is to be bolstered and our country's status maintained, young persons with exceptional talents must be identified, guided into proper lines of endeavors, and provided with adequate incentive and opportunity for training. Although this national anxiety is a direct outcome of a perceived inadequacy in science and technology, many persons, including the President of the United States, have explicitly recognized that our need is not only for more trained scientists and technicians but also for more educated persons in many fields.

Of direct and immediate concern to us should be the possibility that a wide discrepancy will be found between what is expected of testing, counseling, and guidance, and what is delivered. Some of us believe, for instance, that counseling can help young persons make more appropriate educational and vocational choices, but the *main* determinants of these choices are solidly imbedded in our social and cultural background, and if great redistributions of talent are to be effected, more than counseling will be needed. (*Counseling News and Views*, 1958, Vol. 10, No. 2, p. 1)

The question of society's *expectations* of what counseling promised as contrasted to what it could actually deliver to recipients was one which would be raised with regularity in the ensuing years.

Shoben (1958) provided yet another perspective on the impact of the federal government on the interests of counseling psychologists. In addition to describing the impact of the NDEA, he also noted the importance of the Cooperative Research Program of the United States Office of Education:

> The former, probably one of the most significant governmental actions with respect to education ever taken, provides, among other things, for (1) the identification of talented youth through systematic testing, (2) the establishment of counseling and guidance services for secondary school youngsters, and (3) the setting up of special institutes in appropriate universities and colleges for training of testing and counseling personnel in the public schools. The Co-operative Research Program provides funds to foster research, surveys, and demonstrations in the field of education, including research in counseling. Together, the two acts define four enterprises in which we have a considerable interest and a social responsibility that has never before been quite so compelling. The successful and wise administration of these laws virtually demands that the competencies of counseling psychologists be available, and the fulfillment of the potentialities for public benefit in the legislation depends in significant part on us. How can we best serve?
>
> From the standpoint of Division 17, we are in the process of establishing direct lines of communications with responsible administrators in the U.S. Office of Education. The first step is to set up an informal committee to consult with these people on various phases of the law's implementation; and while the terms of the Education Act preclude the formalizing of this arrangement, it will enable us to play an influential and genuinely helpful role if we can conduct ourselves in a truly professional way. This condition implies that we must maintain the attitude of responsible and hard-headed altruism that we like to think is characteristic of us, keeping our focus firmly on the potentialities of the law and resisting both the greedy self-interest that is so likely to be evoked by the availability of money and the parochial yearnings for dominance that are often elicited by interdisciplinary undertakings. Educators and others besides psychologists have an appropriate interest in the Education Act, and it is part of our job to work collaboratively with them. (*Counseling News and Views*, 1958, Vol. 11, No. 1, pp. 2-3)

Shoben, in properly noting an opportunity, drew attention to the role which Division 17 could play in serving as a communication channel between counseling psychologists and the U.S. Office of Education.

Schwebel (1984) singled out the launching of Sputnik and its repercussions in American society as an important force affecting the social context in which counseling psychologists work:

Sputnik ushered in a new era, sparked by federal funds for institutes and research attuned to the presumed national need for improved teaching and counseling about mathematics, sciences, and foreign languages. At about the same time, as a reaction to Brown vs. the Topeka Board of Education (the Supreme Court decision striking down as unconstitutional the concept of "separate but equal" education), and the early stages of organized black social action, federal funds were available for institutes to improve professional practices in counseling minorities. (Schwebel, 1984, p. 286)

During this time the social expectations of previously disenfranchised groups began to rise, creating both new populations to serve and a ferment in the fabric of society.

INITIATIVES OF ORGANIZED COUNSELING PSYCHOLOGY

February of 1954 brought a report by Samler (1954) which quoted a U.S. Office of Education memo announcing that:

effective today there is established a Guidance and Pupil-Personnel Section in the Instruction, Organization, and Services Branch of the Division of State and Local School Systems. This Section will be concerned with the conduct of studies and provision of assistance and advice on guidance and pupil personnel matters in elementary and secondary schools. (Samler, 1954, p. 3)

This was welcome news to a profession which had actively lobbied for the reinstatement of a branch specific to guidance with the U.S. Office of Education.

The positive role of the Veterans Administration in the development of counseling psychology continued. Samler (1954, pp. 4-5) reported that 159 professional staff and 73 trainees were at work in the Vocational Counseling Service. Further, the VA had paid the tuition, granting part-time leaves as necessary, for 76 counselors in VA regional offices.

Hahn's (1954) report as Division 17 President in June of 1954 drew attention to the rapid rise of new major problems:

one is surprised with the speed at which new major problems have arisen. The present behemoth is how to meet the expanding and unexpected demand for soundly trained counseling psychologists and psychological counselors. The Veterans Administration's need for Ph.D.s in the hospital program has increased rapidly and soundly, but the appetite for good raw material is insatiable in terms of the supply. The subdoctoral psychological counselor is also in demand not only with government agencies but also with community organizations and secondary schools. In all areas demand is outrunning training facilities and the supply of candidates.

A new emphasis has emerged through the thinking of some that we must either clearly describe and define our special professional status, relative to a unique pattern of function and training, or see ourselves as identical with clinical psychologists except for a course in occupational information. (*Counseling News and Views*, 1954, Vol. 6, No. 3, p. 1)

An emerging national emphasis on the handicapped individual (to reappear 25 years later) raised for Hahn the perpetual problem of subdoctoral training in counseling.

A change in style and format greeted the recipients of Vol. 7, No. 1 of *Counseling News and Views* along with an announcement that the Policy and Planning Board of the APA had proposed that the present number of APA divisions be reduced to six (nothing came of this, except that proposals for reorganization continue to recur!). The establishment of what was to prove to be a very effective new committee for Division 17 was announced, the Committee on Definition. Division 17 President Francis P. Robinson announced that an economy move of the U.S. Office of Education could remove the key position of Chief of the Guidance Section. A small committee under the chairmanship of C. Winfield Scott was set up to see that a history of Division 17 was prepared.

The years 1954-1955 proved to be very active as far as the committee structure of Division 17 was concerned. For example, the Research Committee chaired by William C. Cottle (1954) reported on four matters:

1. A symposium on "Implications of Research on Standardized Tests for College Personnel Work";
2. A proposal for the Research Committee to develop each year an annotated bibliography on some new topic in counseling psychology;
3. A proposal to make the Research Committee a clearing house for all completed masters' theses or projects and for all completed doctoral dissertations supervised by members of Division 17;
4. An agreement with the Sub-Committee on Selection of Counselors of the Committee on Counselor Training to help in the development of criteria for judging counselor effectiveness. (Cottle, 1954, p. 17)

On this fourth matter, criteria were suggested for measuring counselor effectiveness in academic training and in the actual conduct of counseling sessions.

Publication Committee Chair Leona E. Tyler reported that, with few exceptions, counseling psychologists were pleased with the new *Journal of Counseling Psychology*. Division 17 members reported that there was no special problem in getting papers published, and there was a tremendous range of materials counseling psychologists considered relevant to their work.

The titles of other committees which issued reports in 1954-55 give a flavor to the topics important to organized counseling psychology in the middle 1950s: Committee on the Exchange of Current Research Activities, Committee on Counseling Psychology and Relations with Public Schools, Committee on Talent Hunt (to broaden the participation in Division 17 activities), Committee on Psychological Terminology, Committee on Counseling Psychology and Related Disciplines, Committee on Training of Rehabilitation Workers, Counselor Training Committee, and the Joint Committee of Division 5, 7, 12, 15, 16, 17, and 20 on the 1954 APA Program. This is an impressive array of diverse concerns.

The next issue of *Counseling News and Views* (Vol. 7, No. 2) reported still other committees: Advisory Committee to the U.S. Office of Education, History of Division 17 Committee, the ongoing Definition of Counseling Psychology Committee, and the Cooperative Project on Behavior Theory. Editor Walter Johnson of *Counseling News and Views* was moved to note:

> Division Seventeen, always a lusty and vigorous member of the APA Divisional family, has shown evidence of even greater growth and maturity during this year. Its ever-continuing growth in membership is only one indication of development. More important is the increasing responsibility it has been assuming in professional activities which promote human welfare through many and varied channels. This has been a healthy growth, primarily because of the unselfish efforts of the many members with high ethical principles and willingness to put duty and profession above personal interest or gain. (Johnson, 1955, p. 1)

Despite the emerging differences of opinion within organized counseling psychology, this was a very active period of time for the formal organizational structure. This was also a period of active cooperation with the American Personnel and Guidance Association as reflected in the Joint Advisory Committee to the U.S. Office of Education. As Division 17 President Francis P. Robinson (1955) stated, "It has been our feeling that joint action of our two groups would be more effective and efficient when we need to work with outside agencies or work on problems of mutual interest" (*Counseling News and Views*, 1955, Vol. 7, No. 2, p. 5). It is regrettable that this spirit of cooperation on topics of mutual interest has not continued over the years.

Vol. 8, No. 1 of *Counseling News and Views* for November of 1955 is of interest as it announced the appearance of the report of the Committee on Definition (to be published the next year in the *American Psycholo-*

gist) and the fact that $1,000.00 had been set aside for a "professional project," later to be the Greyston Conference of 1964.

Vol. 8, No. 3 of *Counseling News and Views* reported the appearance of a new Committee on Bibliographic Services which had been assigned the task of developing, preparing, and making available a card file of *Psychological Abstracts* items relevant to counseling psychology. The chair of the committee was Barbara A. Kirk, someone who subsequently contributed three decades of dedicated service to organized counseling psychology.

The Stanford Conference on Education and Training for Psychological Contributions to Mental Health (Strother, 1957) occurred in August of 1955 to explore the general question of: What kind of training can psychology best give in the area of mental health? This conference was held in the context of the supposed unique interest of counseling psychologists in the normal person and in the promotion of positive mental health. Samler (1964) quoted Seeman (undated) as identifying "at least three aspects which make counseling psychology at home with the concepts of the conference." Those aspects were "consistent interest in working with the normal person, a sensitivity to sociological and environmental factors in adjustment, and an interest in measurement and quantification" (Samler, 1964, p. 53).*

An interim report of the Committee on Divisional History by the chair, C. Winfield Scott (1956), indicated the problem associated with their task:

> With a slow pace reminiscent of the march of history itself, the Committee has been progressing toward the development of an interpretive history. It has completed a careful study of all pertinent records in the Secretary's office and at APA headquarters. Incidentally, it has found that permanent files contain only a small proportion of the original committee reports and presumably of the important correspondence. However, the Executive Committee has decided that the shortage is not serious and that no effort need be made to remedy the situation.

> Official records, such as minutes of meetings and special reports; communications from the Secretary; and that excellent secondary source, *Counseling News and Views*, provide a good basis of fact and evolving thought for use by the Committee. Correspondence with "Founding Fathers" and, perhaps, analysis of membership data should round out the historical picture adequately. (*Counseling News and Views*, 1956, Vol. 8, No. 3, pp. 10-11)

---

*This and all other quotations from this source are reprinted by permission of the publisher and A. S. Thompson and D. E. Super (Eds.), *The professional preparation of counseling psychology: Report of the 1964 Greyston Conference.* (New York: Teachers College Press, © 1964 by Teachers College, Columbia University. All rights reserved.)

Access to primary historical documents remains a difficult obstacle in compiling a history of counseling psychology three decades later. The task is aided, however, by access to four resources: *Counseling News and Views*, until it ceased publishing in 1968, *The Counseling Psychologist* since its inception in 1969, the *Journal of Counseling Psychology* since 1954, and the *Annual Review of Psychology* since 1950.

When interpreted in light of the later (in 1959) action of the APA Education and Training Committee in establishing a group to review the status of counseling psychology, the report of the Division 17 Program Committee for 1955-56 might have been a premonition that all was not well. The time allocated by the APA to Division 17 for the 1956 APA Convention had been assigned to the business meeting, social hour, presidential address, four discussion groups, four symposia, and *two* paper-reading sessions. Only *nine* papers had been submitted. As Shoben (1956a) remarked, "With so little to choose from, it is obvious that paper-reading sessions of high quality are unlikely to result" (p. 4).

Organized counseling psychology had been engaged in addressing substantive issues (training and practicum standards, specialty definition) in the profession for a decade. The next topic to emerge after study was criteria for evaluating internship facilities in university counseling centers (Super, 1956). This statement noted that internship quality is difficult to evaluate because of the fact that there is such a diversity of installations.

The June, 1957 issue of *Counseling News and Views*, Vol. 9, No. 3, reported with regret that the Bibliographic Service would not come to fruition and had to be abandoned. The reason was a lack of financial support by members of Division 17. Only 88 subscriptions were received, not enough to provide a viable base of support. The total membership of Division 17 for 1956-57 was 774 members, according to the dues and special assessments statement (*Counseling News and Views*, 1957, Vol. 10, No. 1, p. 18).

Volume 10, No. 2 of *Counseling News and Views* for February of 1958 carried two statements of importance to counseling psychologists, one on issues in the nationwide testing of students and one on policy regarding the nation's human resources problems. This latter statement indicated that the full utilization of human potentialities depends upon two factors: the country's decision to turn educated talent toward national uses and the goal of promoting maximum growth of human talent through education. The focus of the statement was on the second factor.

One important matter of significance regarding these two statements is that together they occupied five pages of a 36-page issue of *Counseling News and Views*, were quite relevant to the established interests of counseling psychology (as evidenced by their appearance in *Counseling News and Views* as well as their inherent content), yet both were formal documents of the American Personnel and Guidance Association! During this period of time, at least, positive initiative had shifted from Division 17 to other professional organizations.

While this period in the history of counseling psychology has been characterized as rife with disagreement on the status and proper focus of the specialty, it was also a time for pride in accomplishment. In *Counseling News and Views*, Vol. 11, No. 1, Shoben (1958) captured this theme:

> All of us are entitled to a very proper pride in the way that counseling psychology has extended its range in the past few years. In a remarkably short time, we have made our usefulness apparent to a variety of hospitals and community agencies over the nation, won a genuinely professional niche for ourselves in the VA, and have recently attained a kind of endorsement by the National Institute of Mental Health, which, under its policy of broadened support for psychology, is now prepared to make training grants to doctoral programs in our specialty very much like those available to clinical psychology.
>
> These advancements reflect, I think, both our own growing professional maturity and the increasing awareness in society generally that psychology has much to do with issues that confront our nation both domestically and internationally. Dimly, perhaps, but more and more definitely, there seems to be an emerging idea that America's strength and happiness depend on the extent to which it can realize the potentialities of its people. With our emphasis on developmental and facilitative, rather than fundamentally therapeutic and remedial procedures, this objective is in large measure our very serious and important business. (*Counseling News and Views*, 1958, Vol. 11, No. 1, p. 1)

Shoben (1958) also drew attention to the historical and philosophical roots of counseling psychology which exist in education:

> In our concern for our more recent extensions of our service into medical and agency settings, we may be tempted understandably to forget our origins and their implications for the distinctly facilitative character of counseling psychology. Such a lapse of our historical sense would be particularly unfortunate at the present moment. (*Counseling News and Views*, 1958, Vol. 11, No. 1, pp. 1-2)

The "present moment" was referring to the previously described federal NDEA and Cooperative Research initiatives. The failure to become deeply involved in this federal initiative must be viewed ultimately as an opportunity lost by counseling psychology.

Shoben (1959) returned to the theme of the potential importance of the NDEA to counseling psychology:

> Perhaps our most important responsibility of the moment is contributing to the success of the National Defense Education Act.

Not only does this legislation make possible tremendous benefits to American education; it is the first federal law in our history to recognize explicitly the vital role of testing and counseling functions in the educational enterprise. As counseling psychologists, we are confronted by a central challenge: Are we the socially responsible and cooperative profession that we have held ourselves out to be? To meet this challenge, we must make sure that we understand the law and that we find creative ways to contribute to its effective implementation. (*Counseling News and Views*, 1959, Vol. 11, No. 2, p. 1)

Given the historical centrality of diagnostic assessment in the work of the counseling psychologist, particularly in educational and vocational planning, Shoben's reminder of the vital role of testing and counseling in the enterprise of education might have spurred the Division to greater action. He even outlined in the balance of his message how counseling psychologists could become involved in programs funded under NDEA.

In a final portion of his presidential message, Shoben (1959) drew attention to the relative dearth of research reports as follows:

For the last few years, we have had very little at the APA meetings in the way of exciting research reports from counseling psychologists. (See Grummon's bleak little fantasy on pp. 5-6 of the last issue of *CN&V*.) A quick check of the references to Berdie's chapter on Counseling in the 1959 *Annual Review* suggests that as many as from one-half to two-thirds of the items were authored by other than Division 17 members. (*Counseling News and Views*, 1959, Vol. 11, No. 2, p. 6)

This warning about the paucity of research being conducted by counseling psychologists echoed Grummon's (1958) bleak assessment that "only 4% of the association's membership had research as their principal job function" (p. 6). The observation by Shoben that over one-half and maybe even two-thirds of the citations in the *Annual Review of Psychology* treatment of counseling for 1959 were authored by noncounseling psychologists would seem to reflect the statistic quoted by Grummon; namely, the lack of time allocated by counseling psychologists to research.

The issue of the proper content for graduate education in psychology recurred again in late 1958 at the Miami Conference on Graduate Education in Psychology. Of the 120 psychologists in attendance, 25 were counseling psychologists. There were five general topics:

1. For what roles, as perceived by society, should we educate psychologists?
2. What is common in the roles of psychologists, and what should be the common core of training?

3. How do we train psychologists for the differences in doctoral specialties? How far should specialization go?
4. What is the function of subdoctoral training, and what should be its components?
5. How may graduate education be facilitated or hampered by controls?

In Bordin's (1959) report, the conference provided for a:

well informed and articulate exchange of views among clinicians, experimentalists, educational, school and social psychologists, and all of the other nuances of specialization, of content interests, methodology, practice, and work locale, to be found in psychology. (Bordin, 1959, p. 15)

In terms of outcomes of the conference, there was a tendency to move away from a "standardized conception of the education of psychologists," though this sentiment was counterbalanced by the concern that it might appear that "psychology had not yet reached that 'bed rock' level of science where certain principles and the research on which they rest must form the foundation for all psychological endeavor." (Bordin, 1959, p. 15)

Confronting the fact that the need for psychological services exceeds the ability of Ph.D.-level psychologists to meet that need, the attendees at the Miami Conference endorsed the expansion of subdoctoral training programs. They also endorsed the notion that "the psychologist should bring to his service work some of the detachment and critical analysis that represents the research attitude" (Bordin, 1959, p. 17). Clinical observation can lead to the posing of searching questions.

Tyler (1959a), in a commentary on the Miami Conference, also touched on the research attitude:

Research is not a specialty field within psychology but the defining characteristic of all psychologists. Research, broadly conceived, is now regarded as a central feature of the training and activity of any psychologist, regardless of his area of specialization and regardless of the services he expects to render to society. Research should be conceived much more broadly than it has sometimes been in the past to include many varieties of methods through which dependable knowledge can be gained. The continuum of research methodology includes, along with the traditionally accepted methodologies, the clinical and naturalistic devices by which first order hypotheses are generated out of raw observations. That is to say, it includes the first order reduction of data, and it has disciplined ground rules for such reduction. This is in contrast to the notion that scientific thinking starts only after questions have been formulated. (Tyler, 1959a, p. 18)

Psychologists, as a central feature of their role, are defined as having a research mission.

Tyler's report contains training recommendations which were intended to enhance research productivity:

> Research training is paramount. To strengthen this aspect of students' experience a number of specific things were proposed:
>
> a. Broaden methodology courses, using problems and examples from the clinic, the school, and the factory as well as the laboratory.
> b. Begin participation in research as early as possible. Do not confine it to thesis activity.
> c. Provide for the supervision of theses in the clinical area by faculty members who have themselves had clinical experience.
> d. Recognize at least three kinds of research—creative, useful but not original, inquiring and critical but not definitive. (Tyler, 1959a, p. 19)

Research activity "as early as possible" incorporated into doctoral training in counseling psychology has been the exception rather than the rule.

The membership of Division 17 continued its upward growth during this period. Estimated membership for 1959 was 940. Among important activities that year was the preparation of a questionnaire covering counseling center characteristics (staff, case load, budget, etc.) by Thomas M. Magoon of the University of Maryland in conjunction with a meeting of the directors of university counseling centers. This questionnaire initiated a still ongoing process of self-examination, assisting counseling centers in maintaining and improving the quality of service.

Vol. 12, No. 1 of *Counseling News and Views* marked the first official statement by Division 17 President Leona Tyler, who went on to become President of the American Psychological Association. Division 17's most prestigious recognition, the Leona Tyler Award, is named in honor of her contributions as scholar and leader. In her view:

> Counseling psychology is a body of knowledge that should be put at the service of a wide variety of counselors—in schools, in churches, in industry, and in many other settings. Counseling psychologists are professional workers whose daily activities cover a wide range of duties, from psychotherapy to administration. (Tyler, 1959b, p. 1)

In choosing where to place an emphasis, she singled out efforts to stimulate research and make its findings more available, to improve counseling in the public schools, to determine the special interests of counseling psychologists, and to explore what the major *functions* of Division 17 are and should be.

Tyler (1960) indicated that a trend discernible in psychology as the decade of the 1960s began was an effort to establish closer relationships with education and the public schools. She identified two ways to bring psychological knowledge to bear on the problems of education:

> One is to increase the number of professional psychologists who work in school settings. The flourishing APA Division of School Psychologists and the widespread interest in training programs for this specialty show that the idea is being accepted. The other way is to bring a larger amount of usable psychological knowledge into the education of all teachers, school administrators, and other special-ized workers.
>
> Because psychology has become both a science and a profession, its relationships with other occupational groups are of two kinds, and it is often difficult to keep them both in mind. I am convinced that it is just as important to make the body of knowledge we call *psycholo-gy* freely available as to persuade society to use the special skills of the persons we call *psychologists.* (Tyler, 1960, p. 1)

Except for the continued role of diagnostics for educational and voca-tional choice, a decade was to pass before counseling psychologists became involved in the public schools in a major way (Mosher & Sprinthall, 1970, 1971).

Vol. 13, No. 1 of *Counseling News and Views* reported (Seashore, 1960) on the developing saga of the establishment of the committee composed of Tyler et al. (1980) to prepare a response to the report by Berg et al. (1980):

> A special committee composed of Leona Tyler, chairman, C. Gilbert Wrenn, and David Tiedeman has the task of defining *The Current Status of Counseling Psychology.* This assignment arises from a report prepared by a special committee, composed of Irwin Berg, chairman, Harold Pepinsky, and E. Joseph Shoben, appointed by the Education and Training Board of the APA. This report has not been released generally but has now become available to interested persons. While these distinguished men are colleagues in Division 17, their report was not prepared in the name of Division 17 but rather as the collaboration of a committee of individual psychologists. Division 17 was not cognizant that the study was under way. The chairman of the current E & T Board has now asked Division 17 to react to the Berg-Pepinsky-Shoben report. Your Executive Committee expects our committee to prepare an independent appraisal of the status of our field. When this report is finished, we presume the E & T Board will review its association-wide problems of education and training in the light of the two reports. (p. 1)

In light of the publicity at the time, the importance to the profession of the issues of status and focus, and the eminence of the six authors

(Leona Tyler, David V. Tiedeman, C. Gilbert Wrenn, Irv Berg, Harold Pepinsky, and E. J. Shoben, Jr.), it remains an oddity in the history of counseling psychology that three of the four provocative reports they generated during the several-year period of time between 1959 and 1962 remained unpublished for 20 years, and the fourth was only published as an appendix to a conference report (Thompson & Super, 1964) four years later.[4]

As part of a continuing Division 17 concern with strengthening doctoral training programs, Shoben (1960) was asked to investigate why counseling psychology, though technically eligible, received *no* support for its doctoral training programs in 1959 from the National Institute of Mental Health. He concluded that the dearth of counseling psychology students arose not from lack of financial support but because such small numbers applied. Further, counseling psychology training programs overlapped extensively with clinical psychology. Finally, no funds were ever authorized for the financing of counseling psychology internship agencies.

Muthard (1961) reported the discouraging news that the *Annual Review of Psychology* intended to discontinue its practice of regularly publishing reviews of counseling psychology. After 1963, such reviews were to occur "at irregular intervals."

As one approach to stimulating more research in counseling psychology, a subcommittee of the Scientific Status of Counseling Psychology Committee investigated sources of research support:

> The committee is working on the assumption that many of our members lack basic information about the identity of government, foundation, and private sources of research support, but perhaps more importantly they are largely unaware of the procedures for applying for assistance, the widely varying criteria for acceptance employed by different sources, and the orientations peculiar to various sources regarding the problem area, size, etc., of research they will most readily support.
>
> Consequently, our task would seem to involve:
> (1) identification, descriptions, and/or classification of and pertinent notations about sources of research support; (2) suggesting methods of communicating this information to Division 17 members; (3) *possibly* assisting them in best utilizing these sources; and (4) by these means, generally catalyzing greater interaction between our professional group and research—supporting groups to better solve mutual concerns. (Jacobs, 1961, p. 15)

Irrespective of whether their basic assumption was correct, this initiative represented a very proactive approach to improving the quality and amount of scientific research in counseling psychology.

Beck (1961), in commenting upon problems of graduate study in counseling psychology, concluded there were not enough graduate faculties in psychology to offer what was needed and that there was merit to Grossman's (1961) idea of professional schools. The problem of turning out adequate numbers of counseling psychologists was ultimately addressed more satisfactorily once professional schools were established.

Waldrop (1961) reported on a bylaws revision which was necessary to establish a closer liaison with the major boards of APA. In the process, four new standing committees were created: Scientific Affairs, Professional Affairs, Education and Training, and Fellowship. One intent of the revision was to establish vehicles for the participation of more members in organized activities of Division 17.

Waldrop's (1962a) presidential message served to draw an analogy between psychology at the start of the 1960s and the stalemate in which medicine found itself in the 1870s:

> Specifically there is confusion and/or doubt in the minds of many about the efficacy of a central professional organization, about the methods of treatment in psychological practice, about the directions and kinds of research needed in psychology, and about the relationship between and among these—organization, practice, research both basic and applied. And instead of attempts to improve cross-communication, we hear, in effect, that the "practice-minded" and the "laboratory oriented" should go their separate ways, each group to proliferate the public image of psychology and to create instead, "images"; each to champion whatever self-concept it can live with that developed out of the activities of its group members. Or as a Fellow in another division newsletter wrote, "As a matter of fact every division of APA could be combined with any other. All of us overlap in our interests." I should hope so! We were, after all, psychologists. (Waldrop, 1962a, p. 2)

He called for finding and accepting a basic core of studies and proficiencies for all psychologists. In a subsequent statement Waldrop (1962b) indicated that:

> the problems of the majority of our population lie in the normal range of day-to-day frustrations encountered in adapting to life and its demands. The competent application of psychological knowledge to the problems and difficulties encountered by any person from their earliest periods of self-determination is the province of the practicing counseling psychologist. (Waldrop, 1962b, p. 3)

It is also the province of the educator and researcher in counseling.

In a comprehensive survey of counseling psychology during the time between the Northwestern Conference in 1951 and the Greyston Conference in 1964, Robinson (1964) covers much of the terrain which this present document does in its treatment of the second and third periods in the history of the specialty. The interested reader is referred to Robinson's excellent summary of central matters in the 1950s and early 1960s.

CONSTELLATIONS OF SUBSTANTIVE THEORETICAL DEVELOPMENTS

Representative substantive theoretical developments as reflected in major books, articles, and monographs will now be presented for each of the constellations of theories which have influenced counseling psychology significantly. Table 3.1 contains examples of important contributions to personality theory and theories of counseling and psychotherapy from 1954 up to and including 1962. Influential on counseling psychology during its third period were client-centered therapy, which was benefiting from a major program of research, and the emergence of two new approaches to conceptualizing aspects of the human condition and changing behavior: the rational-emotive theory and therapy founded by Albert Ellis and the transactional analysis approach founded by Eric Berne.

Table 3.1

**Representative Contributions to Personality Theory
and Theories of Counseling and Psychotherapy
in the Third Historical Period
(1954-1962)**

Psychoanalysis (Freudian)

Alexander, Franz	The scope of psychoanalysis (1961)
Freud, Sigmund	The standard edition of the complete psychological works of Sigmund Freud (1953-1964)
Jones, Ernest	The life and work of Sigmund Freud (1953-1957)

Psychoanalysis (Neo-Freudian)

Fromm, Erich	The sane society (1955)

Adlerian Psychotherapy (Adlerian Theory and Psychotherapy)

Adler, A.	What life should mean to you (1958) Understanding human nature (1959)
Ansbacher, H. L., & Ansbacher, R.	The individual psychology of Alfred Adler (1956)

Table 3.1 (Continued)

Dreikurs, R.	The psychological interview in medicine (1954)
	Adlerian psychotherapy (1956a)
	Goals in psychotherapy (1956b)
	Early experiments with group psychotherapy (1959)
	Group psychotherapy and group approaches: Collected papers (1960)
	The Adlerian approach to therapy (1961)
Way, L.	Adler's place in psychology (1962)
White, R. W.	Adler and the future of ego psychology (1957)

Behavior Theory and Therapy

Eysenck, H. J. (Ed.)	Behavior therapy and the neuroses (1960)
Wolpe, J.	Psychotherapy by reciprocal inhibition (1958)

Client-Centered Therapy

Rogers, C. R.	The necessary and sufficient conditions of therapeutic personality change (1957a)
	Personal thoughts on teaching and learning (1957b)
	The characteristics of a helping relationship (1958a)
	A process conception of psychotherapy (1958b)
	A theory of therapy, personality, and interpersonal relationships, as developed in the client-centered framework (1959)
	Significant trends in the client-centered orientation (1960)
	On becoming a person (1961)

Humanistic and Existential Theory and Therapy

Binswanger, L.	Grundformen und Erkenntnis menschlichen daseins (1962)
Buber, M.	I and thou (1958)
Gendlin, E.	Experiencing and the creation of meaning (1962)
Heidegger, M.	Sein und zeit (1960)
May, R.	Existential psychology (1961)
May, R. et al.	Existence (1958)
Ruitenbeek, H. (Ed.)	Psychoanalysis and existential philosophy (1962)

Table 3.1 (Continued)

Rational-Emotive Theory and Therapy

Ellis, A.   Outcome of employing three techniques of
                                              psychotherapy (1957a)
                                         Rational psychotherapy and individual
                                              psychology (1957b)
                                         Rational psychotherapy (1958)
                                         Reason and emotion in psychotherapy (1962)

Transactional Analysis

Berne, E.   Ego states in psychotherapy (1957)
                                         Transactional analysis: A new and effective
                                         method of group therapy (1958)
                                         Transactional analysis in psychotherapy (1961)

Table 3.2 presents examples of important contributions to vocational psychology, occupational choice, and career development from 1954 up to and including 1962. This third period in the history of counseling psychology was influenced by the rapid growth of the life space/life span theory, the emergence of two new theories (Roe's occupational psychology and Holland's vocational typology), and the appearance of a classic study in the trait and factor approach, E. K. Strong, Jr.'s *Vocational Interests 18 Years After College* (Strong, 1955).

Table 3.2

**Representative Contributions to Vocational Psychology,
Occupational Choice, and
Career Development in the Third Historical Period
(1954-1962)**

Psychoanalytic/Psychodynamic

Bell, H. M.   Ego-involvement in vocational decisions (1960)
Crites, J. O.   Ego strength in relation to vocational interest
                            development (1960)
                       Parental identification in relation to vocational
                            interest development (1962)
Nachmann, B.   Childhood experiences and vocational choice in
                            law, dentistry and social work (1960)
Segal, S.   A psychoanalytic analysis of personality factors in
                            vocational choice (1961)
Sommers, V. S.   Vocational choice as an expression of conflict in
                            identification (1956)

Table 3.2 (Continued)

Trait and Factor

Strong, E. K., Jr.	Vocational interests 18 years after college (1955)
Scott, T. B., Dawis, R. V., England, G. W., & Lofquist, L. H.	A definition of work adjustment (1960)
Carlson, R. E., Dawis, R. V., England, G. W., & Lofquist, L. H.	The measurement of employment satisfaction (1962)

Life Space/Life Span (Donald Super and Associates)

Super, D. E.	Career patterns as a basis for vocational counseling (1954) The dimensions and measurement of vocational maturity (1955) The psychology of careers (1957)
Super, D. E., & Bachrach, P.	Scientific careers and vocational development theory (1957)
Super, D. E., Crites, J. O., Hummel, R. C., Moser, H. P., Overstreet, P. L., & Warnath, C. F.	Vocational development: A framework for research (1957)

Occupational Psychology (Anne Roe and Associates)

Roe, A.	The psychology of occupations (1956) Early determinants of vocational choice (1957)

Vocational Typology (John Holland and Associates)

Holland, J. L.	A theory of vocational choice (1959)

Super (1984a) described himself as progressing through an evolution of thinking (as did many graduate students of his era in the 1930s) which encompassed behaviorism, Freudianism, Jungianism, and neo-Freudianism. He ended up as a self-described "eclectic neo-behaviorist" who found the self-concept and personal construct theories of Rogers (1951), Snygg and Combs (1949), and Kelly (1955) influential in his personal thinking and in the field of career development as a whole.

Super's earliest studies of work, occupations, and psychometrics (Super, 1939, 1940) were soon followed by the first edition of his text, *The Dynamics of Vocational Adjustment* (Super, 1942). In a subsequent text,

Appraising Vocational Fitness, he applied psychometrics to vocational counseling (Super, 1949). Following interaction with Ginzberg and associates (Super, 1951a, 1953) he rewrote completely his first text (Super, 1957), reported on the Career Pattern Study (Super, Crites, Hummel, Moser, & Overstreet, 1957) and contributed to two collections on career development (Super, Starishevsky, Matlin, & Jordaan, 1963; Tiedeman & O'Hara, 1963). The studies and reports in the 1950s initiated an ongoing focus on the concept of vocational or career maturity. The contributions on vocational development began the inaugural issue for *The Counseling Psychologist* as Volume I, No. 1 (Super, 1969). The expanded focus on "a life span/life space" approach to career development began in the early 1970s (Super, 1976). The intent of this formulation was to bring "lifestage and role theory together to convey a comprehensive picture of multiple role careers, together with their determinants and interactions" (Super, 1984a).

Roe's initial interest in occupational psychology grew out of her work on clinical studies of artists and scientists (Roe, 1984). Her influential book entitled *The Psychology of Occupations* appeared in 1956 (Roe, 1956). It was grounded in the personality theory of Maslow (1954) on basic needs which she applied to occupations. Finding available classifications of occupations not to be of use, she created a logical principle of classification based on factor analyses of interests (Roe, 1984). Selecting occupational groups based on primary focus of activity, she also considered the level of difficulty and responsibility involved in various occupations. Her initial 8 X 8 classification system was modified as a consequence of consultation with Donald E. Super and associates to an 8 X 6 scheme (Roe, 1984). Subsequent research (Roe, 1957, 1966; Roe & Siegelman, 1964; Roe & Klos, 1972; Siegelman & Roe, 1979) has served to support and extend the basic formulations.

Weinrach (1980, 1984) has traced the origin and evolution of Holland's influential typology theory of careers to experiences Holland had as an interviewer in the military during World War II; as a counselor for college students, the physically disabled, and psychiatric patients; and to a series of reviews he conducted of the Strong Vocational Interest Blank. His original theoretical statement appeared in 1959, and the important book, *The Psychology of Vocational Choice*, in 1966.

Principal contributions he has made include the Vocational Preference Inventory (Holland, 1958), the *Self-Directed Search* (Holland, 1977), and the *Vocational Exploration and Insight Kit* (Holland et al., 1980). Extensions of his original theoretical formulations include a model for the delivery of vocational guidance services (Holland et al., 1972) and the expanded system for classifying occupations (Holland, 1973b). The basic typology theory that vocational interests are one aspect of personality is reported in detail in *Making Vocational Choices: A Theory of Careers* (Holland, 1973a). He has identified explicit links between personality characteristics and corresponding job titles, arguing that each individual resembles one of six personality types, and occupational environments also may resemble and be classified into six types.

OTHER THEORETICAL AND RESEARCH ADVANCEMENTS

Hobbs and Seeman (1955) reviewed the literature on counseling under four headings: professional problems, descriptive reports, theoretical contributions, and research contributions. As with Wrenn (1954), the literature on both counseling and psychotherapy was covered if the work reported occurred in nonmedical settings.

Under the heading of professional problems, Hobbs and Seeman observed that for the past several years "counseling as a professional field saw rapid development" (Hobbs & Seeman, 1955, p. 379). In contrast, the year they reviewed was one of "consolidation" with little "professional change and development."

Conflict remained over the boundaries of various helping professions. On this subject, two documents of importance appeared, one by psychiatry (Huston, 1954) on the relationship between psychiatry and psychology, and one by psychology (APA, 1954) on the relationship between psychology and other professions. Both documents took expected positions and did not serve to settle the continuing concerns over domain.

The authors noted progress in related fields such as student personnel work, pastoral counseling, and social work. Tyler's (1953) influential counseling text appeared and was commented upon. After reviewing debate on a number of approaches to conceptualizing counseling, Hobbs and Seeman presented the central dilemma of counseling theory and practice in 1954:

> If one works deductively from any fairly rigorous theory, there is so much attenuation by the time he gets to the individual interview that the enterprise can be justified only as a token of what we may hope some day to accomplish. On the other hand, if he works inductively from clinical materials, he winds up with a theoretical formulation (such as those of Freud and Rogers) which is practical and useful but lacking in the degree of theoretical rigor attained in the hypothetic-deductive systems at their best. (Hobbs & Seeman, 1955, p. 384)

They cited Pepinsky and Pepinsky (1954) who noted the inability of the field to generate deductive consequences which would lead to confirmation of one approach and rejection of another. Literature from the group counseling movement was introduced with the comment that it contained "even greater variability in methods than does individual counseling" (Hobbs & Seeman, 1955, p. 386). In addition to the influences of the various theories of counseling, variability may be traced to the influences of sociometry, group dynamics, and educational practice. Group counseling was "a gathering point for ideas rooted in psychology, sociology, and education" (Hobbs & Seeman, 1955, p. 386).

The theoretical literature of greatest historical significance was Super's (1954) programmatic outline which served to guide subsequent theory development and research in the psychology of vocational development. The later text by Super on the psychology of careers (Super, 1957) as well as the career pattern study (Super et al., 1957) may be traced to this seminal work.

After examining research on counseling process and counseling outcome, the reviewers found little of significance. The literature on client response to counseling was more productive. A typical approach was to compare client reactions to different theoretical approaches to counseling. Client-centered counseling was usually one of the approaches contrasted. This approach to inquiry was to recur over the next decade, though seldom considering variables of counselor personality and theoretical approach together.

The counselor as a focus of research was in its infancy. Investigators explored such questions as how well the counselor understands the client (Dymond, 1953), what factors or variables differentiate counselors from other workers in education and psychology (Cottle & Lewis, 1954), and what the relationship is between counselor behavior and client behavior (Aronson, 1953).

It is constructive to consider the characterization of the literature by Hobbs and Seeman as it reflects the approaches to research and the challenges yet unmet of the middle 1950s. Research in counseling was increasingly being guided by psychological concepts. While counseling had been found to produce changes in the desired direction, much remained to be learned. Control procedures needed much improvement, as did criterion measures. Programmatic research of sizable scope was badly needed. Super's (1954) long-term career pattern study represented a viable model for other researchers and a much needed beginning on programmatic research for the counseling psychology profession.

Shoben (1956b) reviewed the literature on counseling. In a brief historical review, he recognized the distinction made at the Ann Arbor Conference in 1949-1950 between counseling psychologists trained at the doctoral level and psychological counselors who are "subdoctorally trained technicians." This distinction was subsequently influential in shaping the document on training at the Northwestern Conference (APA, 1952a).[5]

Two problems of the profession were singled out by Shoben for extended discussion: jurisdictional questions with other professions, and the motives and attributes basic to the professional tasks of counseling psychology. On the subject of jurisdictional questions with other professions, this had been a very active year for relations between psychology and medicine, especially those with psychiatry. The issues raised were informative, and the interested reader is advised to refer directly to the original sources which are identified.

On the problem of understanding the professional tasks of counseling psychologists, Shoben indicated that the outgrowth of professional psychology from basic science was relevant:

> Almost peculiar to psychology is the strain associated with attempts to reconcile and harmonize the older traditions of psychology as science with the immediate and practical demands of psychology as service. It must be remembered that professional psychology did not arise, like medicine, as a separate discipline drawing on basic sciences, but as an outgrowth of a basic science itself in response to social need. This difference creates problems that may be quite special to applied psychology and for which few models in older profession-science relationships may be available. The other instigator of this kind of self-examination appears to be the often harrowing responsibility of direct work with people who are either poignantly troubled or who are seeking help in making such basic decisions as those affecting career choice, marriage, or considerable investments of time and money in educational ventures. Under such conditions, it is no wonder that the counseling psychologist finds himself concerned with such troublesome questions as these: What skills or knowledge do I have that enable me to help my clients? What can I do in these situations that other psychologists cannot? What personal characteristics does my job demand? When am I behaving in accordance with relevant observation and wise professional principles (whatever they may be), and when am I responding to personal need or in terms of some implicit or explicit bias about the professional issues at stake? How do I know how well I am serving my clients? (Shoben, 1956b, p. 147-148)*

This view of counseling psychology as an outgrowth of basic science is one which is not often articulated in the literature. The kinds of questions Shoben poses which arise from direct work with clients remain with the profession today. The varieties of human experience are such that psychologists will be confronted with problems to help solve irrespective of the state of the theoretical literature, or the previous research on the problem, or the conflicts presented by the client.

The remaining literature is grouped under studies of the counselor, the counseling process and its outcomes, psychological measurement in counseling, work and occupations, and a concluding summary evaluation. Earlier Shoben (1953) had made the distinction between therapeutic and diagnostic problems in counseling, further stating that questions of counseling outcome and predictive knowledge may be considered separately.

---

*This and all other quotations from this source are reproduced, with permission, from the *Annual Review of Psychology*, Vol 7. © 1957 by Annual Reviews Inc.

What Shoben characterized as perhaps the most important publications of that year were Meehl's *Clinical vs. Statistical Predictions* (Meehl, 1954) and the challenge it received from McArthur's (1954) classical rebuttal. Both Meehl and McArthur recognized diversity in clinical skill and the fact that there exists a wide range of predictive ability among clinicians. They differed fundamentally on whether clinical or statistical prediction was the most efficacious, and why. These two contributions to the literature have much to offer psychologists struggling with counseling and clinical problems of the 1980s. This section of the Shoben review is a valuable introduction to basic literature in the prediction field.

Shoben characterized the counseling process and outcome literature as containing "less vitality and novelty," and as lacking the same kind of "conceptual or empirical ingenuity" reflected, for example, in the previous contributions by Pepinsky and Pepinsky (1954), Mowrer (1953), and Rogers and Dymond (1954). The number of textbooks in counseling continued to rise. A frequently quoted and hotly debated contribution by Hans Eysenck (Eysenck, 1952) claimed that patients who receive psychotherapy and patients who do not improve equally. Rosenzweig (1954) led a host of rebuttals. The topic of psychological measurement in counseling was highlighted for Shoben by the appearance of Thorndike and Hagen's (1955) textbook on measurement and evaluation in psychology and education.

The *Edwards Personal Preference Schedule* (Edwards, 1954) went on to become one of the most frequently quoted contributors to the counseling psychology literature. Its utility as an approach to measurement in counseling research in the 1950s, 1960s, and early 1970s accounted for its frequent use. Shoben's prediction that it possessed much "potential value for both clinical and research use" has certainly been borne out.

In the area of work and occupations, Roe (1954) organized the accumulated data on occupations and related it to personality studies as part of the construction of a new classification of occupations. She subsequently expanded this classification system into one of the most important contributions to the occcupational psychology literature.

Beilin (1955) argued that the theories of vocational development by Ginzberg et al. (1951) and Super (1951) were special cases of general human development theory. Age and experience, for example, both have an association to changes in how an individual relates to work in its many facets.

In evaluating the theory and research he reviewed, Shoben observed "a continuation and a maturing" of professionalization which characterized counseling psychology's brief history. Professional issues had become substantive ones, capable of sustained inquiry. Problem areas remained, however, on important dimensions of the field:

> The research output seems to be in bits and pieces rather than integrated and deriving its motive force from some unifying and

fundamental idea or from some conflict between such ideas. Scholarship appears workmanlike but lacking in sweep, and one suspects that scholarly attainment is not highly prized. (Shoben, 1956b, p. 169)

This final comment that scholarly work is not highly prized is one which is shared by others (see Granger, 1959; Brayfield, 1963) and which has continued to plague counseling psychology as it has tried to develop a scientific base. The reward structure in service units in universities and in nonacademic settings does not mandate research. Further, promotion in most universities does not require sustained, programmatic research. This is regrettable and has hampered seriously the construction of a strong scientific base for counseling psychology.[6]

Shaw (1957) was invited by the *Annual Review of Psychology* to focus on the topic of counseling just as Shoben (1956b) had been. He singled out Kelly's (1955) psychology of personal constructs as a major contribution of the period he reviewed. Over a quarter of a century later Kelly's theory continues to be important to personality, developmental, clinical, and counseling psychologists.

This was the first literature review to contain a section on developmental counseling. After noting Sanford's (1955) concept of creative health and Super's (1955a) concepts of vocational development and maturity, Shaw indicated that:

By means of such concepts mental illness can be comprehended as an interruption or retardation of growth. If mental illness is considered the province of the clinical psychologist and creative health the domain of the counseling psychologist, but both are construed as developmental phenomena, then counseling psychologists and clinical psychologists share the common enterprise of what might be called developmental counseling. (Shaw, 1957, p. 357)

The concept of developmental counseling as "opening up new opportunities for constructive life experiences and maturation of personal resources" (Shaw, 1957, p. 357) began to appear in the counseling psychology literature. Shaw cited papers by Cohen (1955), Needleman (1955), Stotsky (1955), and Stubbins and Napoli (1955) as within the developmental perspective. This developmental perspective is somewhat different, however, from the research tradition based upon Piaget (1932) which utilizes such concepts as structural organization of thinking and sequencing of educational experiences. Research in the tradition of Piaget did not begin to appear in the counseling psychology literature until at least 15 years later (Mosher & Sprinthall, 1970, 1971; Rest, 1974; Whiteley, 1978; Whiteley & Associates, 1982).

On the subject of theoretical and conceptual trends, Shaw identified a number of quite different conceptions of the role of the counselor, including:

The counselor as an object for identification (Martire, 1955);
the counselor in a directive mode (Williamson, 1955, 1956a, 1956b);
the counselor playing different roles in different situations (Robinson, 1955);
the counselor's changing roles from client to client and with the same client over time (Bordin, 1955);
the counselor as a strategist with a flexible role (Shaw, 1955).

This was a very fertile period for generating conceptual definitions of the counselor's role in addition to the prevailing client-centered and psychoanalytic conceptions.

Studies of the counseling process are grouped according to relevance to counselor participation and methodological conceptions about how to study process. Debate over outcome studies continued with Cartwright (1955) joining Eysenck's (1952) questioning of evidence. Shaw (1957) aptly quotes Shoben's earlier statement that "the conclusive evidence of therapeutic effectiveness must come not from argument but from relevant and vigorous research."

The measurement section of the review noted the proliferation of self-concept studies which reflected the importance of the concept to both client-centered and vocational development theories. Two significant volumes appeared (Strong, 1955; Darley & Hagenah, 1955) on the subject of vocational interest measurement. There was widespread professional interest in both the Kuder Preference Record and the Strong Vocational Interest Blank. Prediction studies of psychological adjustment proliferated in the literature, with the Minnesota Multiphasic Personality Inventory used increasingly with normal individuals as well as those with personality problems.

After a section on vocational and rehabilitation counseling (the latter topic an infrequent subject for review in counseling psychology literature) and the observation that the number of counseling textbooks continued to proliferate, Shaw closed with the observation that "the counselor of the future will be viewed in different perspective than the counselor of the present" (Shaw, 1957, p. 377). The reason for this view was the "dawning construction of man as a self-expressive entity" which emerged in the literature of this period. Indeed, some of the concepts introduced at this time such as Sanford's (1955) creative health, Kelly's (1955) conceptual freedom, Murphy's (1955) personal enrichment through participation in the environment, and Super's (1955b) emphasis on personal strengths can be found in professional dialogue and the popular press of the 1980s, especially in the literature on the psychology of health and on better living through self-help.

Tyler's (1958) review provided another perspective on the identity of counseling psychology with her distinction between *profession* and *process*:

As a field of professional specialization within psychology, it parallels clinical and industrial psychology and has its own history, techniques, and system of values. As a process, however, it is important in many of the other fields of specialization in psychology, and in social work, education, pastoral care, and a wide variety of other human situations. Counseling, viewed as a process, is a term that parallels "psychotherapy" rather than clinical psychology. (Tyler, 1958, p. 375)

In choosing to emphasize the process aspect of counseling psychology, and in considering material from social work, pastoral counseling, and education, her review is somewhat different in approach from that of previous reviewers.

A number of major contributions appeared of enduring value, including Donald Super's seminal book on career psychology (Super, 1957), and Nevitt Sanford's pioneering research on personality development during the college years (Sanford, 1956). Both of these contributions have had heuristic value in their own right beyond the substance of the work and have served as models of programmatic research for the profession. These were partial reports of ongoing work which has continued to lead to original contributions over a quarter of a century later. As classics in the field, they merit careful scrutiny by both graduate students and researchers.

As part of a banner period of important contributions to the literature, seven other contributors stand out: Anne Roe's book on occupational psychology (Roe, 1956), Carl R. Rogers' series on becoming a person (Rogers, 1956a, 1956b, 1961), Martin Buber's philosophical treatise on the human condition (Buber, 1958), the framework of research by Super and associates for the career pattern study (Super et al., 1957), Clark Moustakas' explorations of self and personal growth (Moustakas, 1956), Victor Frankl's introduction to logotherapy and existential thought (Frankl, 1955), and the report of the Committee on Definition (APA, 1956) which has already been commented upon.

Vocational choice and career development received careful attention from researchers during this period of time. Tyler (1958) commented upon the centrality of this endeavor to counseling psychology:

Counseling psychologists have always been concerned to a greater or lesser extent with the task of facilitating wise choices. This central task fits in well with our definition of counseling as an identity-developing process because of the central importance of one's work to his self-concept. (Tyler, 1958, p. 378)

The general framework for vocational development originated by Super and his associates has continued to be elaborated upon and subjected to empirical scrutiny in the succeeding decades.

Tyler's sections on counseling in social agencies, in public schools, and in churches is important historically. It is timely also to reread in the 1980s because so many counseling psychologists are seeking employment in areas other than universities and the Veterans Administration.

A section of her review on counseling in neuropsychiatric hospitals reflects the distinctive problems encountered, and research beginning to be conducted, by counseling psychologists as a consequence of the opportunities opened up by the Veterans Administration. She noted that the field of rehabilitation counseling was undergoing rapid expansion.

This period of time covered by Berdie's (1959) second review of the counseling literature for the *Annual Review of Psychology* (April, 1957 to April, 1958) did not contain the type of seminal or groundbreaking work which characterized the early and middle 1950s. The literature did contain numerous follow-up, refinement, and extension studies on earlier original formulations. This type of contribution is extraordinarily important to the long-term strengthening of the substantive base of the profession.

Initiatives set in motion earlier began to bear fruit. This was particularly the case in the area of psychological measurement, which produced a continuing series of studies of intelligence tests, multifactor tests, and interest measures. The third edition of the *Occupational Outlook Handbook* (Wolfbein & Goldstein, 1957) appeared, and Hoppock (1957) came out with a detailed summary of previous occupational research.

In a section of his review which was particularly valuable, Berdie identified relevant research from fields other than psychology. It would be a contribution to the theory, research, and practice of counseling psychology if such a review were conducted on an annual basis.

From having had an opportunity to review systematically the counseling psychology literature on diagnostics in 1950, Berdie was in an advantageous position to characterize changes in this literature:

> This survey of the past year's research activities has led the reviewer to the conclusion that current research directly related to counseling, when compared to that done eight or nine years ago, shows greater sophistication, involves more persons, covers a much broader variety of problems, and tends to provide information of more immediate usefulness to counselors. (Berdie, 1959, p. 365)

He indicated that process research was the most needed and the most difficult to do, particularly that which related the characteristics of counselors, counselees, process, and outcomes.

While a chapter on psychotherapy appeared in the 1960, 1961, and 1962 editions of the *Annual Review of Psychology*, there was not another review of counseling psychology until Brayfield completed one for the 1963 edition. Brayfield characterized counseling psychology as one of the most "self-concerned" of the helping professions. Only half of Division 17's members felt that their primary identification was with the Division, and only 20% devoted more than half their time to counseling. Over an eight-year period there was a trend for new members to be less interested in psychometrics and more interested in psychotherapy. He quoted a Division 17 study (APA, 1959) which indicated that equal numbers of the membership reported that their graduate education had been in clinical, educational or developmental psychology, or in vocational counseling. He also quoted the Granger (1959) study which placed counseling psychologists at the bottom of the psychology prestige hierarchy.

When it is recalled that Brayfield became the Executive Officer of the American Psychological Association, his conclusions that "scientific contributions from counseling psychology are unimpressive" (Brayfield, 1963, p. 319),* and that "counseling psychology is not a distinguished intellectual enterprise" (Brayfield, 1963, p. 320) have greater significance. He recalled the study (Tyler et al., 1980) which indicated that only 139 of the 384 authors (36%) of articles in the first seven years of the *Journal of Counseling Psychology* were Division 17 members.

Brayfield quoted a study then in press with the *Journal of Counseling Psychology* by Brigante, Haefner, and Woodson (1962) which studied the similarities and differences between clinical and counseling psychology as perceived by the two groups themselves. Brayfield's summary was that:

> there was consensus that some role attitudes and behaviors are relatively unique to each specialty. Both specialties perceived the counseling psychologist as working with persons who have educational and vocational problems, giving educational and occupational information, doing personnel selection and placement, working with normals, using objective tests including interest and aptitude, as being Rogerian in orientation, and finding an environment compatible with the personality structure of the person rather than trying to alter his personality. (Brayfield, 1963, pp. 321-322)

A sample of counseling psychologists, if surveyed in the 1980s, would undoubtedly not accept this characterization of their theoretical orientation and would not be as heavily involved in personnel selection.

Brayfield's characterization of counseling psychology in the early 1960s merits consideration in detail because he cites relevant literature to support his viewpoint:

> There is probably considerable agreement on the following: (a) working with normal people (Berg, 1959; Hahn, 1955; Seeman, 1959); (b) counseling may be feasible throughout the life span (Hahn,

---

*This and all other quotations from this source are reproduced with permission, from the *Annual Review of Psychology*, Vol. 14. © 1963 by Annual Reviews Inc.

1955; Super, 1957); (c) emphasis upon the strengths and assets of the counselee (Samler, 1962; Tyler et al., 1980); (d) emphasis upon cognitive activities, especially those involving choice and decision (Tiedeman, 1961; Tyler, 1961; Wrenn, 1958), with rationality and reason stressed (Tiedeman, 1961; Williamson, 1959); (e) situational factors and environmental modifications are important in counseling (Brayfield, 1961a; Salinger, Tollefson, & Hudson, 1960). (Brayfield, 1963, p. 322)

The balance of his review stressed occupational and educational aspects of the role of the counseling psychologist.

Before proceeding with the balance of Brayfield's review, it must be observed that the carefully documented evidence he cited would lead to conclusions much closer to those of Berg et al. (1980) and Berg (1980) on the problems before counseling psychology and its status as the decade of the 1960s began than to those of the officially recognized Tyler et al. (1980) version.

Since Brayfield considered the unique identity of counseling psychology to be in its vocational and educational functions, his review focused on theories and findings on vocational behavior, decision theory, significant aspects of the environment, diagnosis and prediction, counseling (he found very little literature on the counseling interaction as such), and under a miscellaneous category, drew attention to the appearance of Oscar Buros' fifth "magnificent edition" of the *Mental Measurement Yearbook* (Buros, 1959).

SUMMARY

The third historical period in the development of counseling psychology was marked by significant conflict concerning the status and proper focus of the specialty. Coming after a period of successful activity by Division 17, this was not a period of positive accomplishment for organized counseling psychology. The fruits of all but one of the major attempts to address the fundamental problems of the status and proper focus of the profession languished unpublished for 20 years. Further, Division 17 failed to become significantly involved with those activities which blossomed after Sputnik with federal funds. Given the contributions which the Veterans Administration made to counseling psychology with federal funds in the second historical period, the failure to seek actively and receive a role in new federal programs during the third historical period was a significant failure by the organized profession.

It is apparent that the profession of counseling psychology in the middle and late 1950s was beginning to be enriched by careful basic research in many aspects of its substantive base as well as by imaginative new thinking about the nature of the human condition and ways to promote personal change in behavior. The third historical period, therefore, was not devoid of accomplishment, but it was the accomplishment of the conceptualizers and the researchers. Collectively, members of the profession laid the groundwork for many scientific advancements in the 1960s and 1970s.

FOOTNOTES

[1]Wrenn (Note 1) provided an elaboration of the finances of the founding as follows: "You did not mention that something like 25 professional people already in counseling psychology thought enough of the field to put up the money to start the *Journal*. I would have to read my own history of the *Journal* over again to make sure. My memory is that we raised about $2,500 in contributions of $50.00 to $300.00 or $400.00 apiece. At the time, we emphasized to them that it was a contribution that would probably never be returned, that it was their own contribution if they wished to make it. Twenty-five people did, and among those 25 people are some well-known figures in our field. What happened, of course, in the sale of the *Journal* in about 1966 or so to APA was that the money that APA paid to us for our mailing list, background, inventory of back issues and so forth enabled us to pay off each contributor about three times what he had contributed. This was a surprise and a delight, of course. Besides that, he or she had been getting in dividends for the past three or four years of our editorship of the *Journal*. It seems to me rather inspiring that people had faith enough in our field to start the *Journal* with hard cash, and this they did."

[2]The appraisal by Tyler, Tiedeman, and Wrenn (1980) was reprinted from the multilith report by Thompson and Super (1964). It had been drafted in 1960-61.

[3]Tyler (Note 2) provided a clarification of her viewpoint: "I would not have considered the thrust of the report as being 'at variance' with Berg's ideas. I have never believed that an unambiguous differentiation of counseling psychology from other specialties was essential, and I would have agreed with Berg's 'alternative roads' ideas and not objected to a fusion with clinical psychology."

[4]The citations for the four provocative reports created between 1959 and 1962 are Berg, Pepinsky, and Shoben, 1980; Tyler, Tiedeman, and Wrenn, 1980; Berg, 1980; and Tiedeman, 1980.

[5]In a recent communication, Bordin (Note 3) commented upon the importance of the Ann Arbor Conference in historical perspective: "It fed into the movement toward a broadened view of counseling as *psychological* counseling. Moreover, it is noteworthy as one of the few times that NIMH put any money into counseling psychology."

[6]Cottle (Note 4) singled out another factor hampering the development of a strong scientific base; namely, "the promotion of our most competent researchers into administrative jobs, ending their research careers."

Chapter 4
Positive Initiatives by Counseling Psychology: The Fourth Historical Period (1963-1967)

Perhaps the most compelling statement of the problems facing counseling psychology as the fourth period of its history began was provided by Brayfield (1963). As noted in the closing section of the previous chapter, Brayfield characterized counseling psychology as "not a distinguished intellectual enterprise" having "unimpressive" scientific contributions and as one of the most "self-concerned" of the helping professions. Additional studies (APA, 1961b; Porter & Cook, 1964) served to strengthen the earlier findings by Granger (1959) that counseling psychologists were low in the APA status hierarchy.

The fundamental debate which occurred between 1959 and 1962 among Berg, Pepinsky, and Shoben (1980) and Berg (1980) on the one hand, and Tyler, Tiedeman, and Wrenn (1980) and Tiedeman (1980) on the other hand over the status and focus of counseling psychology had not been resolved, in part because all but one of their significant contributions were not published for 20 years, and were therefore denied the widespread and timely circulation they deserved.

Counseling psychology was clearly at a crossroads in 1963 as its fourth historical period began.[1] Division 17 had 1,211 fellows, members, and associates (Robinson, 1964). The Division had increased in size 61% from 1950 to 1960. A principal response by Division 17 to being at a crossroads—increasing membership, uneven status, and diffuse focus—was to organize itself to do something substantive and effective about the situation confronting it. The vehicle for this response was the Greyston Conference (Thompson & Super, 1964).

GREYSTON CONFERENCE

The approach of the Greyston Conference was to examine the work and training of counseling psychologists, then to provide specific recommendations for their improvement. The heart of the conference, and its basic contribution to advancing the profession, were the recommendations arising from participation and discussion. An important source of impetus for those recommendations came from a series of six formal papers.

Francis P. Robinson (1964) traced the development of counseling psychology since the Northwestern Conference. He cited a study by Paterson and Lofquist (1960) that found little differentiation between clinical and counseling training in approved university programs and that the topics covered in the American Board of Examiners in Professional Psychology examinations for the counseling and clinical specialties differed little.

Robinson observed a problem which had made it difficult to strengthen the teaching of psychology in colleges of education; namely, the location of psychology and educational psychology in different colleges:

> a problem not only of inconvenience but of rivalry. The liberal arts college departments have jealously limited what the colleges of education might teach in psychology and yet themselves have not always offered what was needed. Because of this, colleges of education tend to offer technique courses and lack substantive offerings in psychological theory and principles. (Robinson, 1964, p. 40)

Problems of interdepartmental and interdisciplinary rivalries, such as those identified above, must be solved in order to avoid developing a nonpsychologically based orientation to counseling.

Samler (1964) explored the settings in which counseling psychologists work, described what they do, then raised the question about what they should do. With a fitting extension of Brayfield's remark about the profession's self-concern, Samler stated that when "we create our long sought-for identity, soul searching will deserve an honorable place in it" (Samler, 1964, p. 43). After reviewing the descriptive information on counseling psychology including settings in which counseling psychologists work and the positions they hold, what their professional interests are, and summarizing notable statements by Division 17 presidents and official documents, Samler chose to focus on the "common core" of counseling psychology.

The "common core" of counseling psychology refers to a "common methodology" which:

> embraces a two-person counseling relationship, supplemented by group methods, the utilization of assessment devices peculiarly appropriate for the study of vocational potential, assumption of a measure of responsibility by the counselor for the client, involvement with the client's environment (family, school, work), and considerable activity by the counselor on behalf of his client outside of counseling sessions. (Samler, 1964, pp. 61-62)

Research involvement by counseling psychologists was termed "equiv-ocal" principally because of the very great service demands.

The most important portion of Samler's paper addressed the ques-tion: What should counseling psychologists do? His answer to the question had five parts. The first part of his answer was to avoid pre-mature stabilization, the temptation to say: "This is who we are, this is what we do, this is where we stop." The profession in his view needed to keep a:

> special awareness of the forces that affect the change in our society, moving from that awareness to anticipation, and from anticipation to considering what our function as counseling psychologists might be in a changed situation. (Samler, 1964, p. 62)

The counseling psychology profession is influenced in numerous ways by the forces in society. Further, while the general functions performed by counseling psychologists may constitute a "common core" of pro-fessional identity over time, the settings in which those core functions are performed change in response to social forces.

The second part of Samler's answer to the question of what coun-seling psychologists should do was to restore vocational counseling to its central place. Brayfield (1961b) had earlier emphasized that a major element in the unique identity of counseling psychology was vocational counseling. Samler agreed that vocational counseling was the core of the profession but indicated that its "true complexity" must be accepted.

The third and fourth parts of Samler's answer were to recommend modification of the dominant approach to personality change (a reaction to what he characterized as the "prevailing" client-centered philosophy) and to define more closely relationships with other counselors. In order to strengthen counseling in the public schools (APA, 1962), there is a need for "greater psychological sophistication." He noted that only 19% of the persons responsible for counselor education were Division 17 members, and 56% are not even APA members. The point was that other groups share elements of the mission of counseling psychology, and there is a need for careful liaison.

Finally, Samler (hesitantly) urged that counseling psychologists be-come more involved in social action in order to affect and change the environment of their clients more effectively:

> In counseling this may involve finding an on-the-job training oppor-tunity, influencing the establishment of still another curriculum in the secondary school, or helping father and mother to reconcile their differences so that the client will not be torn apart. The general outline of such environmental intervention is well established. (Samler, 1964, p. 66)

The issue Samler addressed directly is how involved counseling psychologists should get in social movements which seek the accomplishment of objectives of their profession.

Darley's (1964) topic at the Greyston Conference was the substantive bases of counseling psychology. This was represented as a curricular issue which must be addressed in the context of the low repute of psychologists in general. Further:

> Federal and state agencies may promote and regulate practices, at various educational levels, resulting in the existence of professional personnel widely variant from APA or APGA standards. Yet the generic term *counseling* must serve to cover this broad spectrum; society's needs may not be ill-served by the spectrum, and society can only be confused in the absence of clear guidelines or buying guides when it seeks to purchase services to meet its needs. All this has been referred to as our "identity problem"—we have no clear identity. (Darley, 1964, p. 70)

Darley remarked that it may be that "our identity is unidentifiable and that our specialization has inadequate boundary lines and fences" (Darley, 1964, p. 70). Approaches to improving this state of affairs were summarized:

> a fusion of training at the doctoral level between clinical and counseling programs; a core program at the doctoral level for the "helping professions" in psychology, from which specialties could emerge; the development of clearly distinctive programs, including the establishment of new kinds of specializations in the field; the restriction of counseling psychology to a particular age range and setting, such as student personnel service at the college level; the allocation of counseling functions to a lower level of training, as in a two-year M.A. program. (Darley, 1964, p. 70)

Darley's view was that the problems of identity, boundary lines, and principal focus were capable of solution.

And the solution offered was to use the APA (1947) core program for graduate training in *clinical psychology*! Such an approach reflected the 1952 statement on standards for training in counseling psychology (APA, 1952a) which called for a core of basic concepts, tools, and techniques which "should be common to all psychologists."[2] For Darley, the relevant portions of the APA (1947) report which described graduate training in clinical psychology were as follows:

> Within *general* psychology it recommended content in general, physiological and comparative psychology, as well as work in the history of psychology and contemporary schools of thought, and

work in developmental and social psychology. Within the area of *psychodynamics of behavior* would be found work in fundamental theories of personality and motivation in both normal and abnormal behavior, plus work in experimental psychodynamics and psychopathology. We may skip the recommendations in diagnostic methods and therapy, though I would point out that these encompass and go beyond what we believe is the content of appraisal and counseling in our field. In the area of *research*, we find course work in experimental psychology, advanced statistics and quantitative methods, and research in dynamic psychology. From related disciplines, the committee wants the clinical psychologist to know something of physiological sciences, social organization and pathology, and cultural impacts on personality development, in addition to some elementary consideration of clinical medicine. (Darley, 1964, p. 72)

In addition to becoming "well-grounded" in psychology, it is necessary to acquire "general minimum competence" in the "specialty of counseling" (undefined). Additional training must come on-the-job and by access to postdoctoral experiences.

Darley quoted Brayfield's (1961b) advocacy of vocational counseling as one alternative open to the profession:

I see two opportunities confronting us: (1) to fulfill our responsibilities as psychologists to establish and develop a body of scientific knowledge as the basis for the psychological service called vocational counseling, and (2) to stimulate the general development of psychology as a science through such endeavors. We need, I believe, to re-establish or reaffirm our roots in basic psychology . . . we should be psychologists first and foremost . . . . I propose that we commit ourselves to the development, as an enterprise with the highest priority, of a science of the psychology of occupational behavior. (Brayfield, 1961, pp. 50-51)

The Brayfield approach provided a way to focus scholarly inquiry and channel psychological service. While professing to "like the sound of this" Darley demurred with a "doubt," but did not fully explain his reasons. Presumably this matter was fully discussed following his presentation.

In a section of the Greyston Report (Thompson & Super, 1964), there is a presentation of issues raised by discussants and participants. Darley's statement was characterized as lacking "confidence in professional identity." Brayfield, in contrast, was quoted as stating that comparatively, counseling psychology was a stable and tranquil field, social and cooperative (rather than entrepreneurial and competitive), and educational and developmental rather than remedial and medical.

The formal recommendations of the Greyston Conference were carefully thought out and have had a positive effect on the profession.[3] The chapter by Thompson and Super (Chapter 3) presents "issues which might normally be bypassed because they are difficult" (p. 27). Since the issues remain two decades later, they will be summarized as presented at the time of the Greyston Conference. Some members of the profession have identity problems, though identity is "no longer an issue for many."[4] APA, its boards and committees, and other national organizations, however, are still unclear on the role of the specialty:

> As a *specialty*, counseling psychology suffers from discrimination. Perhaps the educational, as contrasted with remedial (clinical psychology) and natural science (experimental psychology), origins and affiliations of many counseling psychologists are the cause of xenophobia. Perhaps counseling psychologists have been too modest in speaking for their field. (Thompson & Super, 1964, p. 28)

Lack of understanding and support extends to universities as well, where role models and differentiated programs are sometimes lacking.

Under the heading of "Counseling Psychology or Education?" it was pointed out that about one-half of Division 17 members were from non-APA approved programs:

> In some universities large and well-qualified staffs of counseling psychologists are located in a department which is not the department approved by APA for granting a degree in counseling psychology; the approved department is a department of psychology, and the counseling psychologists are in departments of educational psychology or of guidance in the school of education. This fact impressed conferees as an odd state of affairs.
>
> It is not surprising that many recipients of the doctorate who later join Division 17 are produced by departments which are not on the APA list, for these are the departments staffed by counseling psychologists. Counseling psychologists are produced by counseling psychologists. Here are facts which APA, the Education and Training Board, and Division 17 have failed to confront. (Thompson & Super, 1964, p. 31)

The constellation of problems which are identified here have been addressed more successfully in the intervening years.

Another concern of the conference participants was why education has been more responsive to counseling psychology than has traditional psychology:

> Why is Education more hospitable to counseling psychology than psychology itself? Is counseling psychology really an educational

specialty which should be fostered under educational rather than psychological auspices? Is the service emphasis incompatible with the scientific? Does psychology want to exercise the responsibility which it has assumed, does it want to abdicate, or will it continue to do neither effectively? (Thompson & Super, 1964, p. 31)

This issue is still not resolved fully 20 years later. The ensuing years have brought a decline in two subdoctoral specialties which have been sustained more in education than in psychology: vocational guidance and school counseling.

With the confirmation in recent years that psychology, not education, is the core discipline of the profession, this issue has faded somewhat in significance. The problem remains, however, of sustaining support from both disciplines.

THE SOCIETAL CONTEXT: KEYSTONES OF CONSCIOUSNESS

The societal context for the fourth period in the history of counseling psychology began with President John F. Kennedy's New Frontier in Washington, DC, and a ferment of rising expectations within American society from groups which had been previously disenfranchised. Four years after President Kennedy's tragic death in 1963, the fourth historical period ended at a time when President Lyndon Johnson's Great Society had not yet been eroded by the twin forces of inflation and the divisive effects of the Vietnam War.

During this period of time, American society was characterized by diversity in the popular culture: the Beatles, the time period covered by the film *American Graffiti*, the triumphs of the Green Bay Packers, Ed Sullivan, Arthur Godfrey, the flourishing of Disneyland, and a period of unprecedented growth in education and federal programs to benefit society through governmental action. It was possible to have, in Lyndon Johnson's metaphor, both guns and butter. There was not yet the realization that resources were finite and must be deployed prudently.

Counseling psychologists, who traditionally operated in universities, found the period from the 1950s up through 1967 to be one of major growth in job opportunities as state colleges became comprehensive universities, the community colleges burgeoned in size and numbers, and professional schools were greatly transformed. Except for a period from 1952 through 1958 (when enrollment was down), education enjoyed a period of sustained growth. When the post-World War II burst of veteran enrollments began to decline, there was what Mayhew (1977) called a "cautious expansion of egalitarianism" as previously unserved groups began to view higher education as an entree to the mainstream of American society.

The psychological and social context for counseling psychology in the decade of the 1960s has been characterized as a period of hope, vitality, and cautious activism. Clecak (1983) has reinterpreted these cultural themes into:

> a quest for personal fulfillment, a pursuit of a free, gratified, unalienated self with one or more communities of valued others. Although it was variously defined, the ideal itself was endowed with sufficient energy and resources to explore a range of possibilities, both on its own and with others. (Clecak, 1983, p. 6)

He characterized a dominant thrust of American civilization in the 1960s and 1970s as a "quest for personal fulfillment within a small community (or several communities) of significant others" (Clecak, 1983, p. 9). Assisting people to explore possibilities and potentialities alone and with others is mainstream work for counseling psychology practice.

ORGANIZED ACTIVITIES OF COUNSELING PSYCHOLOGY

Volume 15, No. 3 of *Counseling News and Views* (1963) contained a copy of the bylaws which contained the revised statement of purpose for the Division under four headings:

a. Education and Training

  (1) to formulate appropriate requirements for the scientific and professional education and training of specialists in counseling psychology;
  (2) to cooperate with the American Psychological Association and its boards and committees which are concerned with the education and training of psychologists; and
  (3) to work with other divisions on matters of common concern in the training and education of psychologists.

b. Scientific Investigation

  (1) to encourage surveys of research in the field of counseling psychology, summarizing present knowledge and practices, and to identify problems in special need of investigation; and
  (2) to encourage research by members of the Division and other appropriate groups.

c. Practice

  (1) to extend the application of the knowledge and methods of the science of psychology to counseling in educational in-

stitutions, industrial or business enterprises, health and welfare agencies, consulting, and private practice;

(2) to promote high standards of competence in the practice of counseling psychology;

(3) to encourage the development of organizational patterns and administrative procedures which will facilitate good practice; and

(4) to assist in the formulation, interpretation, and promotion of observance of a code of ethics for counseling psychologists.

d. Dissemination of Information

(1) to organize and promote meetings and conferences;

(2) to encourage the preparation and publication of critical reviews of research, training, and practice in counseling psychology;

(3) to encourage the preparation and publication of technical and professional manuals, reports, guides, etc.; and

(4) to promote public understanding of counseling psychology.

(*Counseling News and Views*, 1963, Vol. 15, No. 3, pp. 4-5)

These bylaws served to establish the committee structure as more consistent with that of APA and other divisions. The immediate challenge was to make the structure effective.

Berg (1964) offered a critique of research in counseling psychology that still has not been effectively answered:

It seems to me much of our research in counseling psychology resembles the labors of Petit the Poet. Many of our studies lack a grand design, tread a conventional pathway, and vanish like Petit's snows of yesterday. Or to put it in Masters' own words, "Tick, tick, tick, what little iambics, while Homer and Whitman roared in the pines." So we have studies which indicate that adding two additional tests to a battery will predict success as a mortician by .48 instead of only .44. There is nothing wrong with such studies, but there's nothing much significant in them either. They do have the virtue of being safe, but they also sin in being dull. They are the "tick, tick, tick" studies. Studies which roar in the pines, by contrast, would be addressed to more basic questions with broader scope. What, for example, is the psychological role of the funeral service in our subculture? Do we need morticians as independent operators in our society? What are society's needs for disposal of the dead? What makes a mortician in terms of personality dynamics, etc.? These are questions to stir the cortex and roil the waters of conventionality. (*Counseling News and Views*, 1964, Vol. 16, No. 1, pp. 1-2)

In Berg's view, the profession had yet to identify a series of topics requiring extensive programmatic research which would truly make a difference. The value of programmatic research is that questions initially addressed ultimately lead to questions researched and refined into new problems demanding additional inquiry. Research out of context, and not pursued to the next series of unanswered questions, is ordained to vanish. The desirable goal for the profession is a situation where "Ideas will flow, and almost certainly they will include ideas about generating new ideas" (Berg, 1964, p. 2). That is the essential definition of focused, programmatic research.

There was an apparent drop-off in organized activity of Division 17 for a number of years following the Greyston Conference. At least a careful reading of *Counseling News and Views* from 1963 until it ceased publishing in 1968 does not reflect the rigorous activity of the late 1940s and middle 1950s. As but one barometer of Division 17 activity, the March, 1965 issue (Vol. 17, No. 1) of *Counseling News and Views* contained only eight pages.

There were a number of exceptions to the drift in the middle 1960s which stand out. The first was the 1965 Cubberley Conference cosponsored by Division 17, Stanford University, the California Counseling and Guidance Association, the California Association of School Psychologists and Psychometrists, the California State Psychological Association, the Northern California Guidance Association, the California State Department of Education, and the Western Association of Counselor Educators and Supervisors. The achievement of such a diverse sponsoring coalition was a notable accomplishment in its own right. It represented counseling psychologists reaching out to problems of the public schools and to school based personnel. The focus of the conference on guidance implications of behavioral science was important as it enabled the following important questions to be addressed:

> What new avenues are opening to the school counselor or psychologist for solving pupil problems?
> How can decision-making ability be improved?
> How can disruptive school behavior be reduced?
> What ethical problems arise for the counselor in his efforts to change student behavior?
>
> (*Counseling News and Views*, 1965, Vol. 17, No. 1, p. 6)

The substantive papers from this conference were published (Krumboltz, 1966b), broadening the potential contribution of counseling psychology to issues before the public schools.

The second exception to the drift was the Invitational Conference on Government-University Relations in the Professional Preparation and Employment of Counselors. Under the direction of John F. McGowan, the intent of the conference was to examine the "problems created by government demands upon universities for the education of specialized personnel" (*Counseling News and Views*, 1965, Vol. 17, No. 1, p. 6). The model for examination was the impact of the enormously increased demand for counselors stemming from congressional legislation. A final goal was to prepare guidelines to accomplish more effective relations between universities and the federal government.

A third exception to the drift was the Bromwoods Conference, cosponsored by the Central Midwest Regional Educational Laboratory and Washington University. The purpose of the conference was to evaluate and refocus the research literature in three areas:

1. Research on counselor effectiveness and characteristics of the counselor;
2. characteristics of the client: implications for selection and methods of treatment;
3. assessment of outcome: evaluation of the interaction of client and counselor.

The participants took a detailed look at the relative importance of various personality traits and characteristics of both clients and counselors and at problems of assessing counseling outcome. The intent was to outline a plan for programmatic research in three areas of significance to counseling psychology research. In order to broaden the impact of the reformulations beyond the 45 participants, the proceedings, including major papers, formal discussant papers, and task group reports were published (Whiteley, 1967).

Another exception to the drift was the attempt by Tiedeman (1965) to identify problems facing the profession and to encourage his colleagues to act upon them. In Tiedeman's view, the consensus of the Greyston Conference (Thompson & Super, 1964) on the training of counseling psychologists incorporated a contradiction.

The contradiction is:

that the counseling psychologist is primarily a psychologist and then a counselor. The contradiction rests in the facts that the counselor: (1) brings to bear, not only the insights from psychology, but also those from anthropology, economics, philosophy, political science, and sociology as well; and (2) primarily engages in action, not study, although I presume you realize my insistence that professional action simply must be guided by careful thought. It seems obvious from the presence of these contradictions in our consensus that those who framed the consensus identify with psychology rather than with other occupations and/or knowledge. (*Counseling News and Views*, 1965, Vol. 17, No. 2, p. 5)

Tiedeman's view that insights from anthropology, economics, philosophy, political science, and sociology are relevant to counseling psychology is similar to that articulated earlier by Super (1952a).

In presenting problems before the profession, Tiedeman's format was to raise questions followed by their answers as he viewed them:

1. What is the range of age in which the counselor can operate with benefit of his clients? (I believe that the range is from birth through retirement.)
2. What are the settings in which the counselor operates? (I believe that they are all primarily educational but include hospital, community agency, employment service and other government bureaus, and industry as well as schools and colleges.)
3. What are the procedures which the counselor uses? (I believe that the necessary procedures are more inclusive than mere counseling alone.)
4. What is the primary purpose of the activity of the counselor? (I believe that it is to deepen the awareness of self within the requirements for collaborative activity as experienced while learning in schools, work, recreation, and home.)

(*Counseling News and Views*, 1965, Vol. 17, No. 2, p. 5)

This contribution was very consistent with his long-term view that counseling within education must be broadly defined. Recognizing his divergence from the usual views of Division 17 presidents, he invited the reader to contrast his beliefs noted above with the typical convictions of Division 17 members:

1. The majority of our members are interested in adolescents and young adults.
2. The majority of our members either counsel in college, in the Veterans Administration and other rehabilitation agencies, or engage themselves in the preparation of counselors for school, college, or a rehabilitation agency.
3. The majority of our members seem to think of counseling as *the* procedure in which the division is primarily interested.
4. The majority of our members believe in the purpose of deepening the awareness of self within the requirements of collaborative activity.

(*Counseling News and Views*, 1965, Vol. 17, No. 2, p. 5-6)

His summary statement was that "counseling psychologists share the goal of the counselor but lack his convictions and range of practice and technique" (Tiedeman, 1965, p. 6). Counseling psychology is "too narrowly specialized," and does not represent the "full professional interests of counselors."

Tiedeman went on to offer a specific plan of action for the profession:

1. Let us acknowledge the fact that the membership of the American Personnel and Guidance Association is in a better position than is ours to give definition to the positions of the counselor. For the APGA primary identification is with the position, not the discipline of psychology as is our condition.
2. Let us review with great care an inclination toward acceptance of the report of the immediately finished Invitational Conference on Government-University Relations in the Professional Preparation and Employment of Counselors (John McGowan, Executive Director). This Conference struggled with the issue of a desire for quality in counselors during a time of considerable and grave need for a quantity of counselors.
3. Let us reconsider our aversion to the term "guidance." The term "counseling" is presently too closely linked in general parlance to a specific technique rather than to a framework of professional functions for a counselor. (It's time to stop relying on an analogue of what presumably happens in the mind of a listener in the association of "teacher" and "teaching.") Furthermore, the term "counseling" either fails to convey a goal or too often conveys only the limited goal of "one to one" treatment. The term "guidance" (as an applied behavioral science?) carries a broader meaning as a goal and has the added advantage of then logically permitting examination of *numerous* techniques, including that of counseling, as means of achieving the goal.
4. Let us reaffirm our interest in guidance *to promote the incorporation into educational frames* (think education, not school alone) of procedures designed to cultivate awareness of self within the requirements inherent in collaborative activity . . . .
5. Let us particularly attend to the manner in which we make the foundations of our practice more explicit. In this connection I am personally persuaded that a great deal of our attention should be given, not to the creation of the behavioral sciences, but to the creation of understanding of the process by which people incorporate the insights of historical statements—such as those of the behavioral sciences.

(*Counseling News and Views*, 1965, Vol. 17, No. 2, pp. 6-8)

The central concern of Tiedeman in offering the term "guidance" was quite different than its traditional use in public schools. In his usage, it was a descriptive term of broad scope allowing examination of numerous techniques of helping. It was also narrower in scope than traditional usage in that the setting was usually viewed as educational. Perhaps recognizing his divergence from typical counseling psychology, Tiedeman closed with the statement that he stood to help us improve, and the salutation, *"Your President, Sirs?"* (He closed his presidential statement in *Counseling News and Views*, 1966, Vol. 18, No. 2, with the rhetorical question, Is it time to reform ourselves with a Division of Guidance Psychology?)

As part of a continuing concern with the topic of subdoctoral training in counseling and who directs that training, Gerken (1966) summarized the situation for 1966-67:

Some Professional Identifications of Directors of NDEA Counseling Institutes, 1966-67

Directors of	N	Members of Division 17	Members of APA, not of Division 17	Non-Members of APA
Summer Institutes	46	10 (22%)	11 (24%)	25 (54%)
Academic Year Institutes	19	5 (26%)	7 (37%)	7 (37%)
	65	15 (23%)	18 (28%)	32 (49%)

(*Counseling News and Views,* 1966, Vol. 18, No. 1, p. 6)

Only 51% of NDEA counseling institutes are directed by APA members, and less than half of those (23% of the total directors) are members of Division 17.

Vol. 18, No. 1 of *Counseling News and Views* for March of 1966 reported the discussions leading to the transfer of the *Journal of Counseling Psychology* to the American Psychological Association. Division 17 "unanimously" endorsed the "added professional focus on this major specialty area" which would be accomplished by the shift in management responsibility.

The message by President William C. Cottle (Cottle, 1966) identified a number of issues before the profession:

> Among these are the problems of subprofessional support personnel in counseling; resources for training nonschool counselors; who should be our clients; our place in epidemiological psychology; how to get more of the eligible counseling psychologists to join the Division and strengthen our approaches to national problems; what to do about the conflict between the national and state psychological associations; where do we stand on the perennial argument about psychology as a science or as a profession and, what is our position with reference to "guidance," testing, and computers? (*Counseling News and Views*, 1966, Vol. 18, No. 3, p. 1)

A number of the issues Cottle identified were recurrent ones: subprofessional support personnel, resources for training, attracting more eligible psychologists to join Division 17, etc. Cottle also brought up significant new issues such as the conflict between national and state psychological associations (see Anderson, 1984, for a summary of the 1980s' version of the conflict) and the role of computers in counseling psychology (*The Counseling Psychologist*, 1983, Vol. 11, No. 4).

Cottle's (1966) statement was remarkable in that it also directed the attention of the profession to the responsibility (and opportunity) to expand its client population:

> Too long have we been mainly preoccupied with the role of the counseling psychologist in the school setting, particularly in working with the college-bound or college level student. We need to take a good hard look at our responsibility to make our skills available to the noncollege student and to those persons in nonschool settings who can use our help. We need to find out how we communicate and counsel with persons we call "disadvantaged" because we do not want them to know they are *poor*. The ordinary counseling approaches do not seem adequate, but what research are we doing to see what will be most effective with these groups at all ages and also with college graduates later in life, such as Hahn's "mature, self-actualizing person," who needs our help? (*Counseling News and Views*, 1966, Vol. 18, No. 3, pp. 1-2)

The development of new approaches to cross-cultural counseling and the growth of the literature on counseling minorities in the decade of the 1970s were natural outgrowths of expanding the client groups which were rendered service. The contributions by Smith (1982) and Tanney (1982) are current reflections of counseling psychology's need to expand its base of clients served.

The 1966, Vol. 18, No. 3, issue of *Counseling News and Views* contained the second draft of a report by the Education and Training Committee (1966) on "Recommended roles for counseling psychologists in the development of counselor support personnel." While this draft did not have any "official sanction," it raised important concerns about how to address the problem of a shortage of highly trained counselors. Medicine and engineering were offered as examples of professions which had developed hierarchies of support personnel to perform vital services. Further, counseling psychology was presented as too oriented to the problems of the "middle class"; professionals were either unable or unwilling to deal with the problems of lower-class youth (and adults as well). Gordon (1965) expanded on this problem:

> The counseling process, and its array of associated techniques as represented in the standard textbooks and educational curricula

is one which has been evolved through decades of practical experience and research with middle-class clients and subjects, most in both categories being students. The techniques which have been developed are therefore specifically appropriate to well-motivated applicant-clients who are verbally expressive and quite accepting of middle-class values relative to work and achievement . . . .

Whether it is cause or effect of the middle-class orientation of counseling techniques and procedures, it is true that counselor education, and even more so, clinical psychology, devotes almost all its resources to the preparation of counselors and psychologists for middle-class secondary schools, middle-class agencies, and for universities, thus missing entirely the body of needy, out-of-school nonmiddle-class people. (Gordon, 1965, p. 335)

The expansion of government-funded programs resulted in a situation "demanding a different kind of counselor—one who can work effectively with persons whose problems are far more immediate and earthy than the problems of choosing a college" (Education and Training Committee, 1966, p. 13).

There are four possible courses of action which were identified:

1. Counseling psychologists could simply ignore these new developments, continuing their own activities and offering neither aid nor opposition to programs using counselor support personnel.
2. Counseling psychologists could decry these new developments, insisting that only persons fully trained in approved programs may call themselves counselors and be allowed to perform counseling services.
3. Counseling psychologists could join forces with people in other organizations and try to control, by setting up rigid hierarchies, the functions of several levels of professionals and subprofessionals.
4. Counseling psychologists could offer their services to help programs and agencies which hire counselor support personnel, sharing their relevant skills and at the same time indicating a willingness to learn about new problems.

(Education and Training Committee, 1966, p. 14)

Of these four, the unanimous choice was the fourth alternative, for the following reasons:

Counseling psychologists, in their role as citizens as well as professionals, should be concerned that all members of society have the fullest opportunity to participate in and contribute to that society. We recognize that counseling psychologists have no exclusive knowledge about how best to attain full opportunity for all citizens, but we can do no more, and no less, than contribute our present skills and knowledge while seeking to discover additional ways of promoting the welfare of all our citizens. (*Counseling News and Views*, 1966, Vol. 18, No. 3, p. 14)

This was a more explicit statement of concern and commitment to a much broader range of people and problems in society than had previously been found in the professional literature.

As President of Division 17, Cottle (1967a) reported an invitation from the APA Education and Training Board to appear before them to "help them with some information about the training and work of counseling psychologists." William Bevan, later to become APA President, explained that the Education and Training Board was having trouble differentiating between training programs in clinical and counseling psychology as part of meeting their accreditation function. The Board was considering either dropping the accreditation of counseling psychology, or combining the two into some form of "clinical-counseling" arrangement.

After pointing out that 40% of the members of Division 17 were also members of Division 12, and that the terms "counseling" and "psychotherapy" were often used interchangeably, Cottle (1967a) went on to offer a succinct characterization of counseling psychology:

the bulk of counseling psychologists have been and are working in academic settings or government agencies with clients who are usually within the normal range of behavior; that these are primarily youth and young adults, although more recently older persons and disadvantaged individuals are requiring our services; that the preparation of these counseling psychologists focused on the behavior of the normal individual in school, work, and community settings at various socioeconomic levels; and, that knowledge from other disciplines of sociology, anthropology, social work, economics, and education was necessary and thus our preparation is different from the usual preparation of the clinical psychologist. (*Counseling News and Views*, 1967, Vol. 19, No. 1, pp. 2-3)

He commented that Division 17 would prefer *no* accreditation to some joint combination with clinical psychology. Further, he decried the underrepresentation of counseling psychologists on accreditation teams and the APA Education and Training Board. Over a decade was to pass before organized counseling psychology vigorously responded to the challenge of obtaining adequate representation.

Caracena (1967) commented upon graduate training in counseling psychology specifically in terms of Carl Rogers' harsh evaluation of the basic assumptions of graduate training programs in psychology (Rogers,

1967). The thrust of the critique by Rogers was that "we are doing an unintelligent, ineffectual, and wasteful job of preparing psychologists, to the detriment of our discipline and society" (Rogers, 1967a, p. 55).

Caracena's conclusion, after examining Rogers' sweeping criticism, was as follows:

> To what extent does this sweeping criticism apply specifically to education in counseling psychology? Perhaps it fits us best, for it is counseling psychology which professes values most antithetical to our behavior. Our values of man's autonomy, his originality, his dignity and worth, and his humanity are not readily fostered by nor reflected in many of our training procedures. Rather, we "educate" students too often to conform, to recite. (*Counseling News and Views*, 1967, Vol. 19, No. 1, p. 5)

In applying Rogers' broad program of change to counseling psychology education programs, Caracena offered these propositions:

1. Increase student responsibility for selection of courses
2. More encouragement of student problem solving
3. Minimization of student evaluation
4. Early and continuing experiences of self in human interaction

(*Counseling News and Views*, 1967, Vol. 19, No. 1, pp. 5-9)

After expanding on each proposition, Caracena summarized his position by indicating that "the very principles and values we believe to generate human growth often are forgotten in our practices of procreating our own kind" (Caracena, 1967, p. 9). Changes in individual counseling psychology training programs which resulted from, or were inspired by, the Rogers statement and adaptations or extrapolations from it did not result from any formal action by organized counseling psychology.

Cottle's (1967a) rendition of meeting with the APA Education and Training Board generated a series of responses from counseling psychologists suggesting ways to differentiate between clinical and counseling psychology. There was a spirited critique of the approach of the APA Education and Training Board to accreditation.

Cottle (1967b), under the heading of "Counseling Psychology — 1967," described how counseling psychologists differed from all other psychologists in goals, functions, roles, tools and procedures, settings, and in the nature of clients and needs:

> Of all these characteristics, the *goals* seemed most important in describing us. They were stated as helping an individual develop systematic problem-solving behavior, both cognitive and psychomotor, to help him through the conflict situations in his normal development

from "birth to death." Here the emphasis is on counseling the normal individual at any age by helping him to identify and maximize his strengths through focus on assets, skills, "possibility structures," and obstacles to progress within the individual or the environment, not to change long-established behavior patterns. Our purpose is to help the client acquire a greater range and flexibility of responses. In order to do this we need to eliminate the artificial distinction between counseling and life. We need to define our own professional behavior and to develop training programs for other persons who can follow us and be felt in the structure of society. A major goal is seen to be a focus on the many aspects of career development and the world of work.

Our *functions* are conceived to be an empirical approach to reality, rather than a focus on internal factors alone. We help the individual identify and develop his inadequacies as well as his strengths and provide the experiential setting where he may do these. We accomplish this by constructive intervention, assessment, development of norms, and focus on the world of work and on socialization. We create a climate which fosters individuation of responses. We promote drive induction and promote knowledge of the labor market and occupational demands of the worker. To do this we relate client self-concept to the world of work and relate research on the normal individual to client development in all life settings. One of our functions is seen to be helping the client improve his adaptive skills by reviewing or interpreting client psychometric data and other data *with* him. In this our function is to support his basic orientation and adjustment, not change it. We must stress the positive and the preventive approaches to work with clients.

The roles our members want us to maintain with clients are those of the counselor-interviewer; the group process-dynamics leader; the consultant with parents, teachers, administrators, and other key persons in the community; the designer of learning experiences; the co-explorer of client need structures; the decision stimulator; the fosterer of client harmony with the environment; the *invited* professional who helps reduce a normal client's personal sense of conflict; and the developer of relationship studies with clients. Another series of roles we carry out center around our attempts to help society recognize individual differences and to secure society's assistance to help our clients develop to their full capacities. We need society's help in planning productive life roles for clients and in locating and maintaining other sources of client help. A third series of roles involves identification and exploration of what we do, the description of our self-image in practice, and the interpretation of our unique professional mission to others. Perhaps another role could be in the production of a handbook of counseling psychology or career development psychology.

The *settings* in which we see ourselves working are usually created by the orientation of the counselor toward education and work and seldom include much private practice. Other settings are those of community or private social agencies, business and industry, and government service such as the VA or VRA.

The *tools and procedures* are developed for the collection of client data from many sources and for sharing these data with the client through interview procedures. The interview appears to be our main tool, and its focus is upon collecting, from records and reports, and from observations in school, work, and social settings to help the individual locate his most promising environment. To do this we measure, evaluate, and predict with the help of research and statistics. We modify normal life processes through operant conditioning or behavior therapy to stimulate growth processes and remove inhibitors to growth. We develop case studies focusing on potential for school, work, recreation, and community living.

The nature of our *clients and their needs* is the last way in which our members describe themselves professionally. They are emphatic about placing the focus on the individual, not his problem, and upon the use of the term "counseling" as sharing or collaboration with a client, not treatment or psychotherapy. The primary description of clients and needs centers around sources of school achievement, job satisfaction, vocational choice and success, the development of vocational interest, and psychological and social factors in career development. To do this we explore life stages with a client who is reasonable, rational, and effective when he comes for help. We help him to increase his personal development through awareness and acceptance of self and personal dynamics as well as of his place in the environment. (*Counseling News and Views*, 1967, Vol. 19, No. 2, pp. 2-4)

In Cottle's view, and his view is very consistent with other appraisals at the time, the above statement reflects how counseling psychologists thought of themselves in the middle 1960s.

Enneis (1967), in a new addition to the literature of counseling psychology, described planned and accidental discrimination. While his presentation was related most directly to the use of psychological tests in personnel assessment, it had much broader implications for counseling psychology. He described Title VII of the Civil Rights Act of 1964, which addressed itself to employment practices that discriminated or otherwise adversely affected hiring, classification, or promotion based on an individual's race, color, religion, sex, or national origin. The psychometric movement had become such an integral part of counseling psychology that the impact of Title VII had implications quite pervasive for psychological practice.

Van Atta (1967) proposed a data bank for research on counseling and psychotherapy. In his view, the existence of a pool of data "systematically accumulated" would do much to eliminate the problem of small samples and "samples of convenience" in counseling research. The data bank he proposed was to be designed for data gathering as well as for storage and retrieval. This is one of the good ideas introduced into the literature that did not ultimately come to fruition.

Goldman (1967) provided a detailed explanation of the purposes and procedures of the Board of Trustees of the American Board of Examiners in Professional Psychology. While the ratio of graduates of doctoral programs in counseling to those of clinical psychology had ranged from 1 to 5 in 1957 to 1 to 4 in 1961, the ratio of new counseling diplomates to new clinical diplomates averaged 1 to 15 between 1963 and 1967. In making his point "dramatically," he announced that no counseling psychologist earned diplomate status in 1967 (he might also have pointed out there were no new Fellows named by Division 17 in 1967). An intent of his article was to increase participation in the diplomate program.

CONSTELLATIONS OF SUBSTANTIVE
THEORETICAL DEVELOPMENTS

The fourth period in the history of counseling psychology was note-worthy for the high quality of the continued elaboration of substantive theories of personality development, counseling and psychotherapy, vocational psychology, occupational choice, and career development.

Table 4.1 presents representative contributions to personality theory and theories of counseling and psychotherapy from 1963 up to 1967. This table reveals the appearance of several classics in the psychoanalytic (Freud, 1965; Hartmann, 1964; Rapaport, 1967) and Adlerian (Adler, 1963a, 1964b; Dreikurs, 1963) aproaches. Behavior theory and therapy underwent a period of exceptional innovation (Cautela, 1967; Eysenck, 1964b; Paul, 1966; Wolpe & Lazarus, 1966), careful statement of principles (Bandura, 1969), application to practical therapeutic situations (Ullman & Krasner, 1965), and definition of rationale and implications for counseling (Krumboltz, 1965, 1966a, 1966b).

Building on an active approach to research and theory development which occurred during the second and third historical period, Rogers expanded the client-centered contribution to encompass a more adequate conception of the "fully functioning" person (Rogers, 1963) and offered a detailed statement of what is entailed by a humanistic conception of man (Rogers, 1965). This period also marked the initial appearance of Rogers' expanding interest in encounter groups (Rogers, 1967a).

Eric Berne (Berne, 1964) wrote *Games People Play*, a book that was to become both a classic and best-selling statement of patterns of human interaction from the transactional perspective. Humanistic and existential

Table 4.1

**Representative Contributions to Personality Theory
and Theories of Counseling and Psychotherapy in
the Fourth Historical Period
(1963-1967)**

Psychoanalysis

Freud, Anna	Normality and pathology in childhood (1965)
Greenson, R.	The technique and practice of psychoanalysis (1967)
Hartmann, H.	Essays on ego psychology (1964)
Rapaport, D.	Collected papers (1967)

Adlerian Psychotherapy (Theory)

Adler, A.	The practice and theory of individual psychology (1963a) The problem child (1963b) Problems of neurosis (1964a) Social interest: A challenge to mankind (1964b)
Dreikurs, R.	Individual psychology: The Adlerian point of view (1963) Psychodynamics, psychotherapy, and counseling (1967)
Orgler, H.	Alfred Adler: The man and his work (1965)

Behavior Theory and Therapy

Cautela, J. R.	Covert sensitization (1967)
Eysenck, H. J.	Experiments in behavior therapy (1964a)
Krumboltz, J. D.	Behavioral counseling: Rationale and research (1965) Behavioral goals for counseling (1966a) Revolution in counseling: Implications of behavioral science (1966b)
Paul, G. L.	Insight vs. desensitization in psychotherapy: An experiment in anxiety reduction (1966)
Ullman, L. P., & Krasner, L.	Case studies in behavior modification (1966)
Wolpe, J., & Lazarus, A. A.	Behavior therapy techniques (1966)

Table 4.1 (Continued)

Client-centered Therapy

Rogers, C. R.	The concept of the fully functioning person (1963)
	A humanistic conception of man (1965)
	The process of the basic encounter group (1967b)

Humanistic and Existential Theory and Therapy

Boss, M.	Psychoanalysis and Daseins analysis (1963)
Buber, M.	The knowledge of man (1965)
Frankl, V. E.	Man's search for meaning (1963)
	The doctor and the soul (1965)
	Psychotherapy and existentialism (1967)
Jourard, S. M.	The transparent self (1964)
May, R.	Psychology and the human dilemma (1967)
van Kaam, A.	Existential foundations of psychology (1966)

Transactional Analysis

Berne, E.	Games people play (1964)
	Principles of group treatment (1966)

theory and therapy, as with other approaches during this period, received exceptional attention as an approach to understanding and changing the human condition as a consequence of both classic statements (Frankl, 1963, 1965; Jourard, 1964), expansions of theory (Boss, 1963), and statements of principles (van Kaam, 1966).

The domain of theories of vocational psychology, occupational choice, and career development was likewise in a period of both careful formulations and expanding horizons, as is indicated by Table 4.2. From the psychoanalytic/psychodynamic perspective, for example, Bordin, Nachmann, and Segal (1963) articulated a framework for vocational development, and from the trait and factor approach, Dawis, England, and Lofquist (1964) presented a systematic theory of work adjustment.

From the life space/life span perspective, Super and associates (Super, Starishevsky, Matlin, & Jordaan, 1963) elaborated the conceptual relevance of self-theory to career development, and Super (1964) articulated a developmental approach to vocational guidance. Roe's occupational psychology was undergoing a period of sustained empirical analysis (Roe, 1966; Roe & Baruch, 1967) and theory development (Roe & Siegelman, 1964).

John Holland offered a systematic statement of the typology approach he developed in what has become a classic in vocational psychology, *The Psychology of Vocational Choice* (Holland, 1966). This period in counseling psychology's history also saw the emergence of a new major approach,

Table 4.2

Representative Contributions to Vocational Psychology, Occupational Choice, and Career Development in the Fourth Historical Period (1963-1967)

Psychoanalytic/Psychodynamic

Bordin, E. S., Nachmann, B., & Segal, S. J.	An articulated framework for vocational development (1963)
Galinsky, M. D., & Fast, I.	Vocational choices as a focus of the identity search (1966)
Malnig, L. R.	Fear of paternal competition: A factor in vocational choice (1967)
Segal, S. J., & Szabo, R.	Identification in two vocations: Accountants and creative writers (1964)
Sostek, A. B.	The relation of identification and parent-child climate to occupational choice (1963)
White, J. C.	Cleanliness and successful bank clerical personnel—a brief (1963)

Trait and Factor

Dawis, R. V., England, G. W., & Lofquist, L. H.	A theory of work adjustment (1964)
Williamson, E. G.	An historical perspective of the vocational guidance movement (1964) Vocational counseling (1965)

Life Space/Life Span (Donald Super and Associates)

Super, D. E.	A developmental approach to vocational guidance (1964)
Super, D. E., Starishevsky, R., Matlin, N., & Jordaan, J. P.	Career Development: Self-concept theory (1963)

Table 4.2 (Continued)

Occupational Psychology
(Anne Roe and Associates)

Roe, A.	Cross-classification of occupations (1966)
Roe, A., & Baruch, R.	Occupational changes in the adult years (1967)
Roe, A., Bateman, T., Hubbard, W. D., & Hutchinson, T.	Studies of occupational history. Part I: Job changes and the classification of occupations (1966)
Roe, A., & Siegelman, M.	A parent-child relations questionnaire (1963)
	The origin of interests (1964)

Vocational Typology
(John Holland and Associates)

Holland, J. L.	The psychology of vocational choice (1966)

Development and Decision Making
(David Tiedeman and Robert O'Hara)

Tiedeman, D. V., & O'Hara, R. P.	Career development: Choice and adjustment (1963)

the development and decision-making conceptualizations of David Tiedeman and Robert O'Hara (Tiedeman & O'Hara, 1963). This approach brought together a number of conceptions from the fields of guidance and education and integrated them with insights from the psychology of decision making.

OTHER THEORETICAL AND RESEARCH ADVANCEMENTS

The only reviews of counseling which appeared in the *Annual Review of Psychology* during the fourth period in the history of counseling psychology were those by Patterson (1966) which covered the literature between June 1962 and June 1965, and Segal (1968) which covered the literature up through 1967 (he was also assigned the student development literature). Schmidt and Pepinsky (1965) reviewed the literature on counseling psychology from 1963, and Myers (1966) did it for 1964, both reviews appearing in the *Journal of Counseling Psychology*. Other commentaries on the research literature during this fourth historical period were by Carkhuff (1966) and Whiteley (1967), the latter focusing on selecting counselors, selecting clients, and assessing the outcomes of counseling.

A significant aspect of the Patterson (1966) review is that it excluded much of traditional counseling psychology: studies of self-concept (and other aspects of personality), vocational development theory, tests, and measurements. From a historical point of view, the Patterson review was not in the mainstream of counseling psychology from either the perspective of its historical roots, its central professional identity struggles, or its substantive, theoretical bases of the 1960s.

What the Patterson review did include was valuable, including commentary on texts and other books, activities of the American Personnel and Guidance Association, the preparation of counselors at the subdoctoral level, the use of videotape in counselor preparation, selection procedures in counselor education, and studies of students in NDEA counseling institutes.

His section on research examined literature on topics which were popular then: studies of counselor characteristics and behavior, studies of client characteristics and behavior, investigations of counselor-client interaction, studies of counseling outcomes, and methodological concerns. Patterson noted that a defect in most counseling or psychotherapy studies has been either lack of control or specification of the treatment (counseling) variable.

This was a period when a number of research issues and theoretical problems identified in the 1950s became better understood as a consequence of research in the 1960s. Outcome studies on counseling and psychotherapy appeared (Berger, 1962; Cross, 1964; and Strupp, 1963). Strupp (1964) and Eysenck (1964b) continued to dispute the effectiveness of counseling and psychotherapy.

In a section on new methods and techniques, Patterson indicated that verbal operant conditioning techniques were the most significant development (Ryan & Krumboltz, 1964; Krumboltz & Thoresen, 1964). Excellent reviews of these new techniques at the time were provided by Krasner (1962, 1963, 1965). Also appearing at this time was the first of a series of contributions on the Interpersonal Process Recall (IPR) method of Kagan and his associates (Kagan, Krathwohl, & Miller, 1963).

In a section on theoretical and philosophical issues, Patterson identified the implications of behavior therapy as the major theoretical issue. Those implications had been the subject of lively debate (Rogers, 1964; Skinner, 1964) and extended explication (Wolpe, Salter, & Reyna, 1964; Ullman & Krasner, 1965).

Another important theoretical issue identified by Patterson was the growth and refinement of existential approaches to counseling (Van Kaam, 1965; Bugenthal, 1965) and their confrontation with behavior therapy. London (1964) wrote a significant book on the therapeutic approaches and their moral implications. Rogers (1961b) noted the irreconcilable nature of the existential and behavioral points of view.

Segal's (1968) review began with the identification of Sanford's (1962) book, *The American College*, as presenting "a starting point for reviewing the relationship of increased research focus on college student development to the counseling of college students" (Segal, 1968, p. 497). Segal departed from the format of previous reviews of counseling or counseling psychology in the *Annual Review of Psychology*. He chose instead to "focus on the impact of the research, theory, and practice of counseling on the greater understanding of variables which affect student development" (Segal, 1968, p. 497). The balance of Segal's review touched on differentiation of college and noncollege students, student and college characteristics, and student development during college (academic, vocational, personality).

SUMMARY

The fourth historical period began with counseling psychology at a crossroads. The response was proactive and substantial. The Greyston Conference provided greater clarity on identity, substantive bases, and needed directions for the future. Cottle (1967b) provided further refinement on how counseling psychologists differed from all other psychologists on goals, functions, roles, tools and procedures, settings, and in the nature of clients served.

The cultural themes of quest for personal fulfillment and the exploration of potentialities within the context of a community of significant others created an increased demand for services by counseling psychologists, who began to be employed in a wider variety of settings where they dealt with a wider variety of clients. Research issues and theoretical problems identified in the 1950s became much better understood as a consequence of research in the 1960s. The implications of behavior therapy and the growth of existential approaches to counseling were two major theoretical issues at this time. The fourth period in the history of counseling psychology was noteworthy for the high quality of the continued elaboration of substantive theories of personality development, counseling and psychotherapy, vocational psychology, occupational choice, and career development.

FOOTNOTES

[1] Fretz (Note 1) drew attention to the "strong sense of negativity" that characterized some years in the development of the profession of counseling psychology. His analysis merits attention: "The strong sense of negativity about some years of our profession's development was not universally shared and will not be accepted by some readers. In thinking about my own reaction to some of your material, I arrived at the one hypothesis: that the very existence of *Counseling News and Views* emphasized the problematic features of our professional development. It provided a ready format for a 'noisy minority' while the 'silent majority' might have been going quite comfortably about their pursuit of goals as counseling psychologists. We shall, of course, never know for sure what reality existed, (if there is just one reality!); at any rate, I would prefer some recognition in the

manuscript that, all the while that any crisis of infighting may have been occurring, there were always significant numbers of counseling psychologists who had a good sense of who they were, what they wanted to do, and were busily pursuing the goals of our profession as outlined in our charter."

[2]Thompson (Note 2) reported his understanding that the essence of Darley's position was that "counseling psychology, like clinical psychology, should be based upon a core program of graduate training."

[3]It is beyond the scope of this general history to review the recommendations in detail. They are available in the original source (Thompson & Super, 1964), and because of their significance, have been reprinted in Whiteley (1980c).

[4]As Thompson (Note 3) summarized the situation, "Counseling psychologists are no longer a group of people in search of a professional identity."

Chapter 5
Alternative Directions for the Profession: The Fifth Historical Period (1968-1976)

An important legacy of the previous historical period in counseling psychology's growth as an organized applied-scientific specialty was a much clearer definition of the central thrust of the profession (Thompson & Super, 1964; Cottle, 1967b). The fifth historical period began with the release of the most comprehensive statement yet constructed on the definition of the profession (Jordaan, Myers, Layton, & Morgan, 1968). Whereas the previous statements had limited circulation within the membership of Division 17, or had not been published at all, this statement was one which was published by the Teachers College Press,[1] copyrighted by the American Psychological Association, and much more widely circulated. It began as a project of the Professional Affairs Committee of Division 17 and had the official sanction of the Division Executive Committee. Given its sanction and visibility, it merits examination in detail.

With slight modifications, the definition of "psychologist, counseling" from the 1965 edition of Volume I of the *Dictionary of Occupations* served as the introduction:

PSYCHOLOGIST, COUNSELING. Provides individual and group guidance and counseling services in schools, colleges and universities, hospitals, clinics, rehabilitation centers, and industry, to assist individuals in achieving more effective personal, social, educational, and vocational development and achievement. Collects data about the individual through use of interview, case history, and observational techniques. Selects, administers, scores, and interprets psychological tests designed to assess individual's intelligence, aptitudes, abilities, and interests, applying knowledge of statistical analysis. Evaluates data to identify cause of problem and to determine advisability of counseling or referral to other specialists or institutions. Conducts counseling or therapeutic interviews to assist individual to gain insight into personal problems, define goals, and plan action reflecting his interests, abilities, and needs. Provides

125

occupational, educational, and other information to enable individual to formulate realistic educational and vocational plans. Follows up results of counseling to determine reliability and validity of treatment used. May engage in research to develop and improve diagnostic and counseling techniques. (Jordaan et al., 1968. Also in Whiteley, 1980c pp. 179-180)

Three different but complementary roles were identified: the remedial or rehabilitative, the preventive, and the educative and developmental. The definitions of these three roles are important in understanding the practice of counseling psychology:

Remedial or hehabilitative. This is helping people who are presently experiencing difficulty.

Preventive. This is anticipating, circumventing, or forestalling difficulties which may arise in the future.[2]

Educative and developmental. This is to help plan, obtain, and derive maximum benefit from experiences which will enable them to discover and fulfill their potential. (Adapted from Jordaan et al., 1968. Also in Whiteley, 1980c, p. 181)

In addition to professional practice, counseling psychologists engage in research, teaching, and administrative activities. The settings in which counseling psychologists work and the functions they perform were identified in two tables.

Educational settings predominated (64%) as locations for employment. Teaching and administration functions combined to total 55% of the positions held. Only 38% of counseling psychologists were primarily employed in service positions.

The "point of view" of the counseling psychologist is one of hope and optimism:

individuals can change, can lead satisfying lives, can be self-directing, and can find ways of using their resources, even though these may have been impaired by incapacitating attitudes and feelings, slow maturation, cultural deprivation, lack of opportunity, illness, injury, or old age. (Jordaan et al., 1968. Also in Whiteley, 1980c, p. 181)

In helping individuals change, counseling psychologists use a variety of techniques including exploratory experiences, environmental interventions, and the primary tool of counseling. The counseling role is as "guide, facilitator, informant, question-raiser, commentator, and, above

Table 5.1

Settings in Which Counseling Psychologists Work

	%
Educational settings (colleges and universities, private and public schools)	64
Health-related settings (hospitals, rehabilitation agencies, mental health clinics)	11
Industry and government (excluding hospitals and schools)	13
Community counseling agencies	5
Private practice	5
Other	2

Table 5.2

Positions Held by Counseling Psychologists

	%
Primarily teaching: Professor, department head, other academic positions	32
Primarily service administration: Director or coordinator of a university counseling center, psychological clinic, counseling service, community agency, rehabilitation project, student personnel services	23
Primarily service: Counselor, psychologist, psychotherapist, consultant in colleges, universities, schools, private practice	38
Miscellaneous	7

(Jordaan et al., 1968.* Also in Whiteley, 1980c, p. 186)

*Reprinted and adapted by permission of the publisher from A. S. Thompson and D. E. Super (Eds.), *The professional preparation of counseling psychologists: Report of the 1964 Greyston Conference.* (New York: Teachers College Press, © 1964 by Teachers College, Columbia University. All rights reserved.)

all, a person on whom the counselee can try out ideas and ways of behaving" (Jordaan et al., 1968. Also in Whiteley, 1980c, p. 183). The counseling psychologist was presented as "a data-oriented problem solver."

The Jordaan et al. (1968) contribution concluded with detailed information about job satisfactions and rewards, how one becomes a counseling psychologist, the nature of undergraduate preparation, types of training programs available, and future demand for services and foreseeable trends.

Warnath (1968) argued that medically oriented groups (psychiatry, clinical psychology, and social work) had begun to adapt the concepts of individual strengths and individual differences at the same time that counseling psychology was failing "to exploit our original claim to uniqueness — our concepts of health, strength, and human potential" (Warnath, 1968, p. 5). The strength and uniqueness of counseling psychologists are in "defining ourselves as applied social psychologists who can use expertly the theories and techniques of the clinician and the vocational counselor," but who will also evaluate situations potentially damaging to client development and "work with the situation to reduce its damaging effects."

He addressed the continuing problem of defining counseling psychology and raised the question of whether there was faulty logic in the Tyler, Tiedeman, and Wrenn (1980) report. It is a source of continuing difficulty to build an identity for the profession "on a single type of helping relationship" which has "increasingly limited applications in most work settings." A more "comprehensive" model is needed:

Counseling is *one* technique for helping people, but this technique is not restricted to counseling psychology and, therefore, cannot define the profession. To restrict the definition of Counseling Psychology to an activity which can serve only one person at a time, and only after he has presented his problem, is to lock our profession into the remedial work of several professions and to limit our potential value to the community. Our training programs have emphasized one activity — one form of relationship — and we have tried to sell our uniqueness in carrying out this activity by stressing our use of certain tests and the "normality" of the clients with whom we work.

This is nonsense for several reasons: First, from a practical standpoint, a one-talent group is very quickly relegated to support-personnel status. Second, we have spent 20 years or more trying to define our profession in individual counselor-client terms and have failed. And, third, our paper model is not adequate for Counseling Psychologists who are carrying out service work.

We need a model based on general goals and purposes for the profession, and we need to subordinate questions of techniques and methods to these goals and purposes. One possibility would be Gene Oetting's suggestion in the July, 1967, issue of the *Journal of Counseling Psychology* that we adopt goals related to studying and assisting in the developmental process of individuals within the framework of developmental tasks. I submit that research, consulting, coordinating orientation programs, encouraging new job possibilities in the community, and other relevant activities could be included within the acceptable functions of Counseling Psychologists if a model based on the general goals and purposes of the profession were used. (*Counseling News and Views*, 1968, Vol. 20, No. 3, p. 2)

Warnath recommended a similar approach to Oetting's (1967) suggestion that the profession adopt goals "related to studying and assisting in the developmental process of individuals within the framework of developmental tasks" (Warnath, 1968, p. 3).

Warnath also drew attention to the persistent problems of the communication gap between academicians and service personnel. This gap has several sources:

1. Those who write about counseling and teach counseling theory and techniques do not as a rule offer adequate role models for service work — except as teachers and researchers.
2. The second factor producing a communication gap with our profession relates to consultantships. Although the instructors in counselor education programs act as consultants to service agencies, service personnel are infrequently invited to consult officially with training departments on consumer needs. The status implications in who tells what to whom are not lost on our trainees. But, more importantly, the one-way communication increases the unrelatedness of training to practice.
3. A third communications problem results from the fact that the Division of Counseling Psychology has developed no system for assuring a fair representation on its boards and committees of those engaged primarily in service activities. Service work does not give visibility in the profession. The service worker's research and publications are likely to be designed for local consumption and, hence, do not help to win nominations or elections. As a result, counselors and administrators of service agencies are underrepresented on our boards and committees. Professional problems under discussion within the Division are inevitably given academic and training biases.
4. While we have been modifying our theories of choice and decision making from the trait-factor model to self-concept and developmental models, we have failed to modify our models of counselor practice to take the implications of these developmental theories into account. A difference of opinion about our professional

identity has arisen between the counselor educators and academicians on the one hand, and counseling psychologists in service activities on the other—with some exceptions, of course. The former write, teach, and supervise as if the individual contact with clients was the limit of our professional role. The latter are already committed to act on parts of the environment which are causing general problems and frustrations to potential clients. (Warnath, 1968,p. 3-4)

Tyler (1972) indicated that one special theme which had engaged Division 17 over the years was the search for professional identity. Her conclusion was that questions about the counselor's distinctive *role* are "inherently unanswerable" because counseling is not a role but a function. (She indicated that she was using the terms 'counseling psychologist' and 'counselor' interchangeably.)

Uncertainties about the counselor's role and identity are resolved:

if we characterize counseling in terms of its function in a social system rather than in terms of particular duties and activities. From society's point of view counseling is the essential lubricant that makes it possible for the machine to run smoothly. But since these are human systems and the parts are human beings, a better way of characterizing counseling is to think of it as what keeps a social system from being *only* a smoothly running machine. The counselor is the representative and the advocate of the individuals who make up the system. His function is to help each of them come to terms with the social system in which he finds himself, and we should interpret "come to terms" very broadly. An individual may elect to adapt himself to a social system, to struggle against it, to attempt to change it, or to leave it and enter another. To do any of these things successfully he requires self-knowledge and knowledge of the systems he is dealing with, and he needs very much the assistance and support of other persons who really care about *him*. As social systems get more and more complex, as they have been doing in modern times, the counseling function is more and more necessary. But because of this complexity, the particular sort of service needed most by any one individual or in any one particular place may differ markedly from what is needed by someone else or what is needed in a different place. Thus I am afraid there is no getting around the fact that counseling as a profession must continually struggle with problems of identity and roles. How do counselors differ from teachers, from psychiatrists, from social workers . . .? It all *depends*. In one situation the counselor may look much like a social worker, in another his teaching activities appear to predominate. Perhaps we should think of counseling as the *protean* profession. (Tyler, 1972, p. 6-7)

As social institutions become more complex, counselors are even more necessary, and counseling must be viewed in terms of its role in the social system.

Eight years after the Jordaan et al. (1968) statement, a different view of the profession emerged from the deliberations of a subsequent Committee on Professional Affairs. This different view grew out of the work of the 1974 Division 17 Professional Affairs Committee which had been charged with the task of:

1. defining the current boundaries and relationships between counseling psychology and other specialties;
2. defining the role of counseling psychology as a preventive-developmental function; and
3. more specifically, examining the policies counseling psychologists should adopt in "the teaching of skills to noncounselors. To what extent should we give our profession away?"

(Ivey, 1976. Also in Whiteley, 1980c, p. 196)

In Ivey's view this charge contained an implicit definition of counseling psychology as a specialty. The concern was with educative functions as well as what Ivey characterized as the "traditional" remedial ones:

the teaching function of the counseling psychologist has become clear enough that special attention now must be given to standards to be used when working in educational/preventive functions. Out of the charges, and from the reports of the several subcommittees attacking issues of professional role and function, has evolved a counseling psychologist who is envisioned as a *psychoeducator*, a person who uses many skills, theories, and methods to facilitate human growth. Counseling and psychotherapy remain important skills of the counseling psychologist, but they are only one aspect of a broad new helping role . . . the counseling psychologist as psychoeducator. (Ivey, 1976. Also in Whiteley, 1980c, p. 196)

The educational/developmental role was assigned a primary status with the preventive role secondary and the remedial/rehabilitative role "not discarded, but it becomes subsumed."

The rationale for this revisionary statement is found in the psychoeducator model originally put forward by Authier, Gustafson, Guerney, and Kasdorf (1975). In Ivey's view, this model provides an:

all-inclusive model for the functions of the counseling psychologist. The psychoeducator sees the helping function "not in terms of abnormality (or illness) → diagnosis → prescription → therapy → cure, but rather in terms of client dissatisfaction (or ambition) → goal setting → skill teaching → satisfaction or goal achievement." The person being served "is seen as analogous to a pupil rather than a patient" (Authier et al., 1975, p. 31). Remedial and rehabilitative functions remain important in this model, but the mode of action for change becomes far broader. Prevention activities focus on attainable goals rather than vague descriptions of client or system "need." Most important, systematic educational programs are made available to teach people how to achieve their own uniqueness. (Ivey, 1976. Also in Whiteley, 1980c, p. 197)

While the counseling psychologist performs remedial, preventive, and educative functions, the primary function is no longer counseling (which was primary in the Jordaan et al., 1968, statement).

Counseling was now seen as "only one of a host of skills to educate people for life." Counseling and therapy, "important though they may be, are now limited constructs that fail to take into account the broad new functions of the counseling psychologist" (Ivey, 1976. Also in Whiteley, 1980c, p. 197).

The response of the Division 17 Executive Committee, reminiscent of the official response to the Berg, Pepinsky, Shoben (1980) contribution on counseling psychology in 1960, was essentially to ignore it.[3] The report of the Professional Affairs Committee was "received," then dropped from further official consideration. In retrospect, it would have been a more effective response to articulate the reasons why the Ivey (1976) document was unacceptable to organized counseling psychology.

While the reasons the Division 17 Executive Committee reacted to the Ivey report as it did were never explicitly stated, informal discussion with participants was clear on one point: There was disagreement with Ivey's assertion of primacy for the psychoeducation role and the discounting of counseling as a primary function. There was no explicitly stated disagreement with the content of the psychoeducation role per se. It seemed to be viewed as an elaboration and extension of one of the three roles identified by the earlier Jordaan et al. (1968) report.

The problem caused by essentially ignoring the Ivey report was that the issues of disagreement were not specifically joined. A more effective response would have been to provide greater documentation about the preventive and the remedial/rehabilitative roles. Especially in the preventive area, there have been such major theoretical and research advances in recent years that a fuller and more current explication of that role would have been a constructive addition to the literature.

Finally, a pervasive source of difficulty in resolving the identity issues of counseling psychology has been the recurrent problem of differentiating it from clinical psychology. The problem of differentiation is greatest in the remedial/rehabilitative role. The preventive and educational/developmental roles are much more clearly separate, distinct, and unique contributions of counseling psychology. The challenge still remains to differentiate the remedial/rehabilitative roles more clearly from those of clinical psychology.

ACTIVITIES OF ORGANIZED COUNSELING PSYCHOLOGY

Wrenn (1968) expanded upon the issues raised by Cottle (1967a, 1967b) and clarified how the Evaluation Committee of the APA Education and Training Board functioned. The membership was from clinical and counseling psychology with the chair from general or nonprofessional psychology:

> The Committee has plenty of problems and a good many doubts about the changing nature of its own function, but there has never been a major problem regarding clinical psychologists evaluating counseling psychology programs. Upon every occasion of a visit by representatives of the Committee to a counseling psychology program, a counseling psychologist is a member of the team and generally Chairman of it. I feel that Cottle's concern at this point may apply to the membership of the Board, but not to the membership and problems of the Committee.[4] The Committee is scrupulously careful to see that counseling psychology programs are observed by counseling psychologists, although of course other members of the team may involve clinical or other divisions of psychology. (*Counseling News and Views*, 1968, Vol. 20, No. 1, p. 8)

He indicated that the Committee on Evaluation has always had two or three counseling psychologists on it, corresponding to the ratio of programs to be considered.

Wallace (1968) reported that the Scientific Affairs Committee was addressing itself to the problem of making retrieval, abstracting, and reporting services more "directly germane" to practicing counselors:

> Typically, the counseling psychologist is faced with deciding which of the alternatives of assistance open to him are most likely to help a client achieve his goals. Research literature is often not reported in a format to assist with this applied problem. Although it is unrealistic and unnecessary to suggest that all reported research follow a rigid format, certain key features of such reports might well be specified in sufficient detail so that practitioners could systematically use the results of pertinent previous research. This area of investigation is associated with the content of the recent Invitational Conference on Research Problems in Counseling conducted by the

Central Midwest Regional Educational Laboratory and Washington University. (*Counseling News and Views*, 1968, Vol. 20, No. 2, p. 5)

The Committee was also at work studying the relevance of the ERIC information retrieval program to the counseling field.

The training of professional psychologists was the subject of a conference funded by the National Institute of Mental Health in 1973. Known as the Vail Conference, participants included representation of diverse age groups, cultural backgrounds, and roles within psychology. Thirty-eight pages of recommendations based on the work of the conference may be categorized under five headings: professionalization, the open career systems, social responsivity, expansion of the range of persons trained and served, and evaluation of training services. An analysis of issues in training raised at the Vail Conference which are relevant to counseling psychology has been provided by Fretz et al. (1974). Research training was not a topic subjected to detailed discussion at the conference.

FOUNDING OF *THE COUNSELING PSYCHOLOGIST*

The Counseling Psychologist first appeared in 1969 as a vehicle for critical analysis, reformulation, and commentary on professional issues. The basic idea for this publication was germinated in discussions among Ralph Mosher, Norman Sprinthall, and the present writer during the period 1963-65. We had been unsuccessful at the time in getting support for a research-oriented monograph which would allow greater depth in reporting methodology and facilitating replication of important research advancements.

In 1968, during the presidency of John McGowan and with the support of President-elect John Holland, the decision was made by the Executive Committee to accept a proposal by John M. Whiteley to partially fund a new journal. The balance of funding was envisioned as coming from single-issue sales, nonmember domestic subscribers, international subscribers, and institutional subscribers (largely university libraries). Subsequently, the Book Series in Counseling Psychology was added as an additional source of revenue as well as a means of reaching a broader contemporary and historical audience with extensions and expansions of material originally published in *The Counseling Psychologist*.

The present writer was named founding editor, Arthur Resnikoff was in turn named managing editor, and the initial Editorial Board included Thomas W. Allen, Ralph L. Mosher, Cecil H. Patterson, Thomas M. Magoon, and Carl Thoresen. Wilbur L. Layton, Lenore Harmon, and V. Lois Erickson were added after that to conclude the composition of the founding Editorial Board. Hazel Sprandel served for a number of years as assistant managing editor, working on the myriad problems of production and circulation. Helene Hollingsworth subsequently replaced her as Editorial Assistant.

Each issue of *The Counseling Psychologist* has a different topic of concern. The specific format for the consideration of the major issues varies with the topic. The usual format, however, involves a major treatise on a problem followed by critical analysis by prominent scholars or practitioners; the author of the treatise is then accorded the opportunity for a rejoinder. This format has been so popular that when it is departed from for a specific issue, there are usually letters urging a return to the traditional dialogue. Through Volume VI, the topics covered included:

Vol. I	No. 1 Vocational Development Theory, 1969
	No. 2 Client-Centered Therapy, 1969
	No. 3 Student Unrest, 1969
	No. 4 Behavior Counseling, 1969
Vol. II	No. 1 Black Students in Higher Education, 1970
	No. 2 Encounter Groups, 1970
	No. 3 Existential Counseling, 1971
	No. 4 Deliberate Psychological Education, 1971
Vol. III	No. 1 Individual Psychology, 1971
	No. 2 Integrity Group Therapy, 1972
	No. 3 New Directions in Training, Part I, 1972
	No. 4 New Directions in Training, Part II, 1972
Vol. IV	No. 1 Counseling Women, 1973
	No. 2 The Healthy Personality, 1973
	No. 3 Career Counseling, 1974
	No. 4 Gestalt Therapy, 1974
Vol. V	No. 1 Sex Counseling, 1975
	No. 2 Carl Rogers on Empathy, 1975
	No. 3 Marriage and Family Counseling, 1975
	No. 4 Assertion Training, 1975
Vol. VI	No. 1 Counseling Adults, 1976
	No. 2 Counseling Women II, 1976
	No. 3 Career Counseling II, 1976
	No. 4 Developmental Counseling Psychology, 1977

The genesis of these initial 24 issues of *The Counseling Psychologist* may be traced to a response to one or more of the following:

1. *The appearance of new topics of importance to counseling psychologists.* These new topics of importance often reflected theoretical or research advancements which needed synthesis or elaboration, and have subsequently become part of the substantive

conceptual bases and the central literature of the profession. Included in this category are: Deliberate Psychological Education, Sex Counseling, Assertion Training, Empathy, and Developmental Counseling Psychology.

2. *The opportunity to increase understanding of new client populations.* New client populations and the need to understand them more fully reflected the profession's response to social forces and the changing nature of society: Black Students in Higher Education, Counseling Women I and II, and Counseling Adults.

3. *The necessity and desirability of rethinking, reformulating, and extending the conceptual bases of the initial historical roots of the profession.* From the vocational guidance roots, the issues on Vocational Development Theory and Career Counseling I and II reflect contemporary literature and conceptual formulations. From the mental hygiene roots, The Healthy Personality was a more modern rethinking of basic constructs of health and illness as they relate to counseling psychology's basic concerns. From the roots in counseling and psychotherapy, the issues on Client-Centered Therapy, Behavioral Counseling, Existential Counseling, Individual Psychology, and Gestalt Therapy review the theory, supporting research, and approaches to practice of significant counseling theories.

4. *The extension of substantive new approaches to delivery of services,* irrespective of theoretical approach. New approaches to practice required an analysis of method and supporting research. The issues on Encounter Groups, Integrity Groups, and Marriage and Family Counseling developed from this need by the profession.

5. *The enhancement of the education and training function of the profession.* Such topics as New Directions in Training I and II came from this obligation to enhance training.

It is clearly beyond the scope of this review of the history of counseling psychology to provide an analysis and commentary on each of the substantive issues covered by *The Counseling Psychologist* in the fifth historical period. In terms of Schwebel's (1984) two keystones of consciousness, these 24 issues collectively provide an illumination of one keystone, the relevant theories of human development, behavior change, and counseling theory and practice of the fifth historical period.

THE SOCIETAL CONTEXT

Prevailing social attitudes constitute the second keystone of consciousness affecting the profession of counseling psychology. These changed dramatically during the fifth historical period, especially those affecting counseling psychologists working in educational institutions. The sources of the changes in social attitudes were essentially four:

1. The effects of the Vietnam war and the responses to it by institutions in society, especially education;
2. the changes in attitudes toward authority and loss of trust in institutions in response to the Watergate era;
3. the continuing quest for the ideal self in society which characterized the 1970s; and
4. the search for wellness and pre-occupation with self-help, abetted by the active efforts of some counseling psychologists to "give the profession to the people" through prevention and psychological education.

Mayhew (1977) contends that between 1968 and 1970, profound changes were initiated which were "sharply at variance with the ideals, values, and practices of the past." The previous attitudinal consensus was severely challenged:

> Rationality and intellectuality, meritocracy, selectivity, collegiality and shared authority, campus autonomy, professional expertise and training, and the primacy of professors in instruction and evaluation—all were called into question by the 1970s. (Mayhew, 1977, p. 2)

Where egalitarian sentiments had been previously expressed, and some efforts made to implement reforms based upon them, there was still the assumption that participants in the institutions of society would conform to what were traditional practices and would come to cherish the conventional beliefs which had been the previous pathway to upward mobility and successful enculturation.

Whether it was conformance to orthodox academic arrangements within schools and colleges, or acceptance with minimal questioning of the dictates of the established professions such as law, medicine, and psychology, there was in the 1970s a dramatic challenge to conventional wisdom and the dictates of the established institutions and structures of American society.

The challenges to conventions and the establishment stemming from the Vietnam and Watergate eras were enhanced by the undeniable and justifiable pressure for equality and unfettered opportunity by those who previously had been denied full participation in society, principally women, ethnic minorities, and the physically handicapped.

The search for the ideal self described by Clecak (1983) intensified. In the 1950s and the early 1960s, the role of counseling psychology was seen as rendering service to society. Now the therapeutic quest, the seeking of spiritual salvation by believers and nonbelievers alike, and the Christian revival, all interacting with what Riesman (1964) termed the "reign of abundance," combined to create a very different climate. In characterizing the different quests for the ideal self in the 1970s, Clecak

138

summarized them as representing "genuine manifestations of the common denominator of contemporary meanings of salvation: the quest for personal fulfillment within small effective communities" (Clecak, 1983, p. 107).

CONSTELLATIONS OF SUBSTANTIVE THEORETICAL DEVELOPMENTS

The dominant feature of the substantive theoretical literature during the fifth historical period in counseling psychology is the extent of the explosion of both substantive theoretical and empirical contributions. The proliferation of journals had just begun, and new book publishers were venturing into the counseling psychology market.

Table 5.3 presents representative contributions to the literature on constellations of personality theories and theories of counseling and psychotherapy in the fifth historical period. The growth in the behavioral, rational-emotive, gestalt, and transactional analysis theoretical literature was particularly impressive, though neither the gestalt nor the transactional analysis approaches developed an empirical thrust during this time.

The second constellation of theories of vocational psychology, occupational choice, and career development reflected the steady growth of each of the previously introduced theories as well as the emergence of a new approach. The second constellation of theories is presented in Table 5.4. The new theory introduced during this period of time was that of the social learning model. The general social learning theory of Albert Bandura (Bandura, 1969, 1973, 1977), which had its antecedents in reinforcement theory and classical behaviorism, is presented by Mitchell and Krumboltz (1984) as a basis from which grew the social learning theory of career decision making (Krumboltz, Mitchell, & Jones, 1976; Krumboltz, 1979).[5]

OTHER THEORETICAL AND RESEARCH ADVANCEMENTS

In the second, third, and fourth historical periods, the *Annual Review of Psychology* served as a much better source of commentary on the literature of counseling psychology than it does for the fifth historical period.[6] There were only three relevant reviews (Layton, Sandeen, & Baker, 1971; Pepinsky & Meara, 1973; Whiteley, Burkhart, Harway-Herman, & Whiteley, 1975), and all of them (by assignment) focused on student development and counseling. Layton et al. (1971) selected literature to review, for example, based on "its relevance to the counseling psychologist doing research on students and providing services to them" (Layton et al., 1971, p. 533). The general topics covered were student development, vocational behavior and development, counselor training, counseling research methods, counseling process research, and challenges to counseling.

(*Text continued on page 142*)

Table 5.3

**Representative Contributions
to Personality Theory and Theories of Counseling
and Psychotherapy in the Fifth Historical Period
(1968-1976)**

Psychoanalysis

Erikson, E.	Identity, youth, and crisis (1968)

Adlerian Psychotherapy and Theory

Adler, A.	The science of living (1969)
Allen, T.	The individual psychology of Alfred Adler: An item of history and a promise of a revolution (1971)
Ansbacher, H.	The concept of social interest (1968)
Dreikurs, R.	Psychology in the classroom (1968)
Dreikurs, R., & Grey, L.	Logical consequences: A new approach to discipline (1968)
Grunwald, B.	Strategies for behavior change in schools (1971)
Mosak, H. H.	Life style assessment (1972)
Pew, W.	Life style of Alfred Adler (1972)

Behavior Theory and Therapy

Bandura, A.	Principles of behavior modification (1969) Psychological modeling: Conflicting theories (1971)
Beck, A.	Cognitive therapy and the emotional disorders (1976)
Eysenck, H. J. (Ed.)	Case studies in behaviour therapy (1976)
Franks, C.	Behavior therapy: Appraisal and status (1969)
Goldfried, M., & Davison, G.	Clinical behavior therapy (1976)
Hosford, R. E.	Behavioral counseling (1969)
Hosford, R. E., & de Visser, L.	Behavioral approaches to counseling (1974)
Kanfer, F., & Goldstein, A.	Helping people change (1975)
Kanfer, F. H., & Phillips, J. S.	Learning foundations of behavior therapy (1970)

Table 5.3 (Continued)

Krumboltz, J. D., & Thoresen, C. E. (Eds.)	Behavioral counseling: Cases and techniques (1969)
	Counseling methods (1976)
Lazarus, A. A.	Behavior therapy and beyond (1971)
	Behavior therapy in groups (1968)
Leitenberg, H. (Ed.)	Handbook of behavior modification and behavior therapy (1976)
Mahoney, M. J.	Cognition and behavior modification (1974)
Mahoney, M. J., & Thoresen, C. E.	Self control: Power to the person (1974)
McFall, R. M., & Lillesand, D.	Behavior rehearsal with modeling and teaching in assertion training (1971)
Meichenbaum, D.	Cognitive factors in behavior modification: Modifying what clients say to themselves (1971)
	Therapist manual for cognitive behavior modification (1974)
Rachman, S. J., & Teasdale, J.	Aversion therapy and behavior disorders: An analysis (1969)
Thoresen, C. E. (Ed.)	Behavior modification in education (1973)
Wolpe, J.	The practice of behavior therapy (1st ed.) (1969)
	The practice of behavior therapy (2nd ed.) (1973)
Yates, A.	Behavior therapy (1976)

Client-centered Therapy

Rogers, C. R.	A practical plan for educational revolution (1968)
	Being in relationship (1969a)
	Freedom to learn: A view of what education might become (1969b)
	The person of tomorrow (1969c)
	Carl Rogers on encounter groups (1970)
	On becoming partners: Marriage and its alternatives (1972)
	My philosophy of interpersonal relationships and how it grew (1973)
	Empathic: An unappreciated way of being (1975)

Humanistic and Existential Theory and Therapy

Maslow, A. H.	Holistic emphasis (1970a)
	Motivation and personality (1970b)
May, R.	Love and will (1969)
	Power and innocence (1972)
Spiegelberg, H.	Phenomenology in psychology and psychiatry (1972)

Table 5.3 (Continued)

Rational-emotive Theory and Therapy

Ellis, A.	What *really* causes therapeutic change (1968) The art and science of love (1969) A cognitive approach to behavior therapy (1969) Growth through reason (1971a) Rational-emotive therapy and its application to emotional education (1971b) Humanistic psychotherapy: The rational-emotive approach (1973a) Rational-emotive group therapy (1973b) Experience and rationality: The making of a rational-emotive therapist (1974) The rational-emotive approach to sex therapy (1975) The biological basis of human irrationality (1976)
Ellis, A., & Harper, R.	A guide to rational living (1971) A new guide to rational living (1975)
Maultsby, M., & Ellis, A.	Technique for using rational-emotive imagery (1974)
Morris, K., & Kanitz, J.	Rational-emotive therapy (1975)
Zingle, H., & Mallett, M.	A bibliography of RET materials, articles, and theses (1976)

Gestalt

Carmer, J., & Rouzer, D.	Healthy functioning from the gestalt perspective (1974)
D'Andrea, R.	A handbook on the theory of Gestalt therapy (1973)
Downing, J., & Marmorstein, R.	Dreams and nightmares: A book of Gestalt therapy sessions (1973)
Emerson, P., & Smith, E.	Contributions of gestalt psychology to gestalt therapy (1974)
Fagan, J.	Personality theory and psychotherapy (1974)
Fagan, J., & Shepherd, I. L. (Eds.)	Gestalt therapy now (1970)
Hatcher, C., & Himmelstein, P. (Eds.)	The handbook of gestalt therapy (1976)
Kempler, W.	Principles of gestalt family therapy (1974)
Mermin, D.	Gestalt theory and emotion (1974)
Naranjo, C.	The techniques of gestalt therapy (1973)

Table 5.3 (Continued)

Perls, F.	Gestalt therapy verbatim (1969a) In and out of the garbage pail (1969b)
Polster, E., & Polster, M.	Gestalt therapy integrated (1973)
Purseglove, P. D. (Ed.)	Recognitions in gestalt therapy (1968)
Rhyne, J.	The gestalt art experience (1973)
Rosenblatt, D.	Opening doors: What happens in gestalt therapy (1975)
Stevens, J.	Awareness (1971)
Wallen, R.	Gestalt therapy and gestalt psychology (1970)

Transactional Analysis

Berne, E.	Sex in human loving (1970) What do you say after you say hello? (1972)
Harris, T. A.	I'm OK, you're OK (1969)

James, M.,
  & Jongeward, D.
	Born to win: Transactional analysis with gestalt
	  experiments (1971)

Schiff, J.	Reparenting schizophrenics (1969)
Steiner, C.	Games alcoholics play (1971) Scripts people live (1974)
Wycoff, H.	The stroke economy in women's scripts (1971) Women's scripts (1971)

    The section on student development reflected the increasing sophistication of the human development literature and its growing relevance to the concerns of counseling psychology. Katz (1967) cited the need for longitudinal research designs which allow greater coverage of the life span, since conceptualizing the development of such student characteristics as social, sexual, and vocational maturity must of necessity reflect factors in childhood.

    In an important addition to the literature, Keniston (1970) conceptualized youth as a postadolescent stage for individuals:

1. who have completed the tasks of adolescence as Erikson (1963, 1968) defined them (emancipation from the family, comfort with sexuality, attainment of a sense of identity, and a capacity for intimacy);
2. who assess and reassess their relationship to society while postponing acceptance of adult responsibilities;
3. who enter a period of experimentation with adult roles.

Table 5.4

**Representative Contributions to Vocational Psychology,
Occupational Choice, and Career Development
in the Fifth Historical Period
(1968-1976)***

(*Including several in 1977, 1978, and 1979)

Psychoanalytic/Psychodynamic

Nachmann, B.	Cross currents in the occupational evolution of religious careers (1970)
Neff, W. S.	Work and human behavior (1968)

Trait and Factor

Dawis, R. V., & Lofquist, L. H.	Personality style and the process of work adjustment (1976)
Dawis, R. V., Lofquist, L. H., & Weiss, D. J.	A theory of work adjustment: A revision (1968)
Lofquist, L. H., & Dawis, R. V.	Adjustment to work (1969)
	Application of the theory of work adjustment to rehabilitation and counseling (1972)
	Vocational needs, work reinforcers, and job satisfaction (1975)
	Values as secondary to needs in adjustment (1978)
Willilamson, E. G.	Trait-and-factor theory and individual differences (1972)

**Life Space/Life Span
(Donald Super and Associates)**

Super, D. E.	Vocational development theory (1969)
	Vocational development theory: Persons, positions, processes (1972)
	Measuring vocational maturity for counseling and evaluation (1974)
	Career education and the meanings of work (1976)

**Career Choice
(Eli Ginzberg and Associates)**

Ginzberg, E.	The development of a developmental theory of occupational choice (1970)
	Career guidance: Who needs it, who provides it, who can improve it (1971)

Table 5.4 (Continued)

Toward a theory of occupational choice:
A restatement (1972)

Occupational Psychology
(Anne Roe and Associates)

Roe, A.   Perspectives on vocational development (1972)
Classification of occupations by group and level
(1976)

Roe, A.,   Classification of occupations (1972)
   & Klos, D.

Vocational Typology
(John Holland and Associates)

Holland, J. L.   The self-directed search (1970)
Making vocational choices: A theory of careers
(1973a)
The development and current status of an
occupational classification (1973b)
Vocational guidance for everyone (1974)
The use and evaluation of interest inventories
and simulations (1975)

Holland, J. L.,   Applying a typology to vocational aspirations
   & Gottfredson, G. D.   (1974)
Using a typology of persons and environments to
explain careers: Some extensions and
clarifications (1976)

Holland, J. L.,   An empirical occupational classification derived
   & Others   from a theory of personality and intended for
practice and research (1969)

Development and Decision making
(David Tiedeman and Robert O'Hara)

O'Hara, R. P.   Comment on Super's papers (1969)

Tiedeman, D. V.   A machine for the epigenesis of self-realization
in career development: Career, subsequent
development, and implications (1972)
A person's eye view of career development
education and enactment (1977a)
Towards the career education of all educational
personnel in Illinois (1977b)
A research note on becoming what we do in
career development (1978)
Converting Tiedeman and O'Hara's decision-
making paradigm into "I" power: A symposium
(1979)

Table 5.4 (Continued)

Tiedeman, D. V., & Miller-Tiedeman, A.	Choice and decision processes and career revisited (1979)

Social Learning
(John Krumboltz and Associates)

Krumboltz, J. D.	A social learning theory of career decision-making (1979)
Krumboltz, J. D., Mitchell, A. M., & Jones, G. R.	A social learning theory of career selection (1976)

This was a broader conceptualization of postadolescent and young adult development than had previously appeared in the literature.

This was a period of time when a number of important longitudinal or cross-sectional studies came to fruition. Trent and Medsker (1968) completed their longitudinal study of post-high school youth. Newcomb and Feldman (1969) reported on an extensive review of studies of the impact of the college experience. New instruments based on the personality theories of Henry Murray (Stern, 1970) and Gordon Allport (Newcomb & Feldman, 1969) increased understanding of student development over time. A. W. Astin's (1968a, 1968b) program of longitudinal research on student development began to contribute to the literature. Katz and associates (Katz, 1967) reported their longitudinal study of the freshmen classes at the University of California, Berkeley, and Stanford University. Heath (1968) reported on a series of illuminating studies of psychological maturity, and Chickering's (1969) five-year study of student and institutional characteristics and their interaction in affecting student development appeared, along with his specification of seven major dimensions of growth during the college years. This was an extraordinarily productive period in conceptualizing the process of student development in higher education.

The literature on counseling research was not as impressive during this time period. Thoresen (1969) reported the results of a two-year review of articles in the *Journal of Counseling Psychology*: one-third were not research reports, and descriptive-correlational studies constituted over three-fourths of the articles that reported research. Both Thoresen (1969) and Hosford and Briskin (1969) drew attention to the need for more multivariate designs in counseling research. In counseling process research, Layton et al. (1971) drew attention to the paucity of experimental research on counseling. The literature by Carkhuff and his colleagues (Carkhuff & Alexik, 1967; Carkhuff & Berenson, 1967; Carkhuff, Kratochvil, & Friel, 1968; Holder, Carkhuff, & Berenson, 1967) was introduced as extensive and noteworthy.

Layton et al. (1971) did not undertake a review of the behavior counseling literature since one had just been completed for *The Counseling Psychologist* by Hosford (1969). They did note that the three main behavioral approaches are those derived from classical conditioning, instrumental conditioning, and social learning theory. Krumboltz and Thoresen (1969) were singled out for directing behavioral approaches to problems confronted by counseling psychology. Layton et al. (1971) identified major contributions from the behavioral approach: Mehrabian's (1970) schema for promoting behavior change; Bandura's (1969) emphasis on modeling and social learning in describing the breadth of behavior modification research; Krumboltz and Thoresen (1969) for applying behavior modification methods to educational settings; Ullman and Krasner's (1969) focus on psychologically deviant and other abnormal populations, using applications of behavior modification techniques; and Ayllon and Azrin's (1968) use of operant conditioning in institutional settings.

In the closing sections of their review, Layton et al. (1971) include two new additions: cultures and counter-cultures, and counseling minority group members. The former literature reflected the campus crises of the late 1960s and early 1970s and the growth and flourishing of counter-cultures. The latter body of literature has since come within the mainstream of counseling psychology with subsequent volumes on ethnic psychology, special theoretical and cultural issues on counseling minority group members, and the development of a theory of cross-cultural counseling.

In the reflections with which they closed their review, Pepinsky and Meara (1973) captured the state of the theoretical and research literature in the early 1970s:

there has been increasing alignment of investigative concerns with the theoretical and technical products of basic research work in other areas of psychology, notably in human learning and development, and personality-social psychology. Sophistication in matters of psychometric and statistical analysis, long conspicuous in publications by counseling psychologists, also seem to have been enhanced. (Pepinsky & Meara, 1973, p. 144)*

They also noted that research ethics had arisen as a topic of concern as a consequence of incorporating "precision technologies" such as behavior modification, simulation, and laboratory research into counseling psychology inquiry.

Pepinsky and Meara (1973) reviewed a group of studies which identified a disparity between what counselors think they do (or should do) and

---

*This and all other quotations from this source are reproduced, with permission, from the *Annual Review of Psychology*, Vol. 24. © 1973 by Annual Reviews Inc.

what nonclients, former clients, or clients think should (and does) occur. The literature on counselor education and training was critiqued, particularly the studies of personal characteristics of counselors. Further developments in the influential research were reported by Kagan and associates (Campbell, Kagan, & Krathwohl, 1971; Kagan & Krathwohl, 1967; Kagan & Schauble, 1969; Kagan, Schauble, Resnikoff, Danish, & Krathwohl, 1969; and Resnikoff, Kagan, & Schauble, 1970) as well as by other studies using videotape technology. Applications of videotechnology to counselor education as well as client education and counseling have been basic components of counseling psychology since the early 1970s.

Layton et al. (1971) mentioned the beginning attention in the literature to the training and proper deployment of peer or paraprofessional counselors. Pepinsky and Meara (1973) characterized the state of research in the area:

> Work in this area raises important questions about professional counseling and the training of counselors. Knowledge concerning the effectiveness of paraprofessional help could be enhanced by well-designed, multivariate, longitudinal studies; unfortunately, most of the current research can be classified as one-shot case studies . . . . Another problem with much of the paraprofessional research to date is that there has been no clear demonstration of the precise relationship between therapeutic conditions and counseling outcomes. (Pepinsky & Meara, 1973, pp. 125-126)

While, as the reviewers note, there may be occasions when the efforts of paraprofessionals are just as good as or superior to those of fully trained counselors, the research has not yet been done to demonstrate that. Further, counseling by paraprofessionals needs to be investigated by "solid research design, with treatments clearly delineated and outcome measures expanded" (Pepinsky & Meara, 1973, p. 127).

The literature on cross-cultural counseling, diagnosing and categorizing problems clients bring to counseling, treatment programs to improve academic performance, and vocational counseling was covered. On this latter topic, the appearance of the *Journal of Vocational Behavior* was noted along with a significant book by Holland (1966) on the psychology of vocational choice as well as his new self-administered instrument (Holland, 1970). This was the inaugural detailed treatment by the *Annual Review of Psychology* of his major theoretical advancements as well as the initial appearance of the first of the host of research studies which his work has generated.

Pepinsky and Meara (1973) introduced their section on process-outcome research with the remark that "counseling psychologists have demonstrated themselves to be great borrowers from other psychological specialists" (Pepinsky & Meara, 1973, p. 135). A positive example was the critique of the designs of process and outcome research by Kelley, Smits,

Leventhal, and Rhodes (1970) covering research published in the *Journal of Counseling Psychology* from 1964-68. They used the Campbell and Stanley (1966) category of research designs to determine whether the studies were "pre-experimental" (54%); "one-shot case studies" (31%); "true experimental" (25%); and "quasi-experimental" (14%). Eight percent were categorized as "unscientific" matching studies. While this categorization only addresses some of the problems in evaluating research in this area, it served to raise the consciousness of subsequent investigators to implications of design before they started to work.

Pepinsky and Meara (1973) identified additional significant issues in process-outcome research beyond those of design:

> There remain to be answered even more fundamental questions, such as what the research was designed to accomplish in the first place, how it was conducted, whether the results as analyzed, displayed, and interpreted have anything to do with alleged intentions, and how the reported accomplishment is to be judged on epistemological as well as methodological grounds. That these are not idle concerns is attested to by Meehl (1971) in a discussion of evidence that is legally admissible versus that considered by psychologists to be scientifically acceptable. The latter may offer, e.g., from laboratory experiments, generalized conclusions about conditions that affect everyday human behavior. Lawyers are more prone to accept "fireside inductions," i.e., common-sense beliefs derived from introspection and anecdote, in devising legal sanctions for human conduct. Neither route is satisfactory to Meehl, who believes that "quasi-experiments in the 'real life' setting may often be the optimal data-source." (Pepinsky & Meara, 1973, pp. 135-136)

In commenting on the extensive literature categorized as process and outcome research, Pepinsky and Meara divided the research into two groups. The first group included sociopsychologically oriented research such as the studies conducted by Goldstein and associates (Goldstein, 1962, 1966; Goldstein, Heller, & Sechrist, 1966) which manipulated therapeutic conditions using approaches from experimental, personality, and social psychology. The second group consisted of research in counseling using behavior modification and are studies primarily within educational settings. The study by Tosi, Upshaw, Lande, and Walron (1971) was singled out as well designed. Among the client issues which have been addressed with behavioral counseling in the period covered by this review of the literature are alienation, anxiety, unassertiveness, snake phobia, and self-actualization.

Whiteley et al. (1975) began their review with the observation that the scope and volume of the literature on both counseling and student development had increased dramatically over the past several years. In fact, the literature had become sufficiently extensive on both topics that the authors recommended to the *Annual Review of Psychology* that the areas not be combined again or assigned to the same authors in any given time period. In a sense, this recommendation reflected a very positive accomplishment of theorists and researchers in counseling psychology. Whiteley et al. (1975) remarked that their intial draft had been twice its final length and that it was possible to do books on much less subject matter than had been covered in their review.

The counseling literature was divided into the following categories: empathy and other therapist-offered conditions, self-disclosure, confrontation and self-exploration, training in basic human helping skills, and the interrelated issues of the selection of counselors and the criterion problem.

Training in basic human helping skills, related broadly to counseling skills, had received major attention over the previous decade. A partial listing of these training innovators included, along with their associates, Carkhuff (Carkhuff, 1969a, 1969b, 1971, 1972a, 1972b, 1972c, 1972d), Kagan (Kagan, 1971, 1974; Kagan, et al., 1967), Hosford (1974), Ivey (1971), Gazda (1973), Danish and Hauer (1973), and Brammer (1973).

It is beyond the scope of this historical perspective to undertake a systematic evaluation of these various approaches to teaching human helping skills or to incorporate the new ones developed since the review by Whiteley et al. (1975). There has not been sufficient empirical assessment yet of their comparative effectiveness, though there has been considerable research done within each system. Given the importance to society of developing potent methods for teaching human helping skills to professionals in all allied disciplines, to paraprofessionals, and to the general public, this area needs much more investigation in the immediate future.

The interrelated issues in the selection of counselors and in the criterion problem were approached first in terms of two criticisms of predictive studies in counselor selection: the inadequate definition of the criterion, and the lack of a theoretical rationale for selection of variables. As Whiteley et al. (1975) noted:

> before any progress can be made in a theoretical formulation of the personality dimensions related to effectiveness in counseling, more rigorous consideration must be given to the definition of the criterion—effectiveness—and that definition must be in terms of specifiable counseling behaviors which are clearly and predictably associated with client change. (Whiteley et al., 1975, p. 345)

In reviewing the literature on the criterion problem, they noted that Eysenck's (1952, 1965) questioning of the efficacy of traditional psychotherapy had brought forth a flurry of research activity to demonstrate the effects of psychotherapy and a refocus and reevaluation of the investigative models employed in studying the process and outcome of therapy. The Eysenck challenge led to an increased application of concepts from the behavioral sciences to the theory and practice of counseling and psychotherapy, particularly to the criteria for specifying outcome and measures of change.

Bergin (1971) reviewed Eysenck's (1952, 1965) work and the ensuing 20 years of controversy and productivity it provoked, then concluded that the bases for the issues raised by Eysenck have quietly dissipated and that evidence does exist of significant change in clients receiving the more traditional forms of counseling and psychotherapy.

Bergin (1971) even demonstrated a slight positive relationship between more rigorous design and more positive outcome. Meltzoff (1969) and Meltzoff and Kornreich (1970) asserted that the evidence is conclusive for the effectiveness of psychotherapy. Of adequately designed studies, 84% yielded positive outcomes.

On the student development research literature, Whiteley et al. (1975) noted the great wealth of information being generated on the college student as a consequence of the research model being employed by Alexander and Helen Astin and their associates (Astin, 1970, 1972a, 1972b, 1973; Astin, Astin, Bisconti, & Frankl, 1972; Astin, King, Light, & Richardson, 1973). The heuristic value of their methodological approach has led to considerable subsequent extensions of what is known about college students and the impact of the college experience.

Other aspects of the student development literature singled out for attention included: methodological issues (common designs, longitudinal design, cross-sectional design, time-sequential design, cohort-sequential design, cross-sequential design), statistical issues, philosophical issues (goals of higher education, personality development, occupational development, variations among colleges), and breakdown of the student population (dropouts, residents versus commuters, the disadvantaged student, minority students). The very presence of these well-developed categories within the student development literature reflects both the burgeoning of the literature and the diversity of the approaches to inquiry.

SUMMARY

The fifth historical period began with the most comprehensive statement yet constructed on the definition of the profession. A second definitional statement in 1976 differed in direction from that developed in 1968. The emphasis on a three-part role of remedial/rehabilitative, preventive, and educative/developmental was subsequently reaffirmed by organized counseling psychology.

Prevailing social attitudes changed dramatically as a consequence of the Vietnam War, the Watergate era, the continuing quest for "the ideal self," and the general search for wellness and preoccupation with self-help. This latter social attitude was abetted by those counseling psychologists who emphasized prevention and psychoeducation.

The theoretical and research literature underwent a steady increase in sophistication and methodological rigor, though it lacked the originality of the theoretical formulations of the 1950s.

FOOTNOTES

[1] Thompson (Note 1) drew attention to the contribution to counseling psychology which was made by the Teachers College Press in its publication of the Greyston Conference Report (Thompson & Super, 1964) as well as the comprehensive definitional statement (Jordaan, Myers, Layton, & Morgan, 1968).

[2] Pepinsky's (Note 2) comment remains appropriate: "Regarding 'prevention,' you could make a substantial contribution to our colleagues' awareness by pointing out the most neglected aspect of all. That is to give, in prevention, attention to structural features of the society and to ideas for how existing structure might be modified so as to reduce 'the frequency or severity' of problems."

[3] Pepinsky (Note 3) cautioned that this parallel is not complete. The distinction he makes is between *officially* ignoring a report and *essentially* ignoring it: "You comment that the 'official response' to Ivey's report 'was to essentially (sic) ignore it,' and drew a parallel with the response to Berg et al. (1980). In the latter case, neither the APA (via the E & T Board) nor Division 17 (via the Executive Committee) *officially* ignored the document. John Darley, as Editor of the *American Psychologist*, simply ignored the E & T Board's recommendation to publish the report there. As for Division 17, via its Executive Committee and an ad hoc elite, it certainly did *not* ignore the document! Your own fine prior report makes this abundantly clear. What irritated me at the time was that the original report was *not* disseminated; the one by Tyler et al. (1980) was — e.g., as an appendage to the Greyston Conference Report. The handling of the two reports was quite different!"

[4] Cottle (Note 4) continues to disagree: "This is not so! Bruce Moore and Vic Raimy were the team to evaluate our counseling program at Kansas. We raised hell and they sent Moore and Pepinsky the second time and we were approved."

[5] Bruce Walsh (Note 5) drew attention to the appearance of two influential textbooks during this time frame which cover the general subject matter of theories of vocational psychology, occupational choice, and career development. The textbooks are Samuel Osipow's *Theories of Career Development* and John Crites' *Vocational Psychology*.

[6] Tyler (Note 6) is helpful in understanding the policy of the *Annual Review of Psychology*: "An inference made from the decreasing frequency of *Annual Review* chapters seems wrong to me. There was a definite policy change that called for a rotation of topics over a three-year period, and many other areas besides counseling were affected. Another policy change that makes it impossible to compare successive reviews was to ask each reviewer to pick out only one aspect of the field that he or she was interested in instead of attempting to cover it all."

Chapter 6
Rethinking Professional Identity and the Role of the Specialty: The Sixth Historical Period (1977-1983)

The sixth historical period in the development of counseling psychology began with three elements which were different than those greeting the inaugural years of previous historical eras. The first element was a general consensus on professional identity. While there remained a need for further refinement, extension, innovation, and restatement, there was such a legacy from the first five historical periods that the unique and substantive identity and direction of the profession were no longer an issue.

The second element was the legacy of theoretical and empirical developments which had their origins in the 1940s and 1950s, were systematically pursued in the 1960s and early 1970s, and burgeoned in the remainder of the 1970s. Even though some of the main contributors to counseling psychology theory and practice were not counseling psychologists (the interesting substantive problems confronting the profession attracted many competent researchers from other disciplines), progress had been so substantial that the Brayfield (1963) critique of the lack of research productivity and poor intellectual quality was no longer valid. Further, there was now programmatic research of a systematic nature in such different areas of counseling psychology as client-centered and behavioral counseling, rational-emotive therapy, student development, vocational development, counseling process and outcome research, and career interventions.

The third element was the supportive attitude of society toward the array of preventive and developmental services the profession could render clients. Social attitudes, one of the keystones of consciousness influencing counseling psychology, were as positive going into the sixth historical period as at any time in its history.[1]

In considering this sixth historical period in the history of counseling psychology, it is important to recognize that there are already four important sources of information about this period: an issue of *The Counseling Psychologist* on professional identity (Vol. 7, No. 2), a book on the present and future of counseling psychology (Whiteley & Fretz,

153

1980), an issue of *The Counseling Psychologist* on the next decade (Vol. 10, No. 2), and a book on the coming decade in counseling psychology (Whiteley, Kagan, Harmon, Fretz, & Tanney, 1984). The interested reader is referred to these resources for a more detailed presentation of issues, primary documents, key developments, and opinions concerning this sixth historical period.

INITIATIVES OF ORGANIZED COUNSELING PSYCHOLOGY

There were four initiatives of quite different focus by organized counseling psychology during this period. The first initiative was further refinement of professional identity. This was set in motion by Fretz (1977) and consisted of three separate activities. The first activity was to solicit historical and current views on the profession's identity from individuals whose primary professional identification was "counseling psychologist." The second activity was to obtain the perspectives of allied professionals who work closely with counseling psychologists. The third activity was to commission commentaries on professional identity by two past presidents of Division 17.

The second initiative was to project the role of the profession into the 21st century and, in the process, undertake a proactive approach to shaping counseling psychology in the years to come. The assignment by Whiteley (1980a) to 17 authors was to predict what the world would be like in the year 2000 AD, then to specify what changes would be necessary for counseling psychology to make in order for it to have a vital role at the start of the 21st century.

The third initiative was thrust upon organized counseling psychology; namely, the further defining by the American Psychological Association of the specialties within psychology (Wellner, 1978). The development of these definitional statements had been in progress for a number of years. Division 17 issued a statement in 1975 on the licensing and certification of psychologists (APA, 1975), and in 1977 on the defining characteristics of counseling psychologists (APA, 1977).

Kagan (Note 2) clarified the issues before organized counseling psychology at this time:

> In 1977, we were faced with a dilemma. We had two alternatives. One was to do battle with those who would have preferred to keep counseling psychologists from being licensable; and the second, to ignore licensing and maintain distinctions between clinical and counseling psychology. At the time, our first choice was clearly the direction the membership wanted me to take as president and as representative to the various APA Task Forces in which decisions about definition and programs were being formulated. The issue became one of status—are we as good as they? Are we as worthy of being called "psychologists" as they? Were we helpless or could we

exert influence in APA? And yet, there were those among us, including myself, who realized that in winning that battle we may have damaged our own future. To live within APA as second rate citizens clearly was unacceptable; but in retrospect, winning the battle (so that now graduates of our programs are more easily licensed for independent practice) in my opinion has weakened the potential of counseling psychologists to make an important and unique contribution to the well-being of society.

There has been a shift within counseling psychology toward the independent practice of psychotherapy with clients who are troubled enough to receive health insurance reimbursement. Increasingly, students in counseling psychology programs select courses on the basis of licensing board requirements! Courses in projective techniques are sought out by students as desirable background for independent practice. The distinction between clinical and counseling psychology is in danger of becoming even further blurred as institutional cutbacks in preventative mental health force more people into the independent practice of psychotherapy. It is now going to take extraordinary effort on the part of the leadership of counseling psychology to reaffirm our unique identity.

The key portion of the criteria developed by APA for the designation of doctoral programs in psychology were the following 10 points:

1. Programs that are accredited by the American Psychological Association are recognized as meeting the definition of a professional psychology program. The criteria for accreditation serve as a model for professional psychology training.
2. Training in professional psychology is doctoral training offered in a regionally accredited institution of higher education.
3. The program, wherever it may be administratively housed, must be clearly identified and labeled as a psychology program. Such a program must specify in pertinent institutional catalogues and brochures its intent to educate and train professional psychologists.
4. The psychology program must stand as a recognizable, coherent organizational entity within the institution.
5. There must be a clear authority and primary responsibility for the core and specialty areas whether or not the program cuts across administrative lines.
6. The program must be an integrated, organized sequence of study.
7. There must be an identifiable psychology faculty and a psychologist responsible for the program.
8. The program must have an identifiable body of students who are matriculated in that program for a degree.

9. The program must include supervised practicum, internship, field or laboratory training appropriate to the practice of psychology.

10. The curriculum shall encompass a minimum of three academic years of full-time graduate study. In addition to instruction in scientific and professional ethics and standards, research design and methodology, statistics, and psychometrics, the core program shall require each student to demonstrate competence in each of the following substantive content areas. This typically will be met by including a minimum of three or more graduate semester hours (five or more graduate quarter hours) in each of four substantive content areas: (1) biological bases of behavior: physiological psychology, comparative psychology, neuropsychology, sensation and perception, and psychopharmacology; (2) cognitive-affective bases of behavior: learning, thinking, motivation, and emotion; (3) social bases of behavior: social psychology, group processes, organizational and systems theory; (4) individual differences: personality theory, human development, and abnormal psychology.

(Wellner, 1978, pp. 29-30)

The central points were that the program, wherever housed administratively, must be clearly labeled as a psychology program with an identifiable psychology faculty and a psychologist as program head. Further, each student must complete at least three or more graduate semester hours in each of four substantive content areas: biological bases of behavior, cognitive-affective bases of behavior, social bases of behavior, and individual differences.

This detailed definition has become the basis for the licensing and credentialing of counseling psychologists (Fretz & Mills, 1980a, 1980b), and for determining who is eligible for listing in the National Register of Health Service Providers in Psychology (Wellner, 1978, 1984).

The fourth and final initiative was the Next Decade Project of Division 17 under the leadership of Norman Kagan (Kagan, 1982). The Next Decade Project consisted of four committee reports: perspective and definition (Fretz, 1982), counseling psychology in the marketplace (Tanney, 1982), scientific affairs (Harmon, 1982), and education and training (Myers, 1982).[2] It was intended to provide: (1) a long-range guide for its major standing committees, (2) statements with which to communicate with state licensing boards and their national associations, (3) documents to use with prospective students of counseling psychology about the future of their specialty, (4) documents to communicate to other professions and specialties within psychology about the role and aspirations of counseling psychology, and (5) a process whereby counseling psychologists could consider their roles, aspirations, and opportunities in the next decade. While the impact of this project on the profession can only be assessed over time, the recommendations are clear and explicit; organized counseling psychology has a unique opportunity to strengthen its future.

THEORY AND RESEARCH

Four reviews of counseling topics in the *Annual Review of Psychology* appeared during the sixth period in the history of the field: Super and Hall (1978) on career development; Krumboltz, Becker-Haven, and Burnett (1979) on counseling psychology; Holland, Magoon, and Spokane (1981) on career interventions; and Borgen (1984) on counseling psychology.

Super and Hall (1978) emphasized the exploration and planning aspects of career development. Career refers to a "sequence of positions" held by a person in the context of a life-span approach utilizing constructs from both developmental and differential psychology (Super, 1957; Super, Starishevsky, Matlin, & Jordaan, 1963; and Super & Bohn, 1970). Based on the references cited, this review covered a sweep of literature from 1932 (Brewer, 1932) through 1978. The tremendous growth of the scientific literature on career development is reflected in the categories by which the review was organized:

I. Research in Educational Settings and Criterion and Instrument Development

   A. Vocational maturity
   B. Behavioral measures of career exploration and planning

II. The Nature of Exploration

   A. The dimensions of exploratory behavior

      1. fortuitous and random exploration
      2. intended and other-initiated exploration

   B. Conclusions and research needs in educational settings

      1. settings
      2. vocabulary
      3. logic and empiricism
      4. vocational maturity
      5. behavioral measures of exploration and planning
      6. exploration
      7. planning

A parallel outline can be made of the organization they chose for the literature and research in work settings. This work setting literature covered dimensions ranging from adult career stages and school-to-work transitions to a survey of work programs. A concluding section of Super and Hall (1978) covered research needs in work settings.

While their assigned topic was counseling psychology, Krumboltz et al. (1979) chose to focus upon three specific content areas: altering maladaptive responses, developing skills for career transitions, and preventing problems. The general question they addressed was, What do counseling psychologists know better now than they did four years ago about helping people solve their problems? (Krumboltz et al., 1979, p. 556). The organization of their review was in terms of selected outcomes which counselors may wish to obtain.

While they did not articulate their choice of selected outcomes in terms of Jordaan et al.'s (1968) three roles for counseling psychologists, "altering maladaptive responses" corresponds to the remedial/rehabilitative role, "developing skills for career transitions" is very consistent with the educative/developmental role, and "preventing problems" corresponds directly to the preventive role.

The specification of four categories of maladaptive responses on which counseling psychologists can have an impact, and the theoretical and research literature supporting and guiding their methods of intervention, are a valuable contribution to the literature. They reviewed aspects of social behavior (school conduct and academic behavior, aggression, assertiveness, friendship, and marital problems), emotional behavior (sexual disorders, depression, phobias, and anxiety), health-related outcomes (insomnia, pain control, weight control, and smoking cessation), and a variety of intracounseling behaviors.

On the topic of prevention, Krumboltz et al. (1979) focused on two areas: family problems and school problems. Their commentary on this literature is significant:

> Prevention, unfortunately, continues to occupy last place in the hearts of counseling psychologists, and it is so represented in this review. Studies cannot unambiguously be classified as "preventive" since even obviously remedial procedures may have unanticipated benefits on staff members and nontargeted subjects. In general, preventive work attempts to reduce the frequency or severity of future problems by teaching coping skills or imparting useful knowledge not merely to current sufferers but to persons likely to experience future stress. (Krumboltz et al., 1979, p. 588)

The reviewers are quite correct in stating that prevention occupies "last place" in the hearts of counseling psychologists. The opportunity now exists, however, to elevate prevention to an equal role with remedial/rehabilitative and educative/developmental. The principal sources of this opportunity are the theory and research which have occurred within the last few years in the areas of health psychology, human resources training, and personal wellness.

In the past theories of prevention have not been so well developed; recent progress has been heartening. Murphy and Frank (1979) reviewed two prevention topics which are relevant to counseling psychologists: training in preventive roles and understandings basic to prevention planning. Kessler and Albee (1975) reviewed the literature on primary prevention, citing 381 references in the process. They remarked that this literature was "so enormous and amorphous as to defy adequate coverage" (Kessler & Albee, 1975, p. 557). They went on to say:

> Our reading for a year leads us to the conclusion that practically every effort aimed at improved child rearing, increasing effective communication, building inner control and self-esteem, reducing stress and pollution, etc. — in short, everything aimed at improving the human condition, at making life more fulfilling and meaningful — may be considered to be part of primary prevention of mental or emotional disturbance. (Kessler & Albee, 1975, p. 557)

There is now an extraordinarily large body of relevant knowledge about prevention in the literature of clinical psychology, allied behavioral sciences, and medical sciences which has yet to be integrated into the counseling psychology literature.

The basic literature in counseling psychology, without even getting into the relevant theory development and research in other branches of psychology and related behavioral and medical sciences, has grown dramatically in the 1970s. Krumboltz et al. (1979), for example, covered only three selected aspects of counseling psychology, yet cited 330 relevant contributions.

Holland et al. (1981) covered the literature on career interventions and did so from a different theoretical perspective and emphasis than did Krumboltz et al. (1979). They approached their task by dividing the topic into two categories: career interventions and vocational research. Additional sections on speculations, achievements, and possibilities afforded the authors an opportunity to critique broadly the thrust of contributions to career interventions. In general, they found that "the research and theory about career interventions has culminated in some practical, substantive, and theoretical achievements" (Holland et al., 1981, p. 298). As a synthesis of this important field within counseling psychology, the authors singled out the following positive outcomes:

1. The number and variety of career interventions has greatly increased so that researchers and practitioners have a larger pool of treatments to draw from.
2. Multiple evaluations suggest that divergent treatments (counselors, inventories, workshops, special techniques, workbooks, and so on) usually have positive effects on clients. These positive outcomes usually hold for a wide range of evaluations that use divergent populations and designs which range from elegant to ugly.

3. We have a rough understanding of how career interventions work. An ideal intervention or a series of related interventions would include (a) occupational information organized by a comprehensible method and easily accessible to a client; (b) assessment materials and devices that clarify a client's self-picture and vocational potentials; (c) individual or group activities that require the rehearsal of career plans or problems; (d) counselors, groups or peers that provide support; and (e) a comprehensible cognitive structure for organizing information about self and occupational alternatives.
4. Our understanding of the development of vocational interests and career pathways is more complete.
5. The development and revision of occupational classification systems have had a pervasive substantive and theoretical impact. (Adapted from Holland et al., 1981, pp. 298-299)*

Finally Holland et al. (1981) indicated that: (1) The most promising new theoretical formulation appeared to be Krumboltz's (1979) social learning model; (2) Holland's (1973a) approach to the psychology of careers and career intervention and Lofquist and Dawis' (1969) theory of work adjustment continued to receive the most research attention; and (3) developmental formulations continued to be characterized by appealing, but vague, statements and weak data.

Borgen (1984) reviewed two categories of literature and, in the process, identified some newly developed aspects of counseling psychology. Under "trends and emerging trends," he had sections on cognitive-behavioral psychology; social psychological models; analytic models; human decision making; eclecticism, prescription, and nonspecific effects; shifting questions; supervisor and skill training; breadth of application; and vigor in vocational psychology. Under the category of controversy, conflict, and change, he had sections on developing a profession, scientist-practitioner model, search for integration, liberalizing bases for inference, philosophical underpinnings, and models of causation.

Borgen (1984, in press) characterized the past decade as a time of "stirring and searching" which was a sign of "vigorous health," even though there had been a "crisis of identity as the marketplace and Capitol Hill have pressed a new world view on them and on other professional psychologists" (Borgen, 1984, in press).

Referring to the *Handbook on Counseling Psychology* (Brown & Lent, 1984) and the *Handbook of Vocational Psychology* (Walsh & Osipow, 1983a, 1983b), Borgen stated that the maturation of the field is evident in the appearance of two handbooks which are exemplary

---

*This and all other quotations from this source are reproduced, with permission, from the *Annual Review of Psychology*, Vol. 32. © 1981 by Annual Reviews, Inc.

presentations of counseling psychology. (As an historical note, Cottle, 1967b, called for the development of a *Handbook of Counseling Psychology* or a *Handbook of Career Development Psychology* as something the profession needed. It took years for those two needed compilations to materialize.) Borgen summarized the potential impact of these two handbooks:

> Together, these handbooks provide unprecedented coverage of the recent literature of counseling psychology. Their scholarly reviews give new impact to the empirical studies they summarize and integrate. In addition, these handbooks are packed with sufficient research agendas to keep a generation of investigators busy. (Borgen, 1984)

This sixth historical period also marked the appearance of five new volumes of *The Counseling Psychologist* and the inaugural 10 books in the Book Series in Counseling Psychology. The contents of Volumes VII through XI were as follows:

Vol. VII Rational Emotive Therapy
Professional Identity
The Behavior Therapies Circa 1978
Counseling Men

Vol. VIII Counseling Women III
Ego and Self
Research in Counseling Psychology
The Future of Counseling Psychology

Vol. IX Professional Certification in Counseling Psychology
Adult Transitions
Leisure Counseling
Parenting in Contemporary Society

Vol. X Supervision in Counseling I
Counseling Psychology—The Next Decade
Counseling Psychology in Business and Industry
Research in Counseling Psychology II

Vol. XI Supervision in Counseling II
Counseling Psychology in the Justice System
Family Counseling
Computer Assisted Counseling

The titles of the first ten books in the Book Series in Counseling Psychology are as follows:

Approaches to Assertion Training

Theoretical and Empirical Foundations of Rational-Emotive Therapy

Career Counseling

Developmental Counseling and Teaching

The Present and Future of Counseling Psychology

Counseling Men

The Behavior Therapist

History of Counseling Psychology

Counseling Women

Counseling Adults

While it is beyond the scope of this general historical perspective to review the contents of the issues of *The Counseling Psychologist* that appeared between 1977 and 1983 and the 10 books in the Book Series in Counseling Psychology, their titles give a clear indication of topics which concerned counseling psychologists during this historical time period and collectively provide insight into a keystone of consciousness.

This period is recent enough in the history of counseling psychology that it was deemed premature to single out substantive contributions to the two constellations of theories previously identified.

SUMMARY

The sixth historical period began with three elements which were different than had greeted the inaugural years of previous historical eras: a general consensus on identity, a positive legacy of theoretical and empirical developments with promising programmatic research in progress, and a supportive attitude of society toward the profession.

There were four initiatives of organized counseling psychology: a refinement of identity, a projection of the role of the profession into the 21st century, the further defining of the specialties within psychology, and the Next Decade Project.

The theoretical and research literature of the profession continued to be enhanced by consistent programmatic inquiries in psychometrics, student development, behavior change, vocational psychology, and career development and interventions.

FOOTNOTES

[1] Wrenn's (Note 1) comment is of interest given his important historical role in the development of counseling psychology: "The challenges to the profession are unmistakable. But I think, however, that anybody who read the first three paragraphs of this chapter would feel it was worth all the struggle we have been through over the past 30 or 40 years."

[2] The Next Decade Project, along with various supporting documents, appears in *The Coming Decade in Counseling Psychology* (Whiteley et al., 1984).

Chapter 7
Challenge and Opportunity Building of the Historical Legacy: The Seventh Historical Period (1984—)

There are a number of immediate challenges confronting counseling psychology. The first challenge is to reach out to other psychologists, increase their involvement in issues before the profession, and encourage their participation in organized counseling psychology itself. In 1951 Division 17 was the second largest division of the American Psychological Association (second only to clinical psychology) at a time when APA had a total of 8,554 members. Thirty-two years later, in 1983, APA's membership was 58,183. In the interim Division 17 has gone from 645 members to only 2,556 members and, in the process, slipped to seventh place in overall APA divisional membership. Division 17's growth has neither kept pace with the rate of growth of APA nor grown in comparison with other divisions. In fact, in actual members, Division 17 has declined slightly in membership since reaching a high of 2,659 in 1978.

A second immediate challenge remains in the area of generating more quality scholarly accomplishments. Counseling psychologists need to increase their research productivity. While Brayfield's (1963) critique that counseling psychology has "unimpressive" scientific contributions has been addressed satisfactorily by the accomplishments of the last two decades (in fact, a counseling psychologist was the recipient of one of the 1983 APA Distinguished Scientific Contribution Awards), only 40% of the principal authors cited in the most recent *Annual Review of Psychology* review of counseling psychology (Borgen, 1984, in press) are members of Division 17. More non-Division 17 psychologists were referenced as principal authors of counseling psychology research than were Division 17 psychologists. Approximately 60% of the contributions to the counseling psychology literature in the Borgen review, therefore, were done by members of other divisions of the American Psychological Association or by nonpsychologists.

Division 17 has yet to develop and endorse a statement of the *specific* research competencies which are to result from doctoral training. The

165

initial minimum standards were set too low in the initial policy statements (APA, 1952a, 1952b, 1956). The minimum should *not* have been set at the "ability to review and to make use of the results of research." The minimum should have been set then, and should be set now, at the ability to formulate hypotheses independently, to conduct original inquiry, and to review and make use of the results of research. Historically, there has been all too little time allocated in graduate training to the attainment of research competencies.

A third immediate challenge to the profession is presenting to the broader society our basic mission and the services which we can deliver to clients. A revision and expansion of the Jordaan et al. (1968) statement on counseling psychology would be an effective beginning. Fretz (1982) has already outlined the substance of such a revised statement.

A fourth immediate challenge is anticipating the consequences for client needs of the pervasive shifts which are occurring in the economic structure of society. These shifts are a consequence of the breakup of an established labor intensive industrial society and the emergence of high technology, rather than labor, as the basic force in the economic structure of the future. The implications for educational and vocational development and the assessment of personal skills are numerous and must be approached proactively.

A fifth immediate challenge is to regain involvement in the area of prevention.[1] Initiative has shifted to clinical and community psychology for advancing the theoretical and research base of this fundamental role of counseling psychology. In the Kessler and Albee (1975) review of the literature on primary prevention, counseling psychologists were almost unrepresented. Krumboltz et al. (1979) indicated that prevention has occupied "last place" in the hearts of counseling psychologists. The centrality of prevention to the core role of counseling psychology mandates a fundamental reawakening of interest and activity. Indeed the historical facts are that organized counseling psychology has done little in three key areas which are well within its own conceptual definitions of concern: prevention, community psychology, and health psychology.

The opportunities before counseling psychology are numerous. Counseling psychologists in the contemporary world are confronted more than ever with a myriad of client problems irrespective of what has yet to be learned about a particular problem or how to resolve it. As we move into the final years of the decade of the 1980s, the practicing counseling psychologist has a legacy of long-term programmatic research on which to draw in helping solve client problems. More inquiry is needed, however, and on a broader range of subjects.

In order to detail more clearly the issues involved in satisfactorily addressing each of these areas of immediate challenge, this historical perspective will close by indicating what must be accomplished in order that the profession enter the 21st century with a renewed sense of purpose and more extensive record of accomplishment.

INCREASING PARTICIPATION IN ORGANIZED COUNSELING PSYCHOLOGY

Increasing participation in organized counseling psychology may be approached from a number of directions. Among those directions are: increasing attention to the concerns of private practitioners, expanding the marketplace to include the emerging health care settings, and increasing the representation of underrepresented ethnic minorities.

INCREASING ATTENTION TO THE CONCERNS OF THE PRIVATE PRACTITIONER

Tanney (1984) and others have recognized the obstacles to counseling psychologists working as private practitioners: the substantial equivalency issue, eligibility to independently collect third-party payments, and eligibility for licensure in different states from where training occurred. As Tanney (1984) observed, "Counseling psychologists may have been sleeping when the state laws were enacted or far too impotent to have effected the type of regulation which would have recognized the nature of training as the critical element in licensing for independent practice" (p. 125).

Both observations are correct, and must be addressed. One solution, in Tanney's view, is for counseling psychologists to become more involved in the political process. She has offered a number of timely suggestions on how to proceed which will need implementation if counseling psychology is going to be an effective political force. These suggestions include making state psychological associations aware of the concerns of counseling psychologists, joining the Association for the Advancement of Psychology, continuing to work with the *National Register*, and supporting the Psychology Defense Fund and the Psychology Legal Action Network.

EXPANDING THE MARKETPLACE TO INCLUDE THE EMERGING HEALTH CARE SETTINGS

The analysis of how to increase organized counseling psychology's role in health care settings, therefore creating more roles and employment opportunities for counseling psychologists, begins with Resnick's (1984) observation on the importance of marketplace concerns:

> These are direct service roles for counseling psychologists in CMHCs and HMOs that are appropriate and have potential for expansion. Whether or not we as counseling psychologists involve ourselves, it is quite evident that other applied psychologists have and will continue to do so. The health industry is an expanding market in which our contributions can be significant. (p. 113)

In Resnick's view, HMOs can be a "professionally appropriate and exciting job setting" for counseling psychologists if there is not too much delay in getting involved.

Potential roles for counseling psychologists will vary with the specific type of health care setting. For example, according to Resnick (1984), it is likely that counseling psychologists will be engaged in more direct service (offering principally counseling and psychotherapy) in CMHCs, while in HMOs there will likely develop more opportunities for consultation, training, and preventive mental health roles and programs.

In order for these opportunities to develop, counseling psychologists need to seek greater exposure within health care settings. Resnick (1984) outlines the reasons for this:

> Much of the literature and research base used to build services in an HMO is part of the counseling psychologists' curriculum. Work on developmental theory and life-span development is being discovered anew by our colleagues in health care settings which have also become part of the counseling psychologists' educational and training experiences; in fact, there are many insights on young adulthood and vocational development from the literature that we could add to the health care setting. Given appropriate exposure, counseling psychologists clearly have the training and knowledge which allow them to function effectively in many HMO-type organizations. (p. 110)

It is apparent that counseling psychologists have much to contribute to health care settings and are professionally less constrained by the "narrow confines of a mental health/psychotherapy model than some of our colleagues" (Resnick, 1984, p. 111). He singles out Division 17 for a key advocacy and supportive role if counseling psychologists are to assume appropriate roles within CMHCs and HMOs, a key challenge for organized counseling psychology.

INCREASING THE REPRESENTATION OF UNDERREPRESENTED ETHNIC MINORITIES

Among the many benefits of increasing the number of ethnic minorities in counseling psychology, as identified by Smith (1982), include:

> serving to counter the forces leading to stereotyping and misrepresentation, reducing the "credibility gap" which currently faces graduate training programs and professional organizations, and presenting "viable role models" for minorities who wish to pursue psychology careers. (p. 62)

She went on to observe that the "delivery of counseling services to ethnic minorities may be limited by the weaknesses of the paradigms and theoretical constructs used within the profession" (p. 62). A consequence of the underrepresentation of ethnic minorities within counseling psychology is that the body of professional knowledge is "artificially truncated."

A valuable first step for organized counseling psychology is to respond with effective action to the Parham and Moreland (1981) survey which found that a low application rate to graduate psychology programs stems from anticipated rejection, a lack of course offerings from a nonwhite perspective, and an underrepresentation of nonwhite faculty.

GENERATING MORE QUALITY SCHOLARLY ACCOMPLISHMENTS

The problem of generating more quality scholarly accomplishments is a complex one. Osipow (1984) indicated that the pool of counseling psychologists who engage in (or at least try to publish) research seems to be diminishing. Biskin (1984) identified some of the factors involved:

> In addition to a "weeding out" process, in which poor researchers are not reinforced for engaging in low quality research, other less fortunate causes may be at work. For example, research funding tends to reflect the general level of the economy; it is likely that only the most creative young researchers are receiving new grants to support research efforts. Academia, which supports most of the people who publish in JCP, is also suffering under a financial burden: salaries lag, tenure is no longer guaranteed to productive young faculty members, facilities decay. I suspect that there is less prestige to be gained by affiliating full time with a university than there was even 10 years ago. As a result, I suspect that fewer potential researchers are finding their ways into environments that reward the research enterprise, either by choice or because of the competition for the few desirable positions that seem to be available. This phenomenon is not unique to counseling psychology; it affects many disciplines. (p. 178)

The circumstance where many disciplines are affected by these sources of decline in research output simply indicates the difficulty of changing the situation.

Holland (1982) observed correctly that there is little unemployment among counseling psychologists and that recent graduates are finding employment with comparatively little difficulty. The problem for generating scholarly activity is that these new employment locations do not emphasize, encourage, or reward research. The task is to increase the number of professionals whose serious thought about the problems of the profession is reflected in a program of regular publication. As Holland (1982) stated the problem, "We [currently] have only a small band of active thinkers, researchers, and developers to march against future problems" (p. 10).

Gottfredson (1982) has observed that in forums where professional identity concerns have received attention, there has been a relative exclusion of the research context of the profession. Osipow's (1984) comment that what is researched and published serves to define the profession to the broader public has another meaning as well; namely, that an outside observer would conclude that counseling psychology lacks a commitment to scholarly inquiry.

Hill and Gronsky (1984) document the absence of research and its consumption within the profession and report that there is a continuing debate over what are appropriate research questions and how those questions are to be investigated. Harmon (1982) has drawn attention to the continuing "dissatisfaction" with the scientific underpinnings of counseling psychology. The modal number of post-Ph.D. publications remains zero.

How can this situation of general dissatisfaction be remedied? There are currently 15 specific recommendations which emerged from the Next Decade Project and which collectively offer a promising direction for the profession:

1. That counseling psychology define itself as a professional specialty bringing scientific thinking to bear on human problems, stressing analytical and critical thinking equally with formal research activities.
2. That the Division 17 Scientific Affairs Committee spell out and publicize the several ways in which the scientist/practitioner model is implemented by counseling psychologists and show the importance of scientific thinking in each model (practitioner, researcher, policymaker).
3. That Division 17 devote itself to promoting communication among individuals in each model encompassed by the scientist/ practitioner model, with the goal of enhancing both the practice of counseling psychology and research. (See more specific Recommendations, 5, 7, and 10.)
4. That the Division 17 Educational Committee discuss with the APA Education & Training Board the importance of study in the philosophy of science as well as in research methods and statistics.
5. That Division 17 plan a preconvention or convention invitational workshop in 1982 which will solicit papers and discussion on *the problems* counseling psychologists face in their work which might be resolved by research. The goal should be to develop a long-term (10-year) priority list. Both practitioners and researchers must participate as well as representatives of other areas of psychology and other disciplines.
6. That Division 17, through its Education Committee, stress the importance of problem definition in training counseling psychologists to identify significant problems as well as to apply statistical analysis. Selecting students who show promise of developing these skills must also be stressed.

7. That the Scientific Affairs Committee of Division 17 compare the list of research priorities with recent publications in relevant journals such as the *Journal of Counseling Psychology* and *The Counseling Psychologist* and make their findings available to journal editors in an attempt to identify neglected areas.

8. That the Scientific Affairs Committee of Division 17 arrange yearly APA convention programs designed to present exemplary research in the high priority areas in a way which responds to the needs of the practitioner.

9. That the Scientific Affairs Committee attempt to influence psychological indexes such as *Psychological Abstracts* and PASAR to provide entry terms which meet the needs of counseling psychologists more adequately than they currently do.

10. That Division 17 plan a preconvention or convention invitational workshop in 1983 which will address the question of research designs appropriate to the problems posed at the 1982 workshop on problems and priorities. Careful attention should be given to choosing an impartial, facilitative chair and participants with wide expertise in methodology.

11. That Division 17 give two research awards for research which suggests how to resolve important questions in counseling psychology: one award to a study using qualitative research methods, the second to a study using quantitative research methods.

12. That Division 17 encourage the editor of *The Counseling Psychologist* to devote some space to a Research Forum focused on methodology, giving adequate attention to all methods. (This recommendation is being implemented currently.)

13. That yearly or bi-yearly follow-up conferences be sponsored by Division 17 for the purposes of: (a) assessing progress toward resolving prioritized problems; (b) revising the priority list; (c) exploring new methods applicable to the priority problems; and (d) recognizing research which has had significant impact on practice.

14. That Division 17 commission the Scientific Affairs Committee to initiate discussion with funding agencies no later than 1983 in the interests of making the scientific priorities of counseling psychologists known to them and soliciting support for needed research.

15. That Division 17 find means (publications or other communications) to encourage service agencies to cooperate with researchers in gaining access to client and counselor populations and to encourage researchers to make the value of their research clear to cooperating agencies.

(Harmon, 1982, pp. 32-36)

There are certainly other actions which could be taken to improve the scientific basis of the profession. The bulk of the specific action recommendations, however, which emerged from the Next Decade Project have yet to be implemented. One yardstick by which to measure the extent to which organized counseling psychology meets the immediate challenge of generating more quality scholarly accomplishments is its ability to translate these recommendations into accomplishments.

REPRESENTING COUNSELING PSYCHOLOGY'S MISSION AND CORE SERVICES TO THE BROADER SOCIETY

Representing counseling psychology's mission and core services to the broader profession is a key challenge for the immediate future. This representation will be most effective when it is based upon a clear statement of goals and roles.

Holland (1982) has directed attention to the reasons why a clear statement of goals and roles is needed:

> to design more coherent and appropriate training programs; to decide and focus on what research to perform; to cope with the competition in the marketplace; to represent counseling psychology to the APA, related professions, clients, and funding agencies. Individuals and groups will continue to act on their stereotypes unless we make a concerted attempt to change them. (p. 8)

The "concerted effort" that Holland calls for must be rooted in a satisfactory definition of the profession of counseling psychology.

Fretz (1982) has drawn attention to the problems encountered in achieving a satisfactory definition of the profession: Some counseling psychologists react that "it will cause more trouble than it resolves." Another problem he observed is that "writing a definition that alienates no subspecialty requires so broad a definition" that the result is so general "that it might be seen as equally suitable to 'school psychologist,' 'counselor,' 'social worker,' 'community psychologist' or 'clinical psychologist'" (p. 16). Another problem of note in refining a definitional statement is the division of opinion on whether to include more explicit differentation (territorial boundaries) from allied professional specialties.

Historically, some counseling psychology subspecialties have not encountered identity or job definition problems. Included in this group by Fretz (1982) are professionals involved in career counseling, interest measurement, personal counseling, and psychological measurement. It is necessary to devote the required time and attention to resolving definitional issues if organized counseling psychology is going to be able to represent satisfactorily its mission and core services to the broader society.

ANTICIPATING NEW SPECIAL CLIENT POPULATIONS
AND THEIR NEEDS

A continuing challenge before counseling psychology is to anticipate new client populations and their needs. Dailey (1984) has identified the particular relevance of knowledge which is possessed by counseling psychologists to special populations: personality theory; individual, family, and group counseling; conflict resolution and consultative skills; and methods of gaining more personal control and achieving self-actualization.

In serving new populations, it is necessary to become familiar with the specialized literature in such journals as the *Journal of Gerontology* (aging), *Sports Psychology* (athletics), *Journal of Rehabilitation Counseling* (handicapped), and *Death Education* (the terminally ill). The core areas of counseling psychology training (counseling theory, assessment, career development, and group processes) need to be expanded, in Dailey's (1984) view, to include information about physical handicaps, gerontology, terminal illness, athlete self-image, medical-computer technology, life-span development, physiological/emotional interactions, and bio-medical ethics.

Meeting the challenge of new service populations requires selective modification in the curriculum of counseling psychology training programs. This is less easy than it might appear since the adoption in 1978 of a standard set of core requirements for counseling psychology training. Nonetheless, there remains both flexibility within the core curriculum and electives which may be adapted to preparing future counseling psychologists to meet the needs of special populations.

READDRESSING A CORE ROLE OF COUNSELING
PSYCHOLOGY: PREVENTION

The Jordaan et al. (1968) definition of a core role for counseling psychology as prevention has been recurrent in literature on the focus of the specialty. The documented observation in Chapter 6, therefore, that prevention occupies "last place" in the hearts of counseling psychologists is an indication of the length that the profession must go to realize the potential of this core role. Counseling psychologists, by and large, are not active as researchers in the area of prevention and are not at all prominent in the several recent reviews of the prevention literature which have appeared in the *Annual Review of Psychology*.

The first step for counseling psychology in the area of prevention is to define the conceptual limits much as Robert W. White did for the concept of the "healthy personality" in a special issue of *The Counseling Psychologist*, Vol. 4, No. 2 (White, 1973). A second step is to identify the principal research questions and areas for delivery of services. Once recent developments in the area of prevention have been identified and related to ongoing counseling psychology research and service programs, it will be possible to assess carefully how to meet the challenge to incorporate this core role as a more viable and integral part of the profession.

SUMMARY

Five immediate challenges confronting counseling psychology are presented. The first challenge is to reach out to other psychologists and increase their involvement in issues before the profession, particularly psychologists in private practice and health care, and ethnic minorities. A second challenge is to generate more quality scholarly accomplishments. A third challenge is to represent counseling psychology's mission and core services to the broader society. Meeting this challenge requires further refining definitional statements. A fourth challenge is to anticipate new special client populations and ways to meet their needs. A fifth challenge is to readdress a core role of counseling psychology, prevention, and reintegrate it within the central research and service program of the profession.

FOOTNOTE

[1]Bordin (Note 1) called attention to the developments of community psychology in the 1960s which impacted the area of prevention: "Your omission of the development of community psychology in the 1960s leaves out an important aspect of the dynamic of forces operating on Division 17. I suspect that you will find that community psychology managed to stake out a claim on the preventive and positive goals for psychological interventions, obscuring the fact that especially within the educational community, i.e. the school, counseling psychologists had been articulating and furthering such goals for twenty years."

REFERENCE NOTES

Chapter 1

1. Cottle, W. C. Personal communication, October 1, 1983.
2. Scott, C. W. Personal communication, September 13, 1983 and July 2, 1984.
3. Pepinsky, H. B. Personal communication, October 6, 1983.

Chapter 2

1. Fretz, B. R. Personal communication, September 26, 1983.
2. Pepinsky, H. B. Personal communication, October 6, 1983.
3. Wrenn, C. G. Personal communication, September 24, 1983.

Chapter 3

1. Wrenn, C. G. Personal communication, September 24, 1983.
2. Tyler, L. E. Personal communication, September 8, 1983.
3. Bordin, E. S. Personal communication, August 25, 1983.
4. Cottle, W. C. Personal communication, October 1, 1983.

Chapter 4

1. Fretz, B. R. Personal communication, September 26, 1983.
2. Thompson, A. S. Personal communication, October 6, 1983.
3. Thompson, A. S. Personal communication, October 6, 1983.

Chapter 5

1. Thompson, A. S. Personal communication, October 6, 1983.
2. Pepinsky, H. B. Personal communication, October 6, 1983.
3. Pepinsky, H. B. Personal communication, October 6, 1983.
4. Cottle, W. C. Personal communication, October 1, 1983.
5. Tyler, L. E. Personal communication, September 8, 1983.

Chapter 6

1. Wrenn, C. G. Personal communication, September 24, 1983.
2. Kagan, N. Personal communication, December 12, 1983.

Chapter 7

1. Bordin, E. S. Personal communication, December 19, 1983.

REFERENCES

Abt, L. E., & Bellak, L. (Eds.). Projective psychology: Clinical approaches to the total personality. New York: Knopf, 1950.

Adler, A. Das zartlichkeitsbedurfnis des kindes. In Alfred Adler & Carl Furtmuller (Eds.), *Heilen und Bilden.* München: Reinhardt, 1914.

Adler, A. *Study of organ inferiority and its psychical compensation.* New York: Nervous & Mental Disease Publishing, 1917.

Adler, A. *The education of children* (1930). London: Allen & Unwin, 1957.

Adler, A. *What life should mean to you.* New York: Capricorn Books, 1958.

Adler, A. *Understanding human nature.* New York: Premier Books, 1959.

Adler, A. *The practice and theory of individual psychology.* Paterson, NJ: Littlefield, Adams, 1963. (a)

Adler, A. *The problem child.* New York: Capricorn Books, 1963. (b)

Adler, A. *Problems of neurosis.* New York: Harper & Row, 1964. (a)

Adler, A. *Social interest: A challenge to mankind.* New York: Capricorn Books, 1964. (b)

Adler, A. *The science of living.* New York: Doubleday Anchor Books, 1969.

Adler, A. *The neurotic constitution.* (1926) Freeport, NY: Books for Libraries Press, 1972.

Alexander, F. *The scope of psychoanalysis.* New York: Basic Books, 1961.

Allen, T. The individual psychology of Alfred Adler: An item of history and a promise of a revolution. *The Counseling Psychologist*, 1971, *3*(1), 3-24.

American Psychological Association, Committee on Training in Clinical Psychology. Recommended graduate training program in clinical psychology. *American Psychologist*, 1947, *2*, 539-558.

American Psychological Association, Committee on Ethical Standards for Psychology. Ethical standards for the distribution of psychological tests and diagnostics. *American Psychologist*, 1950, *5*(11), 620-626.

American Psychological Association, Committee on Ethical Standards for Psychology. Ethical standards for psychology. *American Psychologist*, 1951, *6*, 626-661.

American Psychological Association, Division of Counseling and Guidance, Committee on Counselor Training. Recommended standards for training counseling psychologists at the doctoral level. *American Psychologist*, 1952, *7*, 175-181. Also in J. M. Whiteley (Ed.), *The history of counseling psychology.* Monterey, CA: Brooks/Cole, 1980, 70-80. (a)

American Psychological Association, Division of Counseling and Guidance, Committee on Counselor Training. The practicum training of counseling psychologists. *American Psychologist*, 1952, *7*, 182-188. Also in J. M. Whiteley (Ed.), *The history of counseling psychology.* Monterey, CA: Brooks/Cole, 1980, 81-91. (b)

177

American Psychological Association. *Psychology and its relation with other professions*. Washington, DC: American Psychological Association, 1954.

American Psychological Association, Division of Counseling Psychology, Committee on Definition. Counseling psychology as a specialty. *American Psychologist*, 1956, *11*, 282-285. Also in J. M. Whiteley (Ed.), *The history of counseling psychology*. Monterey, CA: Brooks/Cole, 1980, 92-98.

American Psychological Association, Division of Counseling Psychology, Committee on Divisional Functions. *The Division of Counseling Psychology studies its membership*, 1959. (Multilith)

American Psychological Association, Division of Counseling Psychology. *The scope of standards of preparation in psychology for school counselors*, 1961. (Multilith) (a)

American Psychological Association, Division of Counseling Psychology, Committee on Divisional Functions. *The Division of Counseling Psychology studies its membership*, 1961. (Multilith) (b)

American Psychological Association, Division of Counseling Psychology, Committee on School Counselors. The scope and standards of preparation in psychology for school counselors. *American Psychologist*, 1962, *17*, 149-152.

American Psychological Association, Division of Counseling Psychology. The licensing and certification of psychologists—a position statement. *The Counseling Psychologist*, 1975, *5*(3), 135.

American Psychological Association, Division of Counseling Psychology. *The defining characteristics of counseling psychologists*. Washington, DC: APA Division 17, 1977. (Mimeographed)

Anastasi, A. The measurements of abilities. *Journal of Counseling Psychology*, 1954, *1*, 164-168.

Anastasi, A. *Differential psychology: Individual and group differences in behavior*. New York: Macmillan, 1958.

Anderson, H. H., & Anderson, G. L. (Eds.). *Introduction to projective techniques*. New York: Prentice-Hall, 1951.

Anderson, J. E. A note on the meeting of the Joint Constitutional Committee of the APA and AAAP, February 26 and 27, 1944. *Psychological Bulletin*, 1944, *41*, 235-236.

Anderson, R. P. State psychological associations. In J. M. Whiteley, N. Kagan, L. Harmon, B. R. Fretz, & F. Tanney (Eds.), *The coming decade in counseling psychology*. Schenectady, NY: Character Research Press, 1984.

Ansbacher, H. L. The concept of social interest. *Journal of Individual Psychology*, 1968, *24*, 131-149.

Ansbacher, H. L., & Ansbacher, R. (Eds.). *The individual psychology of Alfred Adler*. New York: Basic Books, 1956.

Aronson, M. *A study of the relationships between certain counselor and client characteristics in client-centered therapy*. University Park, PA: Pennsylvania State College, 1953.

Astin, A. W. A program of research on student development. *Journal of College Student Personnel*, 1968, *9*, 299-307. (a)

Astin, A. W. *The college environment*. Washington, DC: American Council on Education, 1968. (b)

Astin, A. W. The methodology of research on college impact, parts one and two. *Sociological Education*, 1970, *43*, 223-254, 437-450.

Astin, A. W. *College Dropouts-a national .profile*. Washington, DC: American Council on Education, 1972. (a)

Astin, A. W. The measured effects of higher education. *Annals of American Academy of Political and Social Sciences*, 1972, *404*, 1-20. (b)

Astin, A. W. The impact of dormitory living on students. *Educational Record*, 1973, *54*, 204-210.

Astin, A. W., King, M. R., Light, J. M., & Richardson, G. T. *The American freshmen: National norms*. Los Angeles: Cooperative Institutional Research Program, 1973.

Astin, H. S., Astin, A. W., Bisconti, A. S., & Frankl, H. H. *Higher education and the disadvantaged student*. Washington, DC: Human Service Press, 1972.

Authier, J., Gustafson, K., Guerney, B., & Kasdorf, J. The psychological practitioner as teacher: A theoretical-historical and practical review. *The Counseling Psychologist*, 1975, *5*(2), 31-50.

Ayllon, T., & Azrin, N. *The token economy*. New York: Appleton-Century-Crofts, 1968.

Bandura, A. *Principles of behavior modification*. New York: Holt, Rinehart & Winston, 1969.

Bandura, A. *Psychological modeling: Conflicting theories*. Chicago, IL: Aldine-Atherton, 1971.

Bandura, A. *Aggression: Social learning analysis*. Englewood Cliffs, NJ: Prentice-Hall, 1973.

Bandura, A. *Social learning theory*. Englewood Cliffs, NJ: Prentice-Hall, 1977.

Beck, A. T. *Cognitive therapy and the emotional disorders*. New York: International Universities Press, 1976.

Beck, C. F. Where are the graduate students? *Counseling News and Views*, 1961, *13*(3), 10-11.

Bedell, R. Report of Committee on Support of Counseling. *Counseling News and Views*, 1952, *5*(1), 11-13.

Beers, C. W. *A mind that found itself*. Garden City, NY: Longmans-Green, 1908.

Beilin, H. The application of general developmental principles to the vocational area. *Journal of Counseling Psychology*, 1955, *2*, 53-57.

Bell, H. M. Message from the president. *Newsletter*, 1948, *1*(1), 1.

180

Bell, H. M. The psychologist as a counselor. *Counseling News and Views*, 1949, *2*(1), 3-4.

Bell, H. M. Ego-involvement in vocational decisions. *Personnel and Guidance Journal*, 1960, *38*, 732-736.

Berdie, R. F. Counseling methods: Diagnostics. *Annual Review of Psychology*, 1950, *1*, 255-266.

Berdie, R. F. Message from the President. *Counseling News and Views*, 1958, *10*(2), 1.

Berdie, R. F. Counseling. *Annual Review of Psychology*, 1959, *10*, 345-370.

Berg, I. A. Measures before and after therapy. *Journal of Clinical Psychology*, 1952, *8*, 46-51.

Berg, I. A. Comments on current books and the passing scene. *Journal of Counseling Psychology*, 1959, *6*, 250-252.

Berg, I. A. The President's message, tick, tick, tick, what little iambics. *Counseling News and Views*, 1964, *16*(1), 1-2.

Berg, I. A. Some alternative roads for counseling psychology: 1962. In J. M. Whiteley (Ed.), *The history of counseling psychology*. Monterey, CA: Brooks/Cole, 1980, 133-135.

Berg, I. A., Pepinsky, H. B., & Shoben, E. J., Jr. The status of counseling psychology: 1960. In J. M. Whiteley (Ed.), *The history of counseling psychology*. Monterey, CA: Brooks/Cole, 1980, 105-113.

Berger, E. M. Zen Buddhism, general psychology and counseling psychology. *Journal of Counseling Psychology*, 1962, *9*, 122-127.

Bergin, A. E. The evaluation of therapeutic outcomes. In A. E. Bergin & S. Garfield (Eds.), *Handbook of psychotherapy and behavioral change: An empirical analysis*. New York: Wiley, 1971, 217-270.

Berne, E. Ego states in psychotherapy. *American Journal of Psychotherapy*, 1957, *11*, 293-309.

Berne, E. Transactional analysis: A new and effective method of group therapy. *American Journal of Psychotherapy*, 1958, *12*, 735-743.

Berne, E. *Transactional analysis in psychotherapy*. New York: Grove Press, 1961.

Berne, E. *Games people play*. New York: Grove Press, 1964.

Berne, E. *Principles of group treatment*. New York: Oxford University Press, 1966.

Berne, E. *Sex in human loving*. New York: Simon & Schuster, 1970.

Berne, E. *What do you say after you say hello?* New York: Grove Press, 1972.

Binet, A. *The mind and the brain*. London: Trubner & Co., 1907.

Binet, A., & Henri, V. La psychologie individuelle. *Annee Psychol.*, 1895, *2*, 411-463.

Binet, A., & Simon, Th. Methodes nouvelles pour le diagnostic du niveua intellectuel des anormaux. *Annee Psychol.*, 1905, *11*, 191-244.

Binswanger, L. *Grundformen und erkenntnis menschlichen daseins*. Munich: Rinehardt, 1962.

Biskin, B. H. Commentaries on research in the 1980s. In J. M. Whiteley, N. Kagan, L. W. Harmon, B. R. Fretz, & F. Tanney (Eds.), *The coming decade in counseling psychology*. Schenectady, NY: Character Research Press, 1984.

Black, J. D. Common factors of the patient-therapist relationship in diverse psychotherapies. *Journal of Clinical Psychology*, 1952, *8*, 302-306.

Blum, M. L., & Balinsky, B. *Counseling and psychotherapy*. New York: Prentice Hall, 1951.

Boone, J. T. In Counseling psychologist (vocational). *Counseling News and Views*, 1952, *5*(1), 16.

Bordin, E. S. A theory of vocational interests as a dynamic phenomenon. *Educa—tional and Psychological Measurement*, 1943, *3*, 49-66.

Bordin, E. S. Diagnosis in counseling and psychotherapy. *Educational and Psychological Measurement*, 1946, *6*, 169-184.

Bordin, E. S. Dimensions of the counseling process. *Journal of Clinical Psychology*, 1948, *4*, 240-244.

Bordin, E. S. A delimitation of the area of research in counseling and guidance. *Newsletter*, 1949, *1*(2), 4.

Bordin, E. S. Counseling methods: Therapy. *Annual Review of Psychology*, 1950, *1*, 267-276.

Bordin, E. S. *Psychological counseling*. New York: Appleton-Century-Crofts, 1955.

Bordin, E. S. Miami Conference. *Counseling News and Views*, 1959, *11*(2), 15-17.

Bordin, E. S., Nachmann, B., & Segal, S. An articulated framework for vocational development. *Journal of Counseling Psychology*, 1963, *10*, 107-116.

Borgen, F. H. Counseling psychology. *Annual Review of Psychology*, 1984, in press.

Boss, M. *Psychoanalysis and daseins analysis*. Translated by L. B. Lefebre, New York: Basic Books, 1963.

Brammer, L. M. *The helping relationship: Process and skills*. Englewood Cliffs, NJ: Prentice Hall, 1973.

Brayfield, A. H. Counseling psychology: Some dilemmas in the graduate school. *Journal of Counseling Psychology*, 1961, *8*, 17-19. (a)

Brayfield, A. H. Vocational counseling today. In E. G. Williamson (Ed.), *Vocational counseling, a reappraisal in honor of Donald G. Paterson*. Minnesota Studies in Student Personnel Work, No. 11. Minneapolis, MN: University of Minnesota Press, 1961. (b)

Brayfield, A. H. Counseling psychology. *Annual Review of Psychology*, 1963, *14*, 319-350.

Brewer, J. M. *Education as guidance*. New York: Macmillan, 1932.

Brigante, T. R., Haefner, D. P., & Woodson, W. B. Clinical and counseling psychologists' perception of their specialties. *Journal of Counseling Psychology*, 1962, *9*(3), 225-231.

Brill, A. A. *Basic principles of psychoanalysis*. Garden City, NY: Doubleday, 1949.

Brown, D., & Brooks, L. (Eds.). *Career choice and development: Applying contemporary theories to practice*. San Francisco: Jossey-Bass, 1984.

Brown, S. D., & Lent, R. W. *Handbook of counseling psychology*. New York: Wiley, 1984.

Buber, M. *Between man and man*. New York: Macmillan, 1948.

Buber, M. *I and thou*. New York: Scribner, 1958.

Buber, M. *The knowledge of man*. New York: Harper & Row, 1965.

Buehler, C. *Der menschliche Lenslauf als psychologisches problemy (The human life course as a psychological subject)*. Leipzig: Hirzel, 1933.

Bugenthal, J. F. *The search for authenticity. An existential analytic approach to psychotherapy*. New York: Holt, Rinehart, & Winston, 1964.

Buros, O. K. (Ed.). *The third mental measurement yearbook, 1949*. New Brunswick, NJ: Rutgers University Press, 1949.

Buros, O. K. (Ed.). *The fifth mental measurement handbook*. Highland Park, NY: Gryphon Press, 1959.

Cameron, D. E. *General psychotherapy*. New York: Grune & Stratton, 1950.

Campbell, D., & Stanley, J. *Experimental and quasi-experimental designs for research*. Chicago: Rand-McNally, 1966.

Campbell, R. J., Kagan, N., & Krathwohl, D. R. The development and validation of a scale to measure affective sensitivity (empathy). *Journal of Counseling Psychology*, 1971, *18*, 407-412.

Caracena, P. F. Graduate education in counseling psychology. *Counseling News and Views*, 1967, *19*(1), 5-9.

Carkhuff, R. R. Counseling research, theory and practice. *Journal of Counseling Psychology*, 1966, *30*, 467-480.

Carkhuff, R. R. *Helping and human relations: A process for lay and professional helpers. Volume I. Selection and training*. New York: Holt, Rinehart, & Winston, 1969. (a)

Carkhuff, R. R. The prediction of the effects of teacher-counselor education: The development of communication and discrimination selection indexes. *Counselor Education and Supervision*, 1969, *8*, 265-272. (b)

Carkhuff, R. R. *The development of human resources*. New York: Holt, Rinehart, & Winston, 1971.

Carkhuff, R. R. *The art of helping*. Amherst, MA: Human Resource Development Press, 1972. (a)

Carkhuff, R. R. *The art of problem solving*. Amherst, MA: Human Resource Development Press, 1972. (b)

Carkhuff, R. R. *The art of training*. Amherst, MA: Human Resource Development Press, 1972. (c)

Carkhuff, R. R. The development of systematic resource development models. *The Counseling Psychologist*, 1972, *3*(3), 4-11. (d)

Carkhuff, R. R., & Alexik, M. Effect of client depth of self-exploration upon high- and low-functioning counselors. *Journal of Counseling Psychology*, 1967, *14*, 350-355.

Carkhuff, R. R., & Berenson, B. G. *Beyond counseling and therapy*. New York: Holt, Rinehart, & Winston, 1967.

Carkhuff, R. R., Kratochvil, D., & Friel, T. Effects of professional training: Communication and discrimination of facilitative conditions. *Journal of Counseling Psychology*, 1968, *15*, 68-74.

Carlson, R. E., Dawis, R. V., England, G. W., & Lofquist, L. G. The measurement of employment satisfaction. *Minnesota Studies in Vocational Rehabilitation*, XIII, 1962.

Carmer, J., & Rouzer, D. Healthy functioning from the Gestalt perspective. *The Counseling Psychologist*, 1974, *4*(4), 20-23.

Carr, A. C. An evaluation of nine non-directive psychotherapy cases by means of the Rorschach. *Journal of Consulting Psychology*, 1949, *13*, 196-205.

Cartwright, D. S. Effectiveness of psychotherapy: A critique of the spontaneous remission argument. *Journal of Counseling Psychology*, 1955, *2*, 291-296.

Cautela, J. R. Covert sensitization. *Psychological Record*, 1967, *20*, 459-468.

Chickering, A. W. *Education and identity*. San Francisco: Jossey-Bass, 1969.

Clecak, P. *America's quest for the ideal self*. New York: Oxford University Press, 1983.

Cohen, L. Vocational planning and mental illness. *Personnel and Guidance Journal*, 1955, *34*, 28-32.

Committee on Counselor Training. In M. Dreese, 1947-1948 Annual report to the membership of the Secretary-Treasurer, Division 17, American Psychological Association. *Newsletter*, 1948, *1*(1), 4.

Committee on Research. In M. Dreese, 1947-1948 Annual report to the membership of the Secretary-Treasurer, Division 17, American Psychological Association. *Newsletter*, 1948, *1*(1), 4.

Cottle, W. C. Personal characteristics of counselors. *Personnel and Guidance Journal*, 1953, *31*, 445-450.

Cottle, W. C. Report of the Research Committee. *Counseling News and Views*, 1954, *7*(1), 17-18.

Cottle, W. C. The president's message. *Counseling News and Views*, 1966, *18*(3), 1-4.

Cottle, W. C. The president's message. *Counseling News and Views*, 1967, *19*(1), 1-4. (a)

Cottle, W. C. Message from the president. *Counseling News and Views*, 1967, *19*(2), 1-4. (b)

Cottle, W. C., & Lewis, W. W., Jr. Personality characteristics of counselors: II. Male counselor responses to the MMPI and GZTS. *Journal of Counseling Psychology*, 1954, *1*, 27-30.

Crites, J. O. Ego strength in relation to vocational interest development. *Journal of Counseling Psychology*, 1960, *7*, 137-143.

Crites, J. O. Parental identification in relation to vocational interest development. *Journal of Educational Psychology*, 1962, *53*, 262-270.

Crites, J. O. *Vocational Psychology*. New York: McGraw- Hill, 1969.

Cronbach, L. J. *Essentials of psychological testing*. New York: Harper, 1949.

Cronbach, L. J. Assessment of individual differences. *Annual Review of Psychology*, 1956, *7*, 173-196.

Cronbach, L. J. *Essentials of psychological testing*. New York: Harper, 1969.

Cross, H. J. The outcome of psychotherapy: A selected analysis of research findings. *Journal of Consulting Psychology*, 1964, *28*, 413-417.

Cutts, N. W. *School psychologists at mid-century*. Washington, DC: American Psychological Association, 1955.

Dailey, A. L. T. New client populations and techniques for the decades ahead. In J. M. Whiteley, N. Kagan, L. W. Harmon, B. R. Fretz, & F. Tanney (Eds.), *The coming decade in counseling psychology*. Schenectady, NY: Character Research Press, 1984.

D'Andrea, R. *A handbook on the theory of Gestalt therapy*. Doctoral dissertation, California School of Professional Psychology, Los Angeles. Ann Arbor, MI: University Microfilms, 1973, No. 73-19.

Danish, S., & Hauer, A. *Helping skills: A basic training program*. New York: Behavioral Publishing, 1973.

Danskin, D. G. Pavlov, Poe, and Division 17. *Counseling News and Views*, 1959, *12*(1), 4-6.

Darley, J. G. The president's message. *Counseling News and Views*, 1949, *2*(1), 2.

Darley, J. G. The substantive bases of counseling psychology. In A. S. Thompson & D. E. Super (Eds.), *The professional preparation of counseling psychologists. Report of the 1964 Greyston Conference*. New York: Bureau of Publications, Teachers College, Columbia University, 1964, 69-75. Also in J. M. Whiteley (Ed.), *The history of counseling psychology*. Monterey, CA: Brooks/Cole, 1980, 168-173.

Darley, J. G., & Hagenah, T. *Vocational interest measurement: Theory and practice*. Minneapolis, MN: University of Minnesota Press, 1955.

Davidson, P. E., & Anderson, H. D. *Occupational mobility in an American community*. Stanford, CA: Stanford University Press, 1937.

Dawis, R. V., England, G. W., & Lofquist, L. H. A theory of work adjustment. *Minnesota Studies on Vocational Rehabilitation, Whole No. 15*. Minneapolis: University of Minnesota Industrial Relations Center, 1964.

Dawis, R. V., & Lofquist, L. H. Personality style and the process of work adjustment. *Journal of Counseling Psychology*, 1976, *23*(1), 55-59.

Dawis, R. V., Lofquist, L. H., & Weiss, D. J. A theory of work adjustment: A revision. *Minnesota Studies in Vocational Rehabilitation (XXIII)*. Minneapolis: University of Minnesota, 1968.

Dictionary of occupational titles. Volume I: Definition of titles. Washington, DC: U.S. Department of Labor, 1965.

Dodge, A. F. *Occupational ability patterns.* New York: Bureau of Publications, Teachers College, Columbia University, 1935.

Dollard, J., & Miller, N. E. *Personality and psychotherapy.* New York: McGraw-Hill, 1950.

Downing, J., & Marmorstein, R. *Dreams and nightmares: A book of Gestalt therapy sessions.* New York: Harper & Row, 1973.

Dreese, M. Report from the president. *Counseling News and Views*, 1952, *5*(2), 3-4.

Dreikurs, R. *The challenge of marriage.* New York: Duell, Sloan, & Pearce, 1946.

Dreikurs, R. *The challenge of parenthood.* New York: Duell, Sloan, & Pearce, 1948.

Dreikurs, R. *Fundamentals of Adlerian psychology.* New York: Greenberg, 1950.

Dreikurs, R. The psychological interview in medicine. *American Journal of Individual Psychology*, 1954, *10*, 99-122.

Dreikurs, R. Adlerian psychotherapy. In F. Fromm-Reichman & J. L. Moreno (Eds.), *Progress in psychotherapy*. NY: Grune-Stratton, 1956. (a)

Dreikurs, R. Goals in psychotherapy. *American Journal of Psychoanalysis*, 1956, *16*, 18-23. (b)

Dreikurs, R. Early experiments with group psychotherapy. *American Journal of Psychotherapy*, 1959, *13*, 882-891.

Dreikurs, R. *Group psychotherapy and group approaches: Collected papers.* Chicago: Alfred Adler Institute, 1960.

Dreikurs, R. Adlerian approach to therapy. In M. I. Stein (Ed.), *Contemporary psychotherapies*. Glencoe, IL: The Free Press, 1961.

Dreikurs, R. Individual psychology: The Adlerian point of view. In J. M. Wepman & R. Heine (Eds.), *Concepts of personality*. Chicago: Aldine, 1963.

Dreikurs, R. *Psychodynamics, psychotherapy and counseling.* Chicago, IL: Alfred Adler Institute of Chicago, 1967.

Dreikurs, R. *Psychology in the classroom.* New York: Harper & Row, 1968.

Dreikurs, R., & Grey, L. *Logical consequences: A new approach to discipline.* New York: Meredith Press, 1968.

Dressel, P. L. Some approaches to evaluation. *Personnel and Guidance Journal*, 1953, *31*, 284-287.

Dymond, R. F. Can clinicians predict individual behavior? *Journal of Personality*, 1953, *22*, 151-161.

Education and Training Committee. Recommended roles for counseling psychologists in the development of counselor support personnel. *Counseling News and Views*, 1966, *18*(3), 11-23.

Edwards, A. L. *Edwards personal preference schedule*. New York: Psychological Corporation, 1954.

Edwards, S. A., & Cronbach, L. J. Experimental design for research in psychotherapy. *Journal of Clinical Psychology*, 1952, *8*, 51-59.

Ellis, A. Requisites for research in psychotherapy. *Journal of Clinical Psychology*, 1950, *6*, 152-156.

Ellis, A. A critique of systematic theoretical foundations in clinical psychology. *Journal of Clinical Psychology*, 1952, *8*, 11-15.

Ellis, A. Outcome of employing three techniques of psychotherapy. *Journal of Clinical Psychology*, 1957, *13*, 334-350. (a)

Ellis, A. Rational psychotherapy and individual psychology. *Journal of Individual Psychology*, 1957, *13*, 38-44. (b)

Ellis, A. Rational psychotherapy. *Journal of General Psychology*, 1958, *59*, 35-49.

Ellis, A. *Reason and emotion in psychotherapy*. New York: Lyle Stuart and Citadel Press, 1962.

Ellis, A. *The art and science of love* (Rev. ed.). New York: Lyle Stuart, 1965.

Ellis, A. What really causes therapeutic change. *Voices*, 1968, *4*(2), 90-97.

Ellis, A. A cognitive approach to behavior therapy. *International Journal of Psychiatry*, 1969, *8*, 896-899.

Ellis, A. *Growth through reason*. Palo Alto, CA: Science and Behavior Books, 1971. (Also Hollywood, CA: Wilshire Books, 1971.) (a)

Ellis, A. *Rational-emotive therapy and its application to emotional education*. New York: Institute for Rational Living, 1971. (b)

Ellis, A. *Humanistic psychotherapy: The rational-emotive approach*. New York: Julian Press & McGraw-Hill Paperbacks, 1973. (a)

Ellis, A. Rational-emotive group therapy. Washington, DC: APGA Film Library, 1973. (b)

Ellis, A. Experience and rationality: The making of a rational-emotive therapist. *Psychotherapy: Theory, research and practice*, 1974, *11*, 194-198.

Ellis, A. The rational-emotive approach to sex therapy. *The Counseling Psychologist*, 1975, *5*(1), 14-21.

Ellis, A. The biological basis of human irrationality. *Journal of Individual Psychology*, 1976, *32*, 145-168.

Ellis, A., & Harper, R. A. *A new guide to rational living*. Englewood Cliffs, NJ: Prentice-Hall, 1961.

Ellis, A., & Harper, R. A. *A new guide to rational living*. Englewood Cliffs, NJ: Prentice-Hall, 1975. (Also, Hollywood, CA: Wilshire Books, 1975.)

Emerson, P., & Smith, E. W. L. Contributions of gestalt psychology to gestalt therapy. *The Counseling Psychologist*, 1974, *4*(4), 8-12.

Enneis, W. H. Discrimination: Planned and accidental. *Counseling News and Views*, 1967, *19*(2), 5-10.

Erikson, E. H. *Childhood and society*. New York: Norton, 1963.

Erikson, E. H. *Identity, youth and crisis*. New York: Norton, 1968.

Eysenck, H. J. The effects of psychotherapy: An evaluation. *Journal of Consulting Psychology*, 1952, *16*, 319-324.

Eysenck, H. J. (Ed.). *Behaviour therapy and the neuroses*. New York: Pergamon, 1960.

Eysenck, H. J. (Ed.). *Experiments in behavior therapy*. New York: Macmillan, 1964. (a)

Eysenck, H. J. The outcome problem in psychotherapy: A reply. *Psychotherapy: Theory, Research, and Practice*, 1964, *1*, 97-100. (b)

Eysenck, H. J. The effects of psychotherapy. *International Journal of Psychiatry*, 1965, *1*, 97-178.

Eysenck, H. J. (Ed.). *Case studies in behaviour therapy*. London: Routledge & Kegan Paul, 1976.

Fagan, J. Personality theory and psychotherapy. *The Counseling Psychologist*, 1974, *4*(4), 4-7.

Fagan, J., & Shepherd, I. L. (Eds.). *Gestalt therapy now*. Palo Alto, CA: Science and Behavior Books, 1970.

Fenichel, O. *The psychoanalytic theory of neurosis*. New York: Norton, 1945.

Fiedler, F. E. The concept of an ideal therapeutic relationship. *Journal of Consulting Psychology*, 1950, *14*, 239-245. (a)

Fiedler, F. E. A comparison of therapeutic relationships in psychoanalytic, non-directive, and Adlerian therapy. *Journal of Consulting Psychology*, 1950, *14*, 436-445. (b)

Fiedler, F. E. Factor analyses of psychoanalytic, non-directive, and Adlerian therapeutic relationships. *Journal of Consulting Psychology*, 1951, *15*, 32-38. (a)

Fiedler, F. E. A method of objective quantification of certain counter transference attitudes. *Journal of Clinical Psychology*, 1951, *7*, 101-107. (b)

Fischer, V. E. *The meaning and practice of psychotherapy*. New York: Macmillan, 1950.

Fletcher, F. M. Review. *Contemporary Psychology*, 1981, *26*(3), 218.

Forer, B. R. Personality factors in occupational choice. *Educational and Psychological Measurement*, 1953, *13*, 361-366.

Frankl, V. E. *The doctor and the soul: An introduction to logotherapy*. New York: Knopf, 1955.

Frankl, V. E. *Man's search for meaning*. New York: Washington Square Press, 1963.

Frankl. V. E. *The doctor and the soul*. New York: Knopf, 1965.

Frankl, V. E. *Psychotherapy and existentialism*. New York: Washington Square Press, 1967.

Franks, C. *Behavior therapy: Appraisal and status*. New York: McGraw-Hill, 1969.

Fretz, B. R. (Ed.). The professional identity of counseling psychology. *The Counseling Psychologist*, 1977, *7*(2), 8-94. Also in J. M. Whiteley & B. R. Fretz (Eds.), *The present and future of counseling psychology*. Monterey, CA: Brooks/Cole, 1980, 1-89.

Fretz, B. R. Perspective and definition. *The Counseling Psychologist*, 1982, *10*(2), 15-19.

Fretz, B. R., & Mills, D. H. *Licensing and certification of psychologists and counselors*. San Francisco: Jossey-Bass, 1980. (a)

Fretz, B. R., & Mills, D. H. Professional certification in counseling psychology. *The Counseling Psychologist*, 1980, *9*(1), 2-17. (b)

Fretz, B. R., Morrill, W. H., Harmon, L. W., Danish, S., Foreman, M., Washington, K. R., Jakubowski-Spector, P., Thoreson, R. W., Meara, N., Warnath, C. F., Howard, M. T., Pietrofesa, J. J., Tanney, M. F., Resnick, H., Southworth, J. A., & Kagan, N. Counseling psychology and the Vail Conference: Analysis of issues in the training of professional psychologists. *The Counseling Psychologist*, 1974, *4*(3), 64-80.

Freud, A. *The ego and the mechanisms of defense*. New York: International Universities Press, 1936.

Freud, A. *Normality and pathology in childhood: Assessments of development*. London: Hogarth Press, 1965.

Freud, S. *Studies of hysteria*. Standard Edition, Vol. 2, 1895.

Freud, S. *The interpretation of dreams*. Standard Edition, Vol. 4, 1900.

Freud, S. *Three essays on sexuality*. Standard Edition, 1905, Vol. 7, 135-248.

Freud, S. *The problem of anxiety* (1926). Translated by H. A. Bunker. New York: Norton, 1936.

Freud, S. *The standard edition of the complete psychological works of Sigmund Freud*. Translated by James Strachey. London: Hogarth Press, 1953-1957.

Fromm, E. *Man for himself*. New York: Rinehart, 1947.

Fromm, E. *The sane society*. New York: Holt, Rinehart, & Winston, 1955.

Fromm-Reichmann, F. *Principles of intensive psychotherapy*. Chicago: University of Chicago Press, 1950.

Galinsky, M. D., & Fast, I. Vocational choices as a focus of the identity search. *Journal of Counseling Psychology*, 1966, *13*, 89-92.

Gazda, G. M. *Human relations development: A manual for educators*. Boston: Allyn & Bacon, 1973.

Gendlin, E. T. *Experiencing and the creation of meaning*. New York: Free Press of Glencoe, 1962.

Gerken, C. Who directs NDEA counseling institutes? II. *Counseling News and Views*, 1966, *18*(1), 6.

Gilbert, W. M. Counseling: Therapy and diagnosis. *Annual Review of Psychology*, 1952, *3*, 351-380.

Ginzberg, E. Z. The development of a developmental theory of occupational choice. In W. H. Van Hoose & J. J. Pietrofesa (Eds.), *Counseling and guidance in the twentieth century*. Boston, MA: Houghton Mifflin, 1970.

Ginzberg, E. Z. *Career guidance: Who needs it, who provides it, who can improve it*. New York: McGraw-Hill, 1971.

Ginzberg, E. Z. Toward a theory of occupational choice: A restatement. *Vocational Guidance Quarterly*, 1972, *20*(3), 169-176.

Ginzberg, E. Z. Career development. In D. Brown & L. Brooks (Eds.), *Career choice and development: Applying contemporary theories to practice*. San Francisco: Jossey-Bass, 1984.

Ginzberg, E. Z., Ginsburg, S. W., Axelrad, S., & Herma, J. L. *Occupational choice*. New York: Columbia University Press, 1951.

Gluck, S. A proposed code of ethics for counselors. *Occupations*, 1952, *30*, 484-490.

Goldfried, M. R., & Davidson, G. C. *Clinical behavior therapy*. New York: Holt, Rinehart, & Winston, 1976.

Goldman, L. The diplomate in counseling psychology. *Counseling News and Views*, 1967, *19*(3), 6-9.

Goldstein, A. P. *Therapist-patient expectancies in psychotherapy*. New York: Macmillan, 1962.

Goldstein, A. P. Psychotherapy research by extrapolation from social psychology. *Journal of Counseling Psychology*, 1966, *13*, 38-45.

Goldstein, A. Behavior therapy. In R. Corsini (Ed.), *Current psychotherapies*. Itasca, IL: Peacock, 1973, 207-249.

Goldstein, A., Heller, K., & Sechrist, L. *Psychotherapy and the psychology of behavior change*. New York: Wiley, 1966.

Goodstein, L. D., Bucheimer, A., Crites, J. O., & Muthard, J. H. *Report of the Ad Hoc Committee on the scientific status of counseling psychology*. APA Division 17, 1959. (Mimeographed)

Gordon, J. E. Project CAUSE, the federal anti-poverty program, and some implications of sub-professional training. *American Psychologist*, 1965, *20*, 334-336.

Gottfredson, L. S. Vocational research priorities. *The Counseling Psychologist*, 1982, *10*(2), 69-84.

Granger, S. G. Psychologists' prestige rankings of 20 psychological occupations. *Journal of Counseling Psychology*, 1959, *6*, 183-188.

Greenson, R. *The technique and practice of psychoanalysis*. New York: International Universities, 1967.

Grossman, D. A note of pessimism to start the year off! *Counseling News and Views*, 1961, *13*(2), 7-11.

Grummon, D. L. By their fruits ye shall know them. *Counseling News and Views*, 1958, *11*(1), 5-6.

Grunwald, B. The application of Adlerian principles in a classroom. *American Journal of Individual Psychology*, 1954, *11*, 131-141.

Grunwald, B. Strategies for behavior change in schools. *The Counseling Psychologist*, 1971, *3*(1), 55-57.

Guthrie, E. R. *The psychology of learning*. New York: Harper, 1935.

Hahn, M. E. Name of our division. *Newsletter*, 1949, *1*(2), 3.

Hahn, M. E. Conceptual trends in counseling. *Personnel and Guidance Journal*, 1953, *31*, 231-235.

Hahn, M. E. Report from the president. *Counseling News and Views*, 1954, *6*(3), 1.

Hahn, M. E. Counseling psychology. *American Psychologist*, 1955, *10*, 279-282. Also in J. M. Whiteley (Ed.), *The history of counseling psychology*. Monterey, CA: Brooks/Cole, 1980, 99-104.

Hahn, M. E., & Maclean, M. S. *General clinical counseling*. New York: McGraw-Hill, 1950.

Haigh, G. Defensive behavior in client-centered therapy. *Journal of Consulting Psychology*, 1949, *13*, 181-189.

Harmon, L. W. Scientific affairs-the next decade. *The Counseling Psychologist*, 1982, *10*(2), 31-37.

Harris, T. *I'm OK, you're OK*. New York: Harper & Row, 1969.

Hartmann, H. *Essays on ego psychology*. New York: International Press, 1964.

Hartmann, H. Ego psychology and the problem of adaptation. In D. Rapaport (Ed.), *Organization and pathology of thought*. New York: Columbia University Press, 1951.

Hatcher, C., & Himmelstein, P. (Eds.). *The handbook of Gestalt theory*. New York: Jason Aronson, 1976.

Heath, D. H. *Growing up in college*. San Francisco: Jossey-Bass, 1968.

Heidegger, M. *Sein und Zeit*. Tübingen: Max Niemeyer, 1960.

Hendrick, I. Work and the pleasure principle. *Psychoanalytic Quarterly*, 1943, *12*, 311-329.

Heron, A. A. A psychological study of occupational adjustment. *Journal of Applied Psychology*, 1952, *36*, 385-387.

Hilgard, E. R. Psychologists' preferences for divisions under the proposed APA by-laws. *Psychological Bulletin*, 1945, *42*, 20-26.

Hill, C. E., & Gronsky, B. R. Research: Why and how? In J. M. Whiteley, N. Kagan, L. Harmon, B. R. Fretz, & F. Tanney (Eds.), *The coming decade in counseling psychology*. Schenectady, NY: Character Research Press, 1984.

Hobbs, N., & Seeman, J. Counseling. *Annual Review of Psychology*, 1955, *6*, 379-404.

Hoffman, A. E. A study of reported behavior changes in counseling. *Journal of Consulting Psychology*, 1949, *13*, 190-195.

Holder, T., Carkhuff, R. R., & Berenson, B. G. Differential effects of the manipulation of therapeutic conditions upon high- and low-functioning clients. *Journal of Counseling Psychology*, 1967, *14*, 63-66.

Holland, J. L. A personality inventory employing occupational titles. *Journal of Applied Psychology*, 1958, *42*, 336-342.

Holland, J. L. A theory of vocational choice. *Journal of Counseling Psychology*, 1959, *6*, 35-45.

Holland, J. L. *The psychology of vocational choice*. Waltham, MA: Blaisdell, 1966.

Holland, J. L. *The self-directed search*. Palo Alto, CA: Consulting Psychologists Press, 1970.

Holland, J. L. A theory-ridden, computerless, vocational guidance system. *Journal of Vocational Behavior*, 1971, *1*(2), 167-176.

Holland, J. L. *Making vocational choices: A theory of careers*. Englewood Cliffs, NJ: Prentice Hall, 1973. (a)

Holland, J. L. The development and current status of an occupational classification. Paper presented at American Personnel and Guidance Association Convention, San Diego, CA, February, 1973. (b)

Holland, J. L. Vocational guidance for everyone. *Educational Research*, 1974, *3*, 9-15.

Holland, J. L. The use and evaluation of interest inventories and simulations. In E. E. Diamond, (Ed.), *Issues of sex bias and sex fairness in career interest measurement*. Washington, DC: U.S. Government Printing Office, 1975.

Holland, J. L. Planning for alternative futures. *The Counseling Psychologist*, 1982, *10*(2), 7-13.

Holland, J. L., & Gottfredson, G. D. *Applying a typology to vocational aspirations*. Center for Social Organization of Schools, Report No. 176. Baltimore, MD: Johns Hopkins University, June, 1974.

Holland, J. L., & Gottfredson, G. D. Using a typology of persons and environments to explain careers: Some extensions and clarifications. *The Counseling Psychologist*, 1976, *6*(3), 20-29.

Holland, J. L., Magoon, T. M., & Spokane, A. R. Counseling psychology: Career interventions research and theory. *Annual Review of Psychology*, 1981, *32*, 279-305.

Holland, J. L., & Others. *An empirical occupational classification derived from a theory of personality and intended for practice and research*. American College Testing Research, Report No. 29. Iowa City, IA: American College Testing Program, 1969.

Holland, J. L., & Others. *A guide to the self-directed career program: A practical and inexpensive vocational guidance system.* Center for Social Organization of Schools, Report No. 126. Baltimore, MD: Johns Hopkins University, 1972.

Holland, J. L., & Others. *The vocational exploration and insight kit (VEIK).* Palo Alto, CA: Consulting Psychologists Press, 1980.

Hoppock, R. *Occupational information.* New York: McGraw-Hill, 1957.

Hosford, R. E. Behavioral counseling—a contemporary overview. *The Counseling Psychologist*, 1969, *1*(4), 1-33.

Hosford, R. E. *A behavioral counseling training curriculum.* Eight-part film series and book. Washington, DC: American Personnel and Guidance Association, 1974.

Hosford, R. E., & Briskin, A. S. Changes through counseling. *Review of Educational Research*, 1969, *39*, 189-207.

Hosford, R. E., & de Visser, L. *Behavioral approaches to counseling.* Washington, DC: APGA Press, 1974.

Hull, C. L. *Aptitude testing.* New York: World Book, 1928.

Hull, C. L. *Principles of behavior.* New York: Appleton-Century-Crofts, 1943.

Husserl, E. *Ideen zu einer reinen phanomenologie und phanomenologichen philosophie.* Haag: Martinus Nijhoff, 1950.

Huston, P. E. The relations of psychiatry and psychology. *American Journal of Psychiatry*, 1954, *110*, 814-816.

Ivey, A. *Microcounseling.* Springfield, IL: Thomas, 1971.

Ivey, A. Counseling psychology, the psychoeducator model and the future. *The Counseling Psychologist*, 1976, *6*(3), 72-75. Also in J. M. Whiteley (Ed.), *The history of counseling psycholgy.* Monterey, CA: Brooks/Cole, 1980, 196-204.

Jacobs, D. F. Subcommittee on sources of research support. *Counseling News and Views*, 1961, *13*(2), 15.

Jacobson, E. *Progressive relaxation.* Chicago: University of Chicago Press, 1938.

James, M., & Jongeward, D. *Born to win.* Reading, MA: Addison-Wesley, 1971.

Johnson, W. F. From the Editor. *Counseling News and Views*, 1955, *7*(2), 1.

Jones, E. *The life and work of Sigmund Freud.* New York: Basic Books, 1953.

Jordaan, J. P., Myers, R. A., Layton, W. C., & Morgan, H. H. *The Counseling Psychologist.* Washington, DC: American Psychological Association, 1968. Also in J. M. Whiteley (Ed.), *The history of counseling psychology.* Monterey, CA: Brooks/Cole, 1980, 179-195.

Jourard, S. M. *The transparent self.* Princeton, NJ: Van Nostrand, 1964.

Jung, C. G. *Symbols of transformation.* (1911) Collected works, Vol. 5, Bollingen Series XX. Princeton, NJ: Princeton University Press, 1967.

Jung, C. G. *The archetypes and the collective unconscious.* (1943) Collected works Vol. 9, Part I. Bollingen Series XX. Princeton, NJ: Princeton University Press, 1968.

Kagan, N. *Influencing human interaction* (a filmed six-hour mental health training series and an accompanying 186-page instructor's manual). East Lansing, MI: Instructional Media Center, Michigan State University, 1971.

Kagan, N. *Influencing human interaction in schools. Unit I, Elements of facilitating communication.* Washington, DC: American Personnel and Guidance Association, 1974.

Kagan, N. Guest editor's introduction. *The Counseling Psychologist*, 1982, *10*(2), 4-5.

Kagan, N., & Krathwohl, D. R. *Studies in human interaction.* East Lansing, MI: Educational Publication Service, 1967.

Kagan, N., Krathwohl, D. R., & Miller, R. Stimulated recall in therapy using videotape—a case study. *Journal of Counseling Psychology*, 1963, *10*, 237-243.

Kagan, N., & Schauble, P. G. Affect simulation in interpersonal process recall. *Journal of Counseling Psychology*, 1969, *16*, 309-313.

Kagan, N., Schauble, P. G., Resnikoff, A., Danish, S. J., & Krathwohl, D. R. Interpersonal process recall. *Journal of Nervous & Mental Diseases*, 1969, *148*, 365-374.

Kanfer, F. H., & Goldstein, A. P. (Eds.). *Helping people change.* New York: Pergamon Press, 1975.

Kanfer, F. H., & Phillips, J. S. *Learning foundations of behavior therapy.* New York: Wiley, 1970.

Katz, J. (Ed.). *Growth and constraint in college students.* Stanford, CA: Institute for the Study of Human Problems, Stanford University, 1967.

Kelley, J., Smits, S. J., Leventhal, R., & Rhodes, R. Critique of the designs of process and outcome research. *Journal of Counseling Psychology*, 1970, *17*, 337-341.

Kelly, G. A. *The psychology of personal constructs.* New York: Norton, 1955.

Kempler, W. *Principles of Gestalt family therapy.* Costa Mesa, CA: Kempler Institute, 1974.

Keniston, K. Post-adolescence (youth) and historical change. In J. Zubin & A. Freedman, (Eds.), *Psychopathy of adolescence.* New York: Grune & Stratton, 1970, 34-50.

Kessler, M., & Albee, G. W. Primary prevention. *Annual Review of Psychology*, 1975, *26*, 557-591.

Krasner, L. The therapist as a reinforcement machine. In H. H. Strupp & L. Luborsky (Eds.), *Research in psychotherapy, II.* Washington, DC: American Psychological Association, 1962, 61-94.

Krasner, L. Reinforcement, verbal behavior and psychotherapy. *American Journal of Orthopsychiatry*, 1963, *33*, 601-613.

Krasner, L. Verbal conditioning and psychotherapy. In L. Krasner & L. P. Ullmann (Eds.), *Research in behavioral modification: New developments and implications.* New York: Holt, Rinehart, & Winston, 1965, 211-228.

Krumboltz, J. D. Behavioral counseling: Rationale and research. *Personnel and Guidance Journal*, 1965, *44*, 383-387.

Krumboltz, J. D. Behavioral goals for counseling. *Journal of Counseling Psychology*, 1966, *13*, 153-159. (a)

Krumboltz, J. D. (Ed.). *Revolution in counseling: Implications of behavioral science.* Boston: Houghton Mifflin, 1966. (b)

Krumboltz, J. D. A social learning theory of career decision-making. In A. Mitchell, G. Jones, & J. Krumboltz (Eds.), *Social learning and career decision making.* Cranston, RI: Carroll, 1979, 19-49.

Krumboltz, J. D., Becker-Haven, J. F., & Burnett, K. F. Counseling psychology. *Annual Review of Psychology*, 1979, *30*, 555-602.

Krumboltz, J. D., Mitchell, A. M., & Jones, G. R. A social learning theory of career selection. *The Counseling Psychologist*, 1976, *6*(1), 71-81.

Krumboltz, J. D., & Thoresen, C. E. The effect of behavioral counseling in group and individual settings on information seeking behavior. *Journal of Counseling Psychology*, 1964, *11*, 321-333.

Krumboltz, J. D., & Thoresen, C. E. *Behavioral counseling: Cases and techniques.* New York: Holt, Rinehart, & Winston, 1969.

Krumboltz, J. D., & Thoresen, C. E. (Eds.). *Counseling methods.* New York: Holt, Rinehart, & Winston, 1976.

Layton, W. L., Sandeen, C. A., & Baker, R. D. Student development and counseling. *Annual Review of Psychology*, 1971, *22*, 533-560.

Lazarus, A. A. Behavior therapy in groups. In G. M. Gazda (Ed.), *Basic approaches to group therapy and group counseling.* Springfield, IL: Thomas, 1968.

Lazarus, A. A. *Behavior therapy and beyond.* New York: McGraw-Hill, 1971.

Leitenberg, H. (Ed.). *Handbook of behavior modification and behavior therapy.* Englewood Cliffs, NJ: Prentice Hall, 1976.

Lindzey, G. Thematic apperception test: Interpretive assumptions and related empirical evidence. *Psychological Bulletin*, 1952, *49*, 1-25.

Lofquist, L. H., & Dawis, R. V. *Adjustment to work.* Englewood Cliffs, NJ: Prentice Hall, 1969.

Lofquist, L. H., & Dawis, R. V. Application of the theory of work adjustment to rehabilitation and counseling. *Minnesota studies in vocational rehabilitation (No. 48).* Minneapolis: University of Minnesota Industrial Relations Center, 1972.

Lofquist, L. H., & Dawis, R. V. Vocational needs, work reinforcers, and job satisfaction. *Vocational Guidance Quarterly*, 1975, *24*, 132-139.

Lofquist, L. H., & Dawis, R. V. Values as secondary to needs in the theory of work adjustment. *Journal of Vocational Behavior*, 1978, *12*, 12-19.

London, P. *The modes and morals of psychotherapy*. New York: Holt, Rinehart, & Winston, 1964.

Magoon, T. M. Personal communication, June 1980. In D. G. Zytowski & D. A. Rosen. The grand tour: 30 years of counseling psychology in the *Annual Review of Psychology*. *The Counseling Psychologist*, 1982, *10*(1), 69-79.

Mahoney, M. J. *Cognition and behavior modification*. Cambridge: Ballinger, 1974.

Mahoney, M. J., & Thoresen, C. E. *Self control: Power to the person*. Monterey, CA: Brooks/Cole, 1974.

Malnig, L. R. Fear of paternal competition: A factor in vocational choice. *Personnel and Guidance Journal*, 1967, *46*, 235-239.

Martire, J. G. Identification in the counseling process. *Journal of Counseling Psychology*, 1955, *2*, 91-95.

Maslow, A. H. *Motivation and personality*. New York: Harper, 1954.

Maslow, A. H. Holistic emphasis. *Journal of Individual Psychology*, 1970, *26*, 39.

Maultsby, M. C., Jr., & Ellis, A. *Technique for using rational-emotive imagery*. New York: Institute for Rational Living, 1974.

May, R. *The art of counseling: How to give and gain mental health*. Nashville: Abingdon-Cokesbury, 1939.

May, R. *The meaning of anxiety*. New York: Ronald Press, 1950.

May, R. *Existential psychology*. New York: Random House, 1961.

May, R. *Psychology and the human dilemma*. New York: Van Nostrand Reinhold, 1967.

May, R. *Love and will*. New York: Norton, 1969.

May, R. *Power and innocence: A search for the sources of violence*. New York: Norton, 1972.

May, R., Angel, E., & Ellenberger, H. F. (Eds.). *Existence*. New York: Simon & Schuster, 1958.

Mayhew, L. B. *Legacy of the seventies*. San Francisco, CA: Jossey-Bass, 1977.

McArthur, C. Analyzing the clinical process. *Journal of Counseling Psychology*, 1954, *1*, 203-207.

McConn, M. Educational guidance is now possible. *Educational Record*, 1935, *16*, 375-411.

McFall, R. M., & Lillesand, D. B. Behavior rehearsal with modeling and coaching in assertion training. *Journal of Abnormal Psychology*, 1971, *77*, 313-323.

McGowan, J. F. In C. G. Wrenn, Conference on preparation and employment of counselors. *Counseling News and Views*, 1965, *17*(1), 7.

Meador, B., & Rogers, C. Client-centered therapy. In R. Corsini, (Ed.), *Current psychotherapies*. Itasca, IL: Peacock, 1973, 119-165.

Meehl, P. E. *Clinical vs. statistical prediction*. Minneapolis, MN: University Press, 1954.

Meehl, P. E. Law and the fireside inductions: Some reflections of a clinical psychologist. *Journal of Social Issues*, 1971, *27*(9), 65-100.

Mehrabian, A. *Tactics of social influence.* Englewood Cliffs, NJ: Prentice-Hall, 1970.

Meichenbaum, D. *Cognitive factors in behavior modification: Modifying what clients say to themselves.* Research Report No. 25. Waterloo: University of Waterloo, 1971.

Meichenbaum, D. *Therapist manual for cognitive behavior modification.* Waterloo: University of Waterloo, 1974.

Meltzoff, J. Effectiveness of psychotherapy is amply demonstrated. *International Journal of Psychiatry*, 1969, *7*, 149-152.

Meltzoff, J., & Kornreich, M. *Research in psychotherapy.* New York: Atherton, 1970.

Mermin, D. Gestalt theory of emotion. *The Counseling Psychologist*, 1974, *4*(4), 15-20.

Miller, C. H. *Foundations of guidance.* New York: Harper & Row, 1961.

Mitchell, A., & Krumboltz, J. D. Social learning approach to career decision making: Krumboltz's theory. In D. Brown & L. Brooks, (Eds.), *Career choice and development: Applying contemporary theories to practice.* San Francisco: Jossey-Bass, 1984.

Morris, K., & Kanitz, J. *Rational-emotive therapy.* Boston: Houghton Mifflin, 1975.

Mosak, H. H. Life style assessment: A demonstration based on family constellations. *Journal of Individual Psychology*, 1972, *28*, 232-247.

Mosak, H., & Dreikurs, R. Adlerian psychotherapy. In R. Corsini, (Ed.), *Current psychotherapies.* Itasca, IL: Peacock, 1973, 35-83.

Mosher, R. L., & Sprinthall, N. A. Psychological education in the secondary schools: A program to promote individual and human development. *American Psychologist*, 1970, *25*, 911-924.

Mosher, R. L., & Sprinthall, N. A. Psychological education: A means to promote personal development during adolescence. *The Counseling Psychologist*, 1971, *2*(4), 3-82.

Moustakas, C. E. (Ed.). *The self: Explorations in personal growth.* New York: Harper, 1956.

Mowrer, O. H. *Learning theory and personality dynamics.* New York: Ronald Press, 1950.

Mowrer, O. H. *Psychotherapy: Theory and research.* New York: Ronald Press, 1953.

Murphy, G. The cultural context of guidance. *Personnel and Guidance Journal*, 1955, *34*, 4-9.

Murphy, L. B., & Frank, C. Prevention: The clinical psychologist. *Annual Review of Psychology*, 1979, *30*, 173-207.

Muthard, J. E. Scientific status of counseling psychology. *Counseling News and Views*, 1961, *13*(2), 14.

Myers, R. A. Research in counseling psychology-1964. *Journal of Counseling Psychology*, 1966, *12*, 371- 379.

Myers, R. A. Education and training-the next decade. *The Counseling Psychologist*, 1982, *10*(2), 39-44.

Nachmann, B. Childhood experiences and vocational choice in law, dentistry, and social work. *Journal of Counseling Psychology*, 1960, *7*, 243-250.

Nachmann, B. Cross currents in the occupational evolution of religion careers. In W. E. Bartlett (Ed.), *Evolving religious careers*. Washington, DC: Center for Applied Research in the Apostolate, 1970.

Naranjo, C. *The techniques of Gestalt therapy*. Berkeley: SAT Press, 1973.

Needleman, S. D. Helping the patients' occupational reintegration. *Personnel and Guidance Journal*, 1955, *33*, 448-450.

Neff, W. S. *Work and human behavior*. New York: Atherton, 1968.

Newcomb, T. N., & Feldman, K. A. *The impact of college on students*. San Francisco: Jossey-Bass, 1969.

Oetting, E. R. Developmental definition of counseling psychology. *Journal of Counseling Psychology*, 1967, *14*(4), 382-385.

O'Hara, R. P. Comment on Super's papers. *The Counseling Psychologist*, 1969, *1*(1), 17-19.

Orgler, H. *Alfred Adler: The man and his work*. New York: Capricorn Books, 1965.

Osipow, S. H. *Theories of Career Development*. New York: Appleton Century Croft, 1973.

Osipow, S. H. Task force on scientific needs: Research needs for the '80s. In J. M. Whiteley, N. Kagan, L. W. Harmon, B. R. Fretz, & F. Tanney (Eds.), *The coming decade in counseling psychology*. Schenectady, NY: Character Research Press, 1984.

Parham, W., & Moreland, J. R. Nonwhite students in counseling psychology: A closer look. *Professional Psychology*, 1981, *12*(4), 499-507.

Parsons, F. *Choosing a vocation*. Boston: Houghton Mifflin, 1909.

Paterson, D. G., & Darley, J. G. *Men, women, and jobs*. Minneapolis, MN: University of Minnesota Press, 1936.

Paterson, D. G., Elliott, R. M., Anderson, L. D., Toops, H. A., & Heidbreder, E. *Minnesota occupational rating scales and counseling profile*. Chicago: Science Research Associates, 1941.

Paterson, D. G., Gerken, C. d'A., & Hahn, M. E. *The Minnesota Occupational Rating Scales*. Chicago: Science Research Associates, 1941.

Paterson, D. G., Gerken, C. d'A., & Hahn, M. E. *Revised Minnesota Occupational Rating Scales*. Minneapolis: University of Minnesota Press, 1953.

Paterson, D. G., & Lofquist, L. H. A note on the training of clinical and counseling psychologists. *American Psychologist*, 1960, *15*, 365-366.

Patterson, C. H. Counseling. *Annual Review of Psychology*, 1966, *17*, 79-110.

Paul, G. L. *Insights vs. desensitization in psychotherapy: An experiment in anxiety reduction.* Stanford, CA: Stanford University Press, 1966.

Pavlov, I. P. *Conditioned reflexes.* Trans. by G. V. Anrep. London: Oxford University Press, 1927.

Pepinsky, H. B. Counseling methods: Therapy. *Annual Review of Psychology*, 1951, *2*, 317-333.

Pepinsky, H. B. Report of the research committee. *Counseling News and Views*, 1952, *5*(1), 9-10.

Pepinsky, H. B. Some proposals for research. *Personnel and Guidance Journal*, 1953, *31*, 291-294.

Pepinsky, H. B. A history of counseling psychology. In R. Corsini (Ed.), *Encyclopedia of psychology.* New York: Wiley, 1984, in press.

Pepinsky, H. B., Hill-Frederick, K., & Epperson, D. L. The *Journal of Counseling Psychology* as a matter of policies. *Journal of Counseling Psychology*, 1978, *25*, 483-498. Also in J. M. Whiteley (Ed.), *The history of counseling psychology.* Monterey, CA: Brooks/Cole, 1980, 47-69.

Pepinsky, H. B., & Meara, N. M. Student development and counseling. *Annual Review of Psychology*, 1973, *24*, 117-144.

Pepinsky, H. B., & Pepinsky, P. *Counseling theory and practice.* New York: Ronald Press, 1954.

Perls, F. S. *Gestalt therapy verbatim.* Moab, UT: Real People Press, 1969. (a)

Perls, F. S. *In and out the garbage pail.* Lafayette, CA: Real People Press, 1969. (b)

Perls, F. S., Hefferline, R. F., & Goodman, P. *Gestalt therapy.* New York: Julian Press, 1951.

Perry, W. G. The findings of the Commission in Counseling and Guidance. *Annals of the New York Academy of Science*, 1955, *63*, 396-407.

Pew, W. Lifestyle of Alfred Adler. Paper presented to the American Society of Adlerian Psychology, Houston, TX, May 28, 1972.

Piaget, J. *The moral judgment of the child.* New York: Harcourt, 1932.

Polster, E., & Polster, M. *Gestalt therapy integrated.* New York: Brunner/Mazel, 1973.

Porter, E. H. *An introduction to therapeutic counseling.* Boston: Houghton Mifflin, 1950.

Porter, T. L., & Cook, T. E. A comparison of students and professional prestige rankings of jobs in psychology. *Journal of Counseling Psychology*, 1964, *11*(4), 385-387.

Pursglove, P. D. (Ed.). *Recognitions in Gestalt therapy.* New York: Funk & Wagnalls, 1968.

Rachman, S. J., & Teasdale, J. *Aversion therapy and behavior disorders: An analysis.* London: Routledge & Kegan Paul, 1969.

Rapaport, D. *Collected papers*. New York: Basic Books, 1967.

Raskin, N. J. An analysis of six parallel studies of the therapeutic process. *Journal of Consulting Psychology*, 1949, *13*, 206-220. (a)

Raskin, N. J. The development of the "Parallel Studies" Project. *Journal of Consulting Psychology*, 1949, *13*, 154-156. (b)

Resnick, H. The counseling psychologist in community mental health centers and health maintenance organizations—Do we belong? In J. M. Whiteley, N. Kagan, L. W. Harmon, B. R. Fretz, & F. Tanney, (Eds.), *The coming decade in counseling psychology*. Schenectady, NY: Character Research Press, 1984.

Resnikoff, A., Kagan, N., & Schauble, P. G. Acceleration of psychotherapy through stimulated videotape recall. *American Journal of Psychotherapy*, 1970, *24*, 102-111.

Rest, J. R. Developmental psychology as a guide to value education: A review of 'Kohlbergian' programs. *Review of Educational Research*, 1974, *44*(2), 241-259.

Rhyne, J. *The Gestalt art experience*. Monterey, CA: Brooks/Cole, 1973.

Riesman, D. *Abundance for what? And other essays*. Garden City, NY: Double-day, 1964.

Robinson, F. P. *Principles and procedures in student counseling*. New York: Harper, 1950.

Robinson, F. P. Letter to colleagues. *Counseling News and Views*, 1955, *7*(2), 5.

Robinson, F. P. Counseling psychology since the Northwestern Conference. In A. S. Thompson & D. E. Super (Eds.), *The professional preparation of counseling psychologists*. New York: Bureau of Publications, Teachers College, Columbia University, 1964, 35-41. Also in J. M. Whiteley (Ed.), *The history of counseling psychology*. Monterey, CA: Brooks/Cole, 1980, 136-142.

Roe, A. A new classification of occupations. *Journal of Counseling Psychology*, 1954, *1*(4), 215-220.

Roe, A. *The psychology of occupations*. New York: Wiley, 1956.

Roe, A. Early determinants of vocational choice. *Journal of Counseling Psychology*, 1957, *4*, 212-217.

Roe, A. Cross classification of occupations. 1966.(Mimeo)

Roe, A. Perspectives on vocational development. In J. M. Whiteley & A. Resnikoff (Eds.), *Perspectives on vocational development*. Washington, DC: American Personnel and Guidance Association, 1972.

Roe, A. *Classification of occupations by group and level*. Bensenville, IL: Scholastic Testing Service, 1976.

Roe, A. Personality development and career choice. In D. Brown & L. Brooks (Eds.), *Career choice and development: Applying contemporary theories to practice*. San Francisco: Jossey-Bass, 1984.

Roe, A., & Baruch, R. Occupational changes in the adult years. *Personnel Administration*, 1967, *30*(4), 26-32.

Roe, A., Bateman, T., Hubbard, W. D., & Hutchinson, T. Studies of occupational history. Part I: Job changes and the classification of occupations. *Journal of Counseling Psychology*, 1966, *13*, 387-393.

Roe, A., Gustad, J. M., Moore, B. V., Ross, S., & Skodak, M. (Eds.). *Graduate education in psychology*. Report of the Conference on Graduate Education in Psychology at Miami Beach, FL. Washington, DC: American Psychological Association, 1959.

Roe, A., & Klos, D. Classification of occupations. In J. M. Whiteley & A. Resnikoff (Eds.), *Perspectives on vocational development*. Washington, DC: American Personnel and Guidance Association, 1972.

Roe, A., & Siegelman, M. A parent-child relations questionnaire. *Child Development*, 1963, *34*, 355-369.

Roe, A., & Siegelman, M. The origin of interests. *The APGA inquiry series, No. 1*. Washington, DC: American Personnel and Guidance Association, 1964.

Rogers, C. R. *Counseling and psychotherapy*. Boston: Houghton Mifflin, 1942. (a)

Rogers, C. R. The use of electrically recorded interviews in improving psychotherapeutic techniques. *American Journal of Orthopsychiatry*. 1942, *12*, 429-434. (b)

Rogers, C. R. The nondirective method as a technique for social research. *American Journal of Sociology*, 1945, *50*, 279-283.

Rogers, C. R. Significant aspects of client-centered therapy. *American Psychologist*, 1946, *1*, 415-422.

Rogers, C. R. *Dealing with social tension: A presentation of client-centered counseling as a method of handling interpersonal conflict*. New York: Hinds, Hayden, and Eldredge, 1948.

Rogers, C. R. A coordinated research in psychotherapy, a non-objective introduction. *Journal of Consulting Psychology*, 1949, *13*, 149-153.

Rogers, C. R. *Client-centered therapy*. Boston: Houghton Mifflin, 1951. (a)

Rogers, C. R. Perceptual reorganization in client-centered therapy. In R. R. Blake & G. V. Ramsey (Eds.), *Perception: An approach to personality*. New York: Ronald Press, 1951, 307-327. (b)

Rogers, C. R. Through the eyes of a client. *Pastoral Psychology*, 1951, *2*(16), 32-40; (7) 45-50; (18) 26-32. (c)

Rogers, C. R. Communication: Its blocking and facilitation. *Northwestern University Information*, 1952, *20*, 9-15.

Rogers, C. R. A research program in client-centered therapy. *Research Publication of the Association of Nervous & Mental Diseases*, 1953, *31*, 106-113.

Rogers, C. R. Becoming a person, Part I. *Pastoral Psychology*, 1956, *7*(61), 6-13. (a)

Rogers, C. R. Becoming a person, Part II. *Pastoral Psychology*, 1956, *7*(63), 16-26. (b)

Rogers, C. R. The necessary and sufficient conditions of therapeutic personality change. *Journal of Consulting Psychology*, 1957, *21*, 95-103. (a)

Rogers, C. R. Personal thoughts on teaching and learning. *Merrill-Palmer Quarterly*, Summer, 1957, *3*, 241-243. (b)

Rogers, C. R. The characteristics of a helping relationship. *Personnel and Guidance Journal*, 1958, *37*, 6-16. (a)

Rogers, C. R. A process conception of psychotherapy. *American Psychologist*, 1958, *13*, 142-149. (b)

Rogers, C. R. A theory of therapy, personality, and interpersonal relationships, as developed in the client-centered framework. In S. Koch (Ed.), *Psychology: A study of a science, Vol. III. Formulations of the person and the social context.* New York: McGraw-Hill, 1959, 184-256.

Rogers, C. R. Significant trends in the client-centered orientation. In D. Brower & L. E. Abt (Eds.), *Progress in clinical psychology. Vol. IV.* New York: Grune & Stratton, 1960, 85-99.

Rogers, C. R. *On becoming a person: A therapist's view of psychotherapy.* Boston: Houghton Mifflin, 1961. (a)

Rogers, C. R. Two divergent trends. In R. May (Ed.), *Existential psychology.* New York: Random House, 1961, 85-93. (b)

Rogers, C. R. The concept of the fully functioning person. *Psychotherapy: Theory, Research and Practice*, 1963, *1*(1), 17-26.

Rogers, C. R. Toward a science of the person. In T. W. Wann (Ed.), *Behaviorism and phenomenology.* Chicago: University of Chicago Press, 1964, 109-140.

Rogers, C. R. A humanistic conception of man. In R. E. Farson (Ed.), *Science and human affairs.* Palo Alto, CA: Science and Behavior Books, 1965, 18-31.

Rogers, C. R. Graduate education in psychology: A passionate statement. *The Clinical Psychologist*, 1967, *20*, 55-62. (a)

Rogers, C. R. The process of the basic encounter group. In J. F. T. Brugental (Ed.), *The challenges of humanistic psychology.* New York: McGraw-Hill, 1967, 261-278. (b)

Rogers, C. R. A practical plan for educational revolution. In R. R. Goulet (Ed.), *Educational change: The reality and the promise.* New York: Citation Press, 1968, 120-135.

Rogers, C. R. Being in a relationship. In C. R. Rogers, *Freedom to learn: A view of what education might become.* Columbus, OH: Charles E. Merrill, 1969. (a)

Rogers, C. R. *Freedom to learn: A view of what education might become.* Columbus, OH: Charles E. Merrill, 1969. (b)

Rogers, C. R. *The person of tomorrow.* Sonoma State College Pamphlet, 1969. (c)

Rogers, C. R. *Carl Rogers on encounter groups.* New York: Harper & Row, 1971.

Rogers, C. R. *On becoming partners: Marriage and its alternatives.* New York: Delacourt, 1972.

Rogers, C. R. My philosophy of interpersonal relationships and how it grew. *Journal of Humanistic Psychology,* 1973, *13*(2), 3-15.

Rogers, C. R. Empathic: An unappreciated way of being. *The Counseling Psychologist,* 1975, *5*(2), 2-10.

Rogers, C. R. *A way of being.* Boston, MA: Houghton Mifflin, 1980.

Rogers, C. R., & Dymond, R. F. (Eds.). *Psychotherapy and personality change.* Chicago, IL: University of Chicago Press, 1954.

Rosenblatt, D. *Opening doors: What happens in Gestalt therapy.* New York: Harper & Row, 1975.

Rosenzweig, S. A transvaluation of psychotherapy-a reply to Hans Eysenck. *Journal of Abnormal and Social Psychology.* 1954, *49,* 298-304.

Ruitenbeek, H. *Psychoanalysis and existential philosophy.* New York: Dutton, 1962.

Ryan, T. A., & Krumboltz, J. D. Effect of planned reinforcement counseling in client decision-making behavior. *Journal of Counseling Psychology,* 1964, *11,* 315-323.

Salinger, M. D., Tollefson, A. L., & Hudson, R. I. The catalytic function of the counselor. *Personnel and Guidance Journal,* 1960, *38,* 648-652.

Salter, A. *Conditioned-reflex therapy.* New York: Creative Age, 1949.

Samler, J. Washington news and views. *Counseling News and Views,* 1954, *6*(2), 3.

Samler, J. An examination of client strength and counselor responsibility. *Journal of Counseling Psychology,* 1962, *9,* 5-11.

Samler, J. Where do counseling psychologists work? What do they do, what should they do? In A. S. Thompson & D. E. Super (Eds.), *The professional preparation of counseling psychologists.* New York: Bureau of Publications, Teachers College, Columbia University, 1964, 43-67. Also in J. M. Whiteley (Ed.), *The history of counseling psychology.* Monterey, CA: Brooks/Cole, 1980, 143-167.

Sanford, F. H. Creative health and the principles of Habeas Mentem. *American Psychologist,* 1955, *10,* 829-835.

Sanford, N. Personality development during the college years. *Journal of Social Issues,* 1956, *12*(4), 74-80.

Sanford, N. (Ed.). *The American college.* New York: Wiley, 1962.

Schiff, J. Reparenting schizophrenics. *Transactional Analysis Bulletin,* 1969, *8,* 47-62.

Schmidt, L. D., & Pepinsky, H. B. Counseling research in 1963. *Journal of Counseling Psychology,* 1965, *12,* 418-427.

Schneidman, E. S. *Thematic test analysis.* New York: Grune & Stratton, 1951.

Schwebel, M. From past to present: Counseling psychology's socially prescribed role. In J. M. Whiteley, N. Kagan, L. W. Harmon, B. R. Fretz, & F. Tanney, (Eds.), *The coming decade in counseling psychology.* Schenectady, NY: Character Research Press, 1984.

Scott, C. W. Committee on Divisional History. *Counseling News and Views,* 1956, *8*(3), 10-11.

Scott, C. W. History of the Division of Counseling Psychology: 1945-1963. In J. M. Whiteley (Ed.), *The history of counseling psychology.* Monterey, CA: Brooks/Cole, 1980, 25-40.

Scott, T. B., Dawis, R. V., England, G. W., & Lofquist, L. G. A definition of work adjustment. *Minnesota Studies in Vocational Rehabilititation,* X, 1960.

Scott, W. S. Characteristics of Division 17 members. *Counseling News and Views,* 1950, *3*(1), 9-14.

Seashore, H. Message from the president. *Counseling News and Views,* 1960, *13*(1), 1-2.

Seeman, J. A study of the process of nondirective therapy. *Journal of Consulting Psychology,* 1949, *13*, 157-168.

Seeman, J. Editorial comment on normality for counselors. *Journal of Counseling Psychology,* 1959, *6*, 2.

Seeman, J., & Rankin, N. J. Research perspectives in client-centered therapy. In O. H. Mowrer (Ed.) *Psychotherapy: Theory, and research.* New York: Ronald Press, 1953.

Segal, S. J. A psychoanalytic analysis of personality factors in vocational choice. *Journal of Counseling Psychology,* 1961, *8*, 202-210.

Segal, S. J. Student development and counseling. *Annual Review of Psychology,* 1968, *19*, 497-508.

Segal, S. J., & Szabo, R. Identification in two vocations: Accountants and creative writers. *Personnel and Guidance Journal,* 1964, *43*, 252-255.

Sells, S. B. Problems of criteria and validity in diagnosis and therapy. *Journal of Clinical Psychology,* 1952, *8*, 23-29.

Severin, D. The predictability of various kinds of criteria. *Personnel Psychology,* 1952, *5*, 93-104.

Shartle, C. L. *Occupational information* (2nd ed.). New York: Prentice-Hall, 1952.

Shaw, F. J. Mutuality and up-ending expectancies in counseling. *Journal of Counseling Psychology,* 1955, *2*, 241-247.

Shaw, F. J. Counseling. *Annual Review of Psychology,* 1957, *8*, 357-376.

Sheerer, E. T. An analysis of the relationship between acceptance of and respect for self and acceptance of and respect for others in ten counseling cases. *Journal of Consulting Psychology,* 1949, *13*, 169-175.

Shoben, E. J., Jr. Some observations on psychotherapy and the learning process. In O. H. Mowrer, (Ed.), *Psychotherapy: Theory and research.* New York: Ronald Press, 1953, 120-139. (a)

Shoben, E. J., Jr. Some problems in establishing criteria of effectiveness. *Personnel and Guidance Journal,* 1953, *31,* 287-291. (b)

Shoben, E. J., Jr. Annual business meeting. *Counseling News and Views,* 1956, *9*(1), 4. (a)

Shoben, E. J., Jr. Counseling. *Annual Review of Psychology,* 1956, *7,* 147-172. (b)

Shoben, E. J., Jr. Message from the president. *Counseling News and Views,* 1958, *11*(1), 1-3.

Shoben, E. J., Jr. Message from the president. *Counseling News and Views,* 1959, *11*(2), 1-6.

Shoben, E. J., Jr. Policies of NIMH with respect to support for counseling psychology. *Counseling News and Views,* 1960, *13*(1), 5.

Siegelman, M., & Roe, A. *Manual, the parent-child relations questionnaire II,* 1979 (Available from the authors).

Skinner, B. F. *The behavior of organisms.* New York: Appleton-Century-Crofts, 1938.

Skinner, B. F. *Science and human behavior.* New York: Macmillan, 1953.

Skinner, B. F. Behaviorism at fifty. In T. W. Wann (Ed.), *Behaviorism and phenomenology.* Chicago, IL: University of Chicago Press, 1964.

Small, L. Personality determinants of vocational choice. *Psychological Monographs,* 1953, *67,* No. 1.

Smith, E. J. Counseling psychology in the marketplace: The status of ethnic minorities. *The Counseling Psychologist,* 1982, *10*(2), 61-68.

Snygg, D., & Combs, A. W. *Individual behavior.* New York: Harper, 1949.

Sommers, V. S. Vocational choice as an expression of conflict in identification. *American Journal of Psychotherapy,* 1956, *10,* 520-535.

Sostek, A. B. The relation of identification and parent-child climate to occupational choice. Unpublished dissertation, Boston University, 1963.

Spiegelberg, H. *Phenomenology in psychology and psychiatry: An historical introduction.* Evanston, IL: Northwestern University Press, 1972.

Steiner, C. *Games alcoholics play.* New York: Grove Press, 1970.

Steiner, C. *Scripts people live.* New York: Grove Press, 1971.

Steiner, L. R. *Where do people take their troubles?* New York: International Universities Press, 1945.

Stern, G. G. *People in context.* New York: Wiley, 1970.

Stevens, J. *Awareness.* Lafayette, CA: Real People Press, 1971.

Stock, D. An investigation into the interrelations between the self-concept and feelings directed toward other persons and groups. *Journal of Consulting Psychology*, 1949, *13*, 176-180.

Stone, D. R. Logical analysis of the directive, non-directive counseling continuum (1950). *Occupations*, 1950, *28*, 2959-2998.

Stotsky, B. A. Vocational counseling in a neuropsychiatric setting. *Journal of Counseling Psychology*, 1955, *2*, 103-107.

Strong, E. K., Jr. *Vocational interests of men and women.* Stanford, CA: Stanford University Press, 1943.

Strong, E. K., Jr. *Vocational interests 18 years after college.* Minneapolis, MN: University of Minnesota Press, 1955.

Strothers, C. R. *Psychology and mental health.* Washington, DC: American Psychological Association, 1957.

Strupp, H. H. The outcome problem in psychotherapy revisited. *Psychotherapy: Theory, Research, & Practice*, 1963, *1*, 1-13.

Strupp, H. H. The outcome problem in psychotherapy: A rejoinder. *Psychotherapy: Theory, Research, & Practice*, 1964, *1*, 101.

Stubbins, J., & Napoli, P. J. Vocational goals for the psychiatric patient. *Personnel and Guidance Journal*, 1955, *33*, 471-475.

Stuit, D. B. Counseling methods: Diagnostics. *Annual Review of Psychology*, 1951, *2*, 305-316.

Sullivan, H. S. *The interpersonal theory of psychiatry.* New York: Norton, 1953. (a)

Sullivan, H. S. *The conceptions of modern psychiatry.* New York: Norton, 1953. (b)

Super, D. E. Occupational level and job satisfaction. *Journal of Applied Psychology*, 1939, *25*, 547-564.

Super, D. E. *Avocational interest patterns: A study in the psychology of avocations.* Stanford, CA: Stanford University Press, 1940.

Super, D. E. *The dynamics of vocational adjustment.* New York: Harper, 1942.

Super, D. E. *Appraising vocational fitness.* New York: Harper, 1949.

Super, D. E. Vocational adjustment: Implementing a self-concept. *Occupations*, 1951, *30*, 88-92. (a)

Super, D. E. Why Division 17? *Counseling News and Views*, 1951, *4*(1), 3-4. (b)

Super, D. E. Of kith & kin. *Counseling News and Views*, 1952, *4*(2), 3-4. (a)

Super, D. E. On the ramparts, inside the workshops, and in the marketplace. *Counseling News and Views*, 1952, *4*(3), 3-5. (b)

Super, D. E. A theory of vocational development. *American Psychologist*, 1953, *8*, 185-190.

Super, D. E. Career patterns as a basis for vocational counseling. *Journal of Counseling Psychology*, 1954, *1*, 12-20.

206

Super, D. E. Transition: From vocational guidance to counseling psychology. *Journal of Counseling Psychology*, 1955, *2*, 3-9. (a)

Super, D. E. Dimensions and measurement of vocational maturity. *Teachers College Record*, 1955, *57*, 151-163. (b)

Super, D. E. Internships in college counseling centers. *Counseling News and Views*, 1956, *9*(1), 16-18.

Super, D. E. *The psychology of careers*. New York: Harper, 1957.

Super, D. E. A developmental approach to vocational guidance. *Vocational Guidance Quarterly*, 1964, *13*, 1-10.

Super, D. E. Vocational development theory. *The Counseling Psychologist*, 1969, *1*(1), 2-30.

Super, D. E. Vocational development theory: Persons, positions, processes. In J. M. Whiteley & A. Resnikoff (Eds.), *Perspectives on vocational guidance*. Washington, DC: American Personnel and Guidance Association, 1972.

Super, D. E. *Measuring vocational maturity for counseling and evaluation*. Washington, DC: American Personnel & Guidance Association, 1974.

Super, D. E. *Career education and the meanings of work*. Washington, DC: U.S. Government Printing Office, 1976.

Super, D. E. Career and life development. In D. Brown & L. Brooks (Eds.), *Career choice and development: Applying contemporary theories to practice*. San Francisco: Jossey-Bass, 1984. (a)

Super, D. E. 1951, 1984 and the 1990s. In J. M. Whiteley, N. Kagan, L. W. Harmon, B. R. Fretz, & F. Tanney (Eds.), *The coming decade in counseling psychology*. Schenectady, NY: Character Research Press, 1984. (b)

Super, D. E., & Bachrach, P. *Scientific careers and vocational development theory*. New York: Bureau of Publications, Teachers College, Columbia University, 1957.

Super, D. E., & Both, M. J., Jr. *Occupational psychology*. Monterey, CA: Brooks/Cole, 1970.

Super, D. E., Crites, J. O., Hummel, R. C., Moser, H. P., Overstreet, P. L., & Warnath, C. F. *Vocational development: A framework for research*. Career Pattern Study, Monograph 1. New York: Bureau of Publications, Teachers College, Columbia University, 1957.

Super, D. E., & Hall, D. T. Career development: Exploration and planning. *Annual Review of Psychology*, 1978, *29*, 333-372.

Super, D. E., Starishevsky, R., Matlin, N., & Jordaan, J. P. *Career development: Self-concept theory*. New York: College Entrance Examination Board, 1963.

Tanney, F. Counseling psychologists in private practice. *The Counseling Psychologist*, 1982, *10*(2), 15-19.

Thompson, A. S., & Super, D. E. (Eds.). *The professional preparation of counseling psychologists. Report of the 1964 Greyston Conference*. New York: Bureau of Publications, Teachers College, Columbia University, 1964.

Thoresen, C. E. Relevance and research in counseling. *Review of Educational Research*, 1969, *39*, 263-281.

Thoresen, C. E. (Ed.). Behavior modification in education. *72nd Yearbook of the National Society of Education*. Chicago: University of Chicago Press, 1973.

Thorndike, E. L. *The psychology of learning*. New York: Teachers College, 1913.

Thorndike, R. L., & Hagen, E. *Measurement and evaluation in psychology and education*. New York: Wiley, 1955.

Thorne, F. C. Directive psychotherapy: XV. Pressure and coercion. *Journal of Clinical Psychology*, 1948, *4*, 178-188.

Thorne, F. C. *Principles of personality counseling*. Brandon, VT: *Journal of Clinical Psychology*, 1950.

Thorne, F. C. Rules of evidence in the evaluation of the effects of psychotherapy. *Journal of Clinical Psychology*, 1952, *8*, 38-42.

Tiedeman, D. V. Decision and vocational development: A paradigm and its implications. *Personnel and Guidance Journal*, 1961, *40*, 15-21.

Tiedeman, D. V. Time for a division of guidance psychology? *Counseling News and Views*, 1965, *17*(2), 4-8.

Tiedeman, D. V. A machine for the epigenesis of self realization in career development: Career, subsequent development, and implications. In J. M. Whiteley & A. Resnikoff (Eds.), *Perspectives on vocational development*. Washington, DC: American Personnel and Guidance Association, 1972.

Tiedeman, D. V. A person's eye view of career development education and enactment. *Illinois Career Educational Journal*, 1977, *34*(2), 13-17. (a)

Tiedeman, D. V. *Towards the career education of all educational personnel in Illinois*. Springfield, IL: Illinois State Board of Education, 100 North First Street, 1977. (b)

Tiedeman, D. V. A research note on becoming what we do in career development. *Vocational Guidance Quarterly*, 1978, *26*, 361-364.

Tiedeman, D. V. Converting Tiedeman and O'Hara's decision-making paradigm into "I" power: A symposium. *Character Potential: A Record of Research*, 1979, *9*, 61-62.

Tiedeman, D. V. Status and prospect in counseling psychology: 1962. In J. M. Whiteley (Ed.), *The history of counseling psychology*. Monterey, CA: Brooks/Cole, 1980, 125-132.

Tiedeman, D. V., & Miller-Tiedeman, A. Choice and decision processes and career revisited. In A. M. Mitchell, G. B. Jones, & J. D. Krumboltz (Eds.), *Social learning and career decision making*. Cranston, RI: Carroll Press, 1979.

Tiedeman, D. V., & O'Hara, R. P. *Career development: Choice and adjustment*. New York: College Entrance Examination Board, 1963.

Tillich, P. *The courage to be*. New Haven: Yale University Press, 1952.

208

Tolman, E. C. *Purposive behavior in animals and men.* New York: Appleton-Century-Crofts, 1932.

Tosi, D. J., Upshaw, K., Lande, A., & Walron, M. A. Group counseling with nonverbalizing elementary students: Differential effects of Premack and social reinforcement techniques. *Journal of Counseling Psychology*, 1971, *18*, 437-440.

Trent, J. W., & Medsker, L. L. *Beyond high school.* San Francisco: Jossey-Bass, 1968.

Tyler, L. E. *The work of the counselor.* New York: Appleton-Century-Crofts, 1953.

Tyler, L. E. Counseling. *Annual Review of Psychology*, 1958, *9*, 375-390.

Tyler, L. E. A brief summary of the conclusions of the Miami Conference. *Counseling News and Views*, 1959, *11*(2), 17-21. (a)

Tyler, L. E. Message from the president. *Counseling News and Views*, 1959, *12*(1), 1. (b)

Tyler, L. E. Message from the president. *Counseling News and Views*, 1960, *12*(2), 1-2.

Tyler, L. E. Research explorations in the realm of choice. *Journal of Counseling Psychology*, 1961, *8*, 195-201.

Tyler, L. E. Reflections on counseling psychology. *The Counseling Psychologist*, 1972, *3*(4), 6-11.

Tyler, L., Tiedeman, D., & Wrenn, C. G. The current status of counseling psychology: 1961. In J. M. Whiteley (Ed.), *The history of counseling psychology.* Monterey, CA: Brooks/Cole, 1980.

Ullman, L. P., & Krasner, L. (Eds.). *Case studies in behavior modification.* New York: Holt, Rinehart, & Winston, 1965.

Ullman, L. P., & Krasner, L. *A psychological approach to abnormal behavior.* Englewood Cliffs, NJ: Prentice-Hall, 1969.

Van Atta, R. E. A general proposal for data banking for research on counseling and psychotherapy. *Counseling News and Views*, 1967, *19*(3), 3-9.

van Kaam, A. Counseling from the viewpoint of existential psychology. In R. L. Mosher, R. F. Carle, & C. D. Kehas (Eds.), *Guidance-an examination.* New York: Harcourt, Brace, & World, 1965, 66-81.

van Kaam, A. *Existential foundations of psychology.* Pittsburgh: Duquesne University Press, 1966.

Viteles, M. S. *Industrial psychology.* New York: Norton, 1932.

Waldrop, R. S. President's message: Dictis facta suppetant. *Counseling News and Views*, 1961, *14*(1), 1-2.

Waldrop, R. S. President's message: Has psyche taken flight from psychology? Or we are losing our professional mind? *Counseling News and Views*, 1962, *14*(2), 1-2. (a)

Waldrop, R. S. President's message. *Counseling News and Views*, 1962, *14*(3), 3. (b)

Wallace, W. L. Progress report of scientific affairs committee. *Counseling News and Views*, 1968, *20*(2), 5.

Wallen, R. Gestalt therapy and Gestalt psychology. In J. Fagen & I. Shepherd (Eds.), *Gestalt therapy now*. Palo Alto, CA: Science & Behavior Books, 1970.

Walsh, W. B., & Osipow, S. H. (Eds.). *Handbook of vocational psychology. Volume I: Foundations*. Hillsdale, NJ: Erlbaum, 1983. (a)

Walsh, W. B., & Osipow, S. H. (Eds.). *Handbook of vocational psychology. Volume II: Applications*. Hillsdale, NJ: Erlbaum, 1983. (b)

Warnath, C. F. Counseling psychology or adjunct psychology? *Counseling News and Views*, 1968, *20*(3), 2-6.

Warner, W. L., Meeker, M., & Elles, K. *Social class in America*. Chicago: Science Reserch Associates, 1949.

Watson, J. B. *Psychology from the standpoint of a behaviorist*. Philadelphia: Lippincott, 1919.

Watson, R. I. Research design and methodology in evaluating the results of psychotherapy. *Journal of Clinical Psychology*, 1952, *8*, 29-31.

Way, L. *Adler's place in psychology*. New York: Collier Books, 1962.

Weinrach, S. G. Have hexagon will travel: An interview with John Holland. *Personnel and Guidance Journal*, 1980, *58*(6), 406-414.

Weinrach, S. G. Determinants of vocational choice: Holland's theory. In D. Brown & L. Brooks (Eds.), *Career choice and development: Applying contemporary theories to practice*. San Francisco: Jossey-Bass, 1984.

Wellner, A. M. (Ed.). *Education and credentialing in psychology: Proposal for a national commission in education and credentialing in psychology*. Washington, DC: American Psychological Association, 1978.

Wellner, A. M. The Council for the National Register of Health Service Providers in Psychology. In J. M. Whiteley, N. Kagan, L. W. Harmon, B. R. Fretz, & F. Tanney (Eds.), *The coming decade in counseling psychology*. Schenectady, NY: Character Research Press, 1984.

White, J. C. Cleanliness and successful bank clerical personnel—a brief. *Journal of Counseling Psychology*, 1963, *10*, 192.

White, R. W. Adler and the future of ego psychology. *Journal of Individual Psychology*, 1957, *13*, 112-124.

White, R. W. The concept of a healthy personality: What do we really mean? *The Counseling Psychologist*, 1973, *4*(2), 3-12.

Whiteley, J. M. (Ed.). *Research in counseling*. Columbus, OH: Merrill, 1967.

Whiteley, J. M. The Sierra Project: A character development program for college freshmen. *Moral Education Forum*, 1978, *3*(4), 1, 3-13.

Whiteley, J. M. (Ed.) Counseling psychology in the year 2000 A.D. *The Counseling Psychologist*, 1980, *8*(4), 2-62. (a)

Whiteley, J. M. A developmental intervention in higher education. In V. L. Erickson & J. M. Whiteley, (Eds.), *Developmental counseling and teaching.* Monterey, CA: Brooks/Cole, 1980, 236-261. (b)

Whiteley, J. M. *The history of counseling psychology.* Monterey, CA: Brooks/ Cole, 1980. (c)

Whiteley, J. M. Future research in counseling psychology: A review of past practices and suggestions for new priorities. In J. M. Whiteley, N. Kagan, L. W. Harmon, B. R. Fretz, & F. Tanney (Eds.), *The coming decade of counseling psychology.* Schenectady, NY: Character Research Press, 1984.

Whiteley, J. M., & Associates. *Character development in college students. Volume 1: The freshman year.* Schenectady, NY: Character Research Press, 1982.

Whiteley, J. M., Burkhart, M. Q., Harway-Herman, M., & Whiteley, R. M. Counseling and student development. *Annual Review of Psychology*, 1975, *26*, 337-366.

Whiteley, J. M., & Fretz, B. R. (Eds.). *The present and future of counseling psychology.* Monterey, CA: Brooks/Cole, 1980.

Whiteley, J. M., Kagan, N., Harmon, L. W., Fretz, B. R., & Tanney, F. (Eds.). *The coming decade in counseling psychology.* Schenectady, NY: Character Research Press, 1984.

Williamson, E. G. In the Preface of D. B. Stuit, G. S. Dickson, T. F. Jordan, & L. B. Schloerb. *Predicting success in professional schools.* Washington, DC: American Council on Education, 1949.

Williamson, E. G. *Counseling adolescents.* New York: McGraw-Hill, 1950.

Williamson, E. G. The working context helps determine professional functions. *Counseling News and Views*, 1952, *4*(2), 8-9.

Williamson, E. G. Counseling: Therapy and diagnosis. *Annual Review of Psychology*, 1953, *4*, 343-360.

Williamson, E. G. The fusion of discipline and counseling in the educative process. *Personnel and Guidance Journal*, 1955, *34*, 74-79.

Williamson, E. G. Counseling in developing self-confidence. *Personnel and Guidance Journal*, 1956, *34*, 398-404. (a)

Williamson, E. G. Preventive aspects of disciplinary counseling. *Educational and Psychological Measurement*, 1956, *16*, 68-81. (b)

Williamson, E. G. Some issues underlying counseling theory and practice. In W. E. Dugan, (Ed.), *The counseling points of view.* Minneapolis, MN: University of Minnesota Press, 1959.

Williamson, E. G. An historical perspective of the vocational guidance movement. *Personnel and Guidance Journal*, 1964, *42*, 854-859.

Williamson, E. G. *Vocational counseling.* New York: McGraw-Hill, 1965.

Williamson, E. G. Trait and factor theory and individual differences. In B. Stefflre & W. H. Grant (Eds.), *Theories of counseling.* New York: McGraw-Hill, 1972.

Wolfbein, S. L., & Goldstein, H. *Occupational outlook handbook* (3rd ed.). U.S. Department of Labor Bulletin No. 1215. Washington, DC: U.S. Government Printing Office, 1957.

Wolpe, J. *Psychotherapy by reciprocal inhibition*. Stanford, CA: Stanford University Press, 1958.

Wolpe, J. *The practice of behavior therapy* (1st ed.). New York: Pergamon Press, 1969.

Wolpe, J. *The practice of behavior therapy* (2nd ed.). New York: Pergamon Press, 1973.

Wolpe, J., & Lazarus, A. A. *Behavior therapy techniques*. New York: Pergamon Press, 1966.

Wolpe, J., Salter, A., & Reyna, L. J. (Eds.). *The conditioning therapies*. New York: Holt, Rinehart, & Winston, 1964.

Wrenn, C. G. *Student personnel work in college*. New York: Ronald Press, 1951.

Wrenn, C. G. Letter to the Committee on the Support of Counseling. *Counseling News and Views*, 1952, *5*(1), 11.

Wrenn, C. G. Counseling methods. *Annual Review of Psychology*, 1954, *5*, 337-356.

Wrenn, C. G. Editorial comment on status of counseling psychology. *Journal of Counseling Psychology*, 1958, *5*, 242.

Wrenn, C. G. The APA evaluation of counseling psychology programs. *Counseling News and Views*, 1968, *20*(1), 8-9.

Wrenn, C. G. Birth and early childhood of a journal. *Journal of Counseling Psychology*, 1966, *13*, 485-488. Also in J. M. Whiteley (Ed.), *The history of counseling psychology*. Monterey, CA: Brooks/Cole, 1980, 41-46.

Wrenn, C. G. Personal reflections on my experiences in counseling psychology and in life. In J. M. Whiteley, N. Kagan, L. W. Harmon, B. R. Fretz, & F. Tanney (Eds.), *The coming decade in counseling psychology*. Schenectady, NY: Character Research Press, 1984.

Wycoff, H. The stroke economy in women's scripts. *Transactional Analysis Journal*, 1971, *1*(3), 16-20. (a)

Wycoff, H. Women's scripts. *Transactional Analysis Journal*, 1971, *1*(3). (b)

Yates, A. *Behavior therapy*. New York: Wiley, 1976.

Zingle, H., & Mallett, M. *A bibliography of RET materials, articles, and theses*. Edmonton: University of Alberta, 1976.

Zytowski, D. G., & Rosen, D. A. The grand tour: 30 years of counseling psychology in the *Annual Review of Psychology*. *The Counseling Psychologist*, 1982, *10*(1), 69-79.

INDEX